Media Policy
Convergence, Concentration and Commerce

edited by

Denis McQuail and Karen Siune

for the

EUROMEDIA RESEARCH GROUP

SAGE Publications
London • Thousand Oaks • New Delhi

Chapter 1 © Karen Siune 1998
Chapter 2 © Els De Bens and Helge Østbye 1998
Chapter 3 © Karen Siune and Olof Hultén 1998
Chapter 4 © Werner A. Meier and Josef Trappel 1998
Chapter 5 © Hans J. Kleinsteuber 1998
Chapter 6 © Wolfgang Truetzschler 1998
Chapter 7 © Bernt Stubbe Østergaard 1998
Chapter 8 © Denis McQuail 1998
Chapter 9 © Kees Brants and Karen Siune 1998
Chapter 10 © Mary J. Kelly 1998
Chapter 11 © Els De Bens and Gianpietro Mazzoleni 1998
Chapter 12 © Claude Sorbets 1998
Chapter 13 © Josef Trappel and Werner A. Meier 1998
Chapter 14 © Mario Hirsch and Vibeke G. Petersen 1998
Chapter 15 © Denis McQuail 1998

First published 1998. Reprinted 2001

SAGE Publications Ltd
6 Bonhill Street
London EC2A 4PU

SAGE Publications Inc.
2455 Teller Road
Thousand Oaks, California 91320

SAGE Publications India Pvt Ltd
32, M-Block Market
Greater Kailash – I
New Delhi 110 048

British Library Cataloguing in Publication data

A catalogue record for this book is available
from the British Library

ISBN 0 7619 5939 4
ISBN 0 7619 5940 8 (pbk)

Library of Congress catalog card number 98–61094

Typeset by Mayhew Typesetting, Rhayader, Powys
Printed in Great Britain by The Cromwell Press Ltd,
Trowbridge, Wiltshire

Contents

Contributors

Kees Brants, lecturer at the Department of Communication Science, University of Amsterdam, The Netherlands.

Els De Bens, professor at the Department of Communications, University of Ghent, Belgium.

Mario Hirsch, journalist, teacher and researcher on economy and policy aspects of mass media, Luxembourg.

Olof Hultén, head of strategic analysis, Corporate Development, Sveriges Television, Stockholm, Sweden.

Mary J. Kelly, lecturer at the Department of Sociology, University College Dublin, Ireland.

Hans J. Kleinsteuber, professor at the Institute of Political Science, University of Hamburg, Germany.

Denis McQuail, emeritus professor of mass communication at the University of Amsterdam, The Netherlands.

Gianpietro Mazzoleni, Department of Communications Science, University of Genoa, Italy.

Werner A. Meier, senior researcher and lecturer at the Department of Mass Communication, University of Zurich, Switzerland.

Helge Østbye, professor of mass communication at the University of Bergen, Norway.

Bernt Stubbe Østergaard, research director at Informedica, Copenhagen, Denmark.

Vibeke G. Petersen, special adviser, Ministry of Culture, Copenhagen, Denmark.

Karen Siune, director of the Danish Institute for Studies in Research and Research Policy, Denmark.

Claude Sorbets, research director, CNRS, Institut d'Etudes Politiques, Bordeaux, France.

Josef Trappel, project manager and consultant with PROGNOS, European Centre for Economic Research and Strategy Consulting, Department for Media and Communication Research, Basel, Switzerland.

Wolfgang Truetzschler, lecturer in communications at the Dublin Institute of Technology, Ireland.

INTRODUCTION

1

Changing Media and Changing Society

Karen Siune

In the late twentieth century we take for granted the centrality of mass-media communication to social life. However, its role in society is highly contested (Raboy and Dagenais, 1992: 1). Under changing conditions, new media structures and other societal changes make it relevant to consider the role of mass media afresh. In *New Media Politics* (McQuail and Siune, 1986), the Euromedia Research Group focused on technological developments regarding mass media and the political reactions which have followed, examining changes in the Western European broadcasting structure and on the types and models of national broadcasting. Later, in *Dynamics of Media Politics* (Siune and Truetzschler, 1991), our focus was on the internal and external forces to which the mass media in Western Europe have responded. Not only national, but also transnational and local media developments were under consideration.

The Euromedia Research Group originally studied policy reactions to change (in the form of media politics). However, media politics turned out to be more the result of a struggle among different types of actors, of which political parties were just one kind, each of them following their own logic. Although it is possible to specify different types of logic attached to different types of actors, to protect national culture versus economic logic, to mention just two of the different logics, some actors share the same logic and, all in all, economic logic seems to dominate over other types.

Dynamics of Media Politics described the forces leading to patterns of development in the media landscape all over Western Europe. The main trends were privatization, internationalization, commercialization and media concentration. Public service broadcasting was now (by the start of the 1990s) just one element in national broadcasting structures, no longer the dominant element.

Changes in media structure are, at the end of the century, still on the agenda as well as changes in media content. But, over time, we have become more concerned about the consequences for society than about these changes in themselves. This book emphasizes the role played by mass media in societies under change, and is especially concerned with the role the media play in the public sphere and in relation to democratic values traditionally held in Western Europe.

Changes in the media landscape are analysed (in Part I of the book) with a growing awareness of old concepts and old ideals under pressure. Old concepts are very often used in public debate even when the content and definitions have changed from their original meanings. This applies very much to the concept 'public service broadcasting' (treated in Chapter 3), but also a concept like commercialization (see Chapter 8). Even a classic sociological concept such as 'culture' is very much under pressure. Changes in concepts, changes in media political actors and their logics, and especially changes in the functions that mass media fulfil will be central in this book.

According to the analyses given in Parts I and II we can raise the question: what kind of future society do we envisage? A number of continuing societal changes, not directly related to mass media, are taking place, including an increased degree of internationalization. What will be the societal roles attached to mass media in future societies? So far we have had a tendency to believe that mass media play a considerable societal role both in relation to individuals and to political systems. But changes in education, in the amount of leisure time and especially in family roles and the roles of political parties have raised doubts about the traditional roles and functions of mass communication. Will the old roles be pursued or will they be dropped?

The content of the media has changed during the past 10 years. On television all over Europe we find less educational programming, and more and more entertainment programmes which, furthermore, seem to become more and more alike everywhere. The backbone of most media is still news, while the rest is more or less entertainment. What remains of the media's function of editorial guidance, traditionally attached to the press? Has 'infotainment', the combination of information and entertainment, made totally obsolete the educational role which, until recently, was attached to public service mass broadcasting? And what about the media's role as cultural transmitter and educator – is it still valid?

Democracy

When we talk about Western societies we traditionally expect them to be democracies. Although democracy can be defined in many different ways, the basic elements of all definitions concern the interplay between the political system and the citizens. The participation of citizens, primarily their role as voters, has for many, including the majority of researchers, been the most important object to study in democratic societies. But we do not only consider the role as voter in a democratic society when we speak of the interplay between ordinary citizens and the political system. Habermas, among others, has shown a broader view of the interplay between citizens and the political system or systems. But Habermas, as well as many other political sociologists, still expects the media to play a central role.

From a sociological point of view we can ask: what about the role of citizens? Is it still the same as it was 20 years ago, and how will it be in the future? And what of the role of voter? Is politics as transmitted by the media still the same as it was 10 years ago? Has there in fact been a decline in politicization? Will mass media in the future be able to fulfil their previous significant function as a source of guidance for political participation? We might fear that the answer is no! If this is the case, is national media policy or the lack of national media politics to blame for this or have the changes in society as such led to new patterns? In this book we try to answer these and other related questions.

Many political scientists have for long ignored the role of the media, but more and more they have come to the reluctant conclusion that, even if they don't like it, mass media have, over the years, played a considerable role in politics. But we still need to ask the question: how much of politics can be explained by the performance of the media? Is democracy today dependent on the interplay with mass media? And, in the future, will it still be mass media and not interactive media like the Internet that will be the main source of information to the majority of citizens? Does the challenge from the interactive media, combined with changes in the user's ability to handle such media, result in new roles very different from the roles that the so-called 'old' mass media, such as television, radio and newspapers, have played so far? The vast expansion of the Internet (discussed in Chapter 6) and the changes in the content of the traditional mass media tend to lead to an affirmative answer. The role of the old media is indeed being challenged! Why is it so? How much is due to changes in the media structure and in their content? How much has the self-perception of the old media roles disappeared among the actors in the media, especially journalists? And has the perception of the democratic role of mass media dissolved among other types of actors such as politicians and industrialists?

Masses in an individualized society

Mass audience has always been the intended goal for all mass media, but are the masses still there? Do a great number of people sit and wait for messages, expecting to be exposed to something which somebody else has decided is worth their attention in societies which are more and more individualized? Has the role of citizen become detached from the role of media consumer? And, secondly, if a potentially great number is being exposed, has it then what we can call 'mass character'? The Euromedia Research Group has dealt with such changes already in the books cited above, but recent changes in the media landscape actualize the question again and it forms a central part of this book.

The structure of broadcasting in Europe has always been much influenced by political initiatives. In contrast, newspaper structure has rather been left to market mechanisms and was consequently neglected from a political science point of view, unless – as illustrated in the Scandinavian tradition – you cared for the development and fall of the 'party press', the party-owned or party-affiliated press. Today it is not sufficient to refer to private ownership and market steering versus licence financing and public service responsibility as the reason for not including newspapers in a sociological analysis of the role of the mass media. Media ownership today cuts across all media types. On the other hand, however, the situation in many countries is still that people spend more time in front of the television than they do reading a newspaper. The number of television channels has increased tremendously and there is no longer, necessarily, the same news coverage or the same type of programmes on all channels that can be received within a nation. Media might have become more individualized with the increase in numbers of channels and they influence society accordingly.

Dynamics

Looking at the changes in the interplay between the media and political systems it is necessary to include all types of media that play a central role in social life. These are defined as media on which citizens spend a certain amount of time, independently of whether it is spent passively on television, radio or newspapers or actively on the computer. Taken together, these media still attract so much of leisure time use that we have to consider them as the main, most important mass media. So far our definition of the most important mass media is not based upon the degree of impact, but the degree of time spent on them. The next question that arises is: what kind of media are considered relevant if we limit attention to those having important influence on peoples' attitudes, behaviour, knowledge and awareness? And which media play, in a wider sense, a role in the interplay of private versus public sphere, in the interplay between system and life-world to use Habermas's elements?

The answer has for some decades been the same both in public and in scientific debate: television is the dominant medium, followed by newspapers. Radio plays a less important role, although radio ranks high measured in time used for consumption. Newspapers come second to television. Has anything happened during the past decade that has changed the role of these media? The number of television channels has increased and the majority are no longer traditional public service oriented (Chapter 3). More and more are privately owned, and an increasing number are owned by individuals or groups with ownership also of other types of mass media (see Chapter 4). Public service monopolies, with national obligations, have disappeared, and the content has increasingly become internationalized and commercialized (Chapter 8). Within the print media new forms of monopolies have emerged.

New technology is only partly at the root of these changes. New technological developments have taken the lead if we look at the amount of time young people spend with electronic media. Computers have taken over in many countries and surfing on the Internet has become more attractive than watching series on television (see Chapter 6). Social changes affecting household everyday life have greatly influenced the use of media and patterns of audience behaviour (Chapter 10): better education, greater competition, changing norms in a wider sense, changing economic conditions leading, for instance, to every second household having a computer which is not only used as a typewriter.

Given the media trends illustrated and/or predicted in our earlier studies, industrialization is now used as a wider concept than the production of hardware; media have become entertainment industries. Now demonopolization is not an issue raised only in relation to state monopolies within broadcasting, but more an issue raised in relation to media concentration. Economic logic is now, even more than cultural logic, behind policy initiatives and globalization is possible thanks to a huge number of satellites. Some consider transnationalization as an issue with very positive aspects, whereas others still worry about the protection of national culture. The issue of culture is still on the agenda.

In the light of all this, we can expect a continuing sequence of political and regulatory initiatives to deal with changes in media structure, content and audience behaviour, although they will take new and rather unpredictable forms. There is likely to be more international intervention, including more European initiatives. There will also be more self-regulation and self-control among senders/professionals. Actors in political institutions will have to adopt new strategies to protect the political role of the media in democracy.

Media politics in the future

We will argue that actors engaged in media politics have, at least from a rational point of view, a need for updated information and awareness of the changes in media structure and media use. Even more, they need updated knowledge about concepts, not forgetting their original content but also being aware of the changes in the values attached to them. At the same time the academic world has to be aware of the actual use of concepts and be aware of the logic characterizing individual actors involved in media politics. What will be considered the 'public interest' in the future from a theoretical versus a political point of view? Do we speak of the same when we say public responsibility? Can we today, even in theory, speak of one great mass public interest?

Some of the crises which we see increasingly debated in public can be related to the distance between culturally prescribed goals and actual generally accepted means of behaviour. But is it relevant to speak about anomie? Finally, we will have to raise the issue of whether politics matters to media. Can the expected changes in media structure and in the use of media in the future for social life in any way be directed by politics, whether national, regional or European?

Bibliography

McQuail, Denis and Siune, Karen (eds) (1986) *New Media Politics.* London: Sage.
Raboy, Marc and Dagenais, Bernard (eds) (1992) *Media, Crises and Democracy: Mass Communication and the Disruption of Social Order.* London: Sage.
Siune, Karen and Truetzschler, Wolfgang (eds) (1991) *Dynamics of Media Politics.* London: Sage.

PART I STRUCTURAL CHANGES

2

The European Newspaper Market

Els De Bens and Helge Østbye

The broadcasting systems of almost all Western European countries share some distinctly European characteristics, especially those which derive from public service broadcasting. When it comes to the newspaper industry, the similarities between the countries are less striking. We find private ownership and an extensive freedom of publication in all countries, but characteristics such as the number of independent newspapers, the existence of newspaper chains, foreign ownership, party political affiliations, the distinction between 'quality' and 'popular' press, state subsidies and the penetration of news-paper readership in society show very distinct differences between the countries of Western Europe. On the other hand, the pressures on the newspaper industry are similar in many countries, and although the starting points are different, some trends seem to be similar, such as increasing concentration, a down-market tabloid trend and a decrease in sales figures and advertising revenue.

In this chapter, we try to give the main outlines of the newspaper market in Western Europe. We cannot go into detail because much comparative data are missing and, at the same time, the available data are often inaccurate and contradictory. Colin Sparks found that there is much con-fusion in this area of media analysis and he came upon very contradictory accounts of the British press (Sparks, 1995: 180). We will illustrate some of our findings with empirical data from many European countries, but our examples cannot include all countries. We mainly look at 'national' daily newspapers and, although regional newspapers are taken into account, most of the data refer to the national daily newspaper market. We do not deal with free-sheets, nor any kinds of periodical publications such as women's magazines, TV weeklies, news magazines and special interest magazines. Many daily newspaper enterprises are, of course, involved in the market of free-sheets and periodical magazines, but our main topic is the analysis of the national daily newspaper market.

In the early years of newspaper development, no huge financial invest-ments were necessary to start a newspaper. This led to a system comprising many newspapers, each aiming at a small segment of society, defined perhaps by geography, social class, language, religion or party politics. Many small newspapers aiming at their own well-defined audience created diversity and pluralism. Towards the end of the nineteenth century, improved printing and typesetting technology made mass production possible. Improved distribution expanded the market for newspapers all over the country, so that several newspapers achieved a national reach. At the same time, new production processes led to a reduction of production costs, an increase in circulation and a widening of social consumption by newspaper readers. The introduction of advertising lowered the price, but at the same time made newspapers dependent on advertising. As newspapers extended their target group, the content was widened and ties with political parties were reduced. Towards the end of the nineteenth century, the tabloid press made its appearance. At the same time and early in the twentieth century, many small independent newspapers were taken over by larger newspaper groups. Competitive conditions in the daily newspaper market became severe, and in all European countries the number of non-chain newspapers has declined over the years. (For the background, mechanisms and evolution of the process of concentration in the newspaper business, see Chapter 13.)

The newspaper in decline?

As a result of continuing press concentration, the number of national daily newspapers as well as regional ones has declined over the years. Changes in the total number of daily newspapers in some European countries are shown in Table 2.1. As we can see from the table, the reduction in the number of newspapers has stopped in some countries. Countries like Norway, Sweden and Denmark still have a high number of newspapers in relation to their small population. In each country, a certain number of newspapers have a national distribution. Most regional newspapers, however, have well-defined geographical areas where they are dominant. In many countries (among them the Scandinavian ones), competition used to exist in these local markets. Several newspapers, representing different political parties and other organized interests, competed. This competition led to the creation of local monopolies.

In most European countries, the national daily newspaper market consists of a very limited number of newspaper titles: for example, in the UK, 10; in France, 8; in Germany, 5; and in Italy, 4. Most of these national newspapers are owned by the major press holdings, the only exception being Germany where only *Die Welt* and *Bild* belong to the Springer Group and where the other national newspapers are published by non-chain enterprises. Competition is strong in the national daily newspaper market which is no longer 'open', making it difficult for new entries to survive.

Table 2.1 *Number of regional and national daily newspapers*

Country	1950	1980	1996
Belgium	51	33	26
Denmark	?	47	42[a]
Finland	?	66	56[a]
France	142	85	69[a]
Germany	225[b]	124	135
The Netherlands	115	77	29
Norway	91	84	85
Sweden	?	93	94[a]
UK	113	100	100

[a] 1994.
[b] 1954.

Sources: For Belgium, Luykx, 1978; De Bens, 1997; for France, Junqua, 1995; for Germany, Schütz, 1996: 325; for Europe, Euromedia Research Group, 1997; Bruck, 1993

In the UK, the national dailies have very high circulation figures: a total circulation of 13,872,000 for only eight press enterprises. The *Sun* has a circulation of 3,929,000 and the *Daily Mirror* 3,097,000 (see Table 2.2). In some other European countries, regional newspapers have a larger market share than the national ones. For example, in France 79.4 per cent of daily circulation is accounted for by regional papers, with *Ouest France* alone having a circulation of 797,090, higher than any national title in 1995.

Concentration of ownership

More important than the reduction in newspaper titles is the reduction in the number of press enterprises that publish newspapers. In most European countries, the majority of newspapers are published by a small number of press holdings. In Belgium, for instance, in 1950 the 51 dailies were published by 33 press enterprises; in 1997, the remaining 26 dailies belong to five press holdings. In some countries, these holdings are strong in specific regions (for example, Germany); in other countries, they dominate the total national press. The largest European daily newspaper groups were as follows in 1995:

Belgium	VUM, RUG, Persgroep, Rossel, IPM, Vers L'Avenir
Denmark	Berlingske officin, Politikens hus, Jyllands Posten
Finland	Sanoma (Erkko family), Aamulehti-Yhtymä (Bonnier), Ketonen
France	Robert Hersant, Amaury, Bayard

Table 2.2   *National newspapers with the largest circulation figures (1995–6)*

Country	Title	Circulation
Austria	*Neue Kronenzeitung*	1,075,000
	Täglich Alles	544,000
Belgium	*Het Laatste Nieuws*	303,993
	Le Soir	182,798
Denmark	*Ekstrabladet*	168,000
	Jyllands Posten	161,000
Finland	*Helsingin Sanomat*	470,600
	Ilta-Sanomat	213,600
France	*Le Parisien Libéré*	451,159
	Le Figaro	391,533
Germany	*Bild-Zeitung*	4,300,000
	Süddeutsche Zeitung	407,000
Greece	*Eleftheros Typos*	110,361
	Nea	107,705
Ireland	*Irish Independent*	160,032
	Irish Times	102,460
Italy	*Corriere della Sera*	674,000
	La Repubblica	622,000
Luxembourg	*Luxemburger Wort*	85,000
The Netherlands	*De Telegraaf*	760,000
	Algemeen Dagblad	401,000
Norway	*Verdens Gang*	386,137
	Aftenposten	279,965
Portugal	*Correio da Manha*	69,000
	Diario de Noticias	63,000
Spain	*El Pais*	420,934
	ABC	321,573
Sweden	*Aftonbladet*	381,000
	Expressen	374,000
Switzerland	*Blick*	335,143
	Tages-Anzeiger	282,222
UK	*Sun*	3,929,000
	Daily Mirror	3,097,000

Source: Euromedia Research Group, 1997

Germany	Springer, WAZ
Italy	Benedetti-Mondadori, Rizzoli-Agnelli, Rusconi, Ferruzzi, Fininvest
The Netherlands	De Telegraaf, Perscombinatie, Wegener, VNU
Norway	Schibsted, A-pressen, Orkla
Sweden	Bonnier, Hjörnegruppen, Svenska Dagbladet
UK	United News, Associated Newspapers, Mirror Group, News International, Hollinger, Pearson

In many European countries, the periodical press is also dominated by large press holdings. For instance, in France Hachette/Filipacchi, Prisma Presse and Editions Mondiales publish 80 per cent of women's and television magazines, family and lifestyle papers. In Germany, Bertelsmann, Bauer and Burda are the market leaders. But also in small countries like Belgium, only two holdings publish 75 per cent of the periodical press. In several countries, the most important newspaper owners have access to the quality newspaper market as well as to the popular press. In the UK, Rupert Murdoch's group News International controls the quality paper *The Times* as well as the tabloid *Sun*. In France, Robert Hersant publishes both a quality paper (*Le Figaro*) and a popular one (*France-Soir*). Axel Springer Verlag in Germany controls *Bild* and *Die Welt*. The same system applies in Scandinavian countries: in Denmark, Berlingske controls *Berlingske Tidende* and *BT*, Politiken, *Politiken* and *Ekstrabladet*; in Finland, Sanoma controls *Helsingin Sanomat* and *Ilta-Sanomat*; in Norway, Schibsted: *Aftenposten* and *VG*; in Sweden, Bonnier: *Dagens Nyheter* and *Expressen*.

All over Europe, small marginal newspapers have been taken over by the large press holdings, and as remaining press groups have increased their market segment, it has become almost impossible for new entries to obtain a share in the daily newspaper market: they have disappeared (for example, *Infomatin* in France, *Super!Zeitung* in Germany, *24 uur* in Belgium) or they have been taken over by one of the major companies (for example, *Today* launched by Eddie Shah, bought by Murdoch and finally stopped in 1996; the *Independent* launched in 1986, bought by the Mirror Group in 1994 and resold in 1998). It becomes obvious that concentration has made it very difficult for outsiders to establish new titles. The market is no longer open. The periodical market, however, seems more 'open' and new 'entries' are still possible. Many daily newspaper groups have entered this market and have developed a profitable business.

Following the gradual opening and extension of commercial radio and television in Europe, the newspaper industry has become more and more integrated with other media. In the UK, Murdoch moved from newspapers into British satellite television (BSkyB). Meanwhile, he has also developed audiovisual activities in the USA (Fox Network), in Asia (Star TV), in Latin America and in Germany, where he took a share of 49.9 per cent (1996) in Vox-TV. Other large newspaper holdings, such as Associated News, United News and Pearson, have also developed audiovisual media activities.

In France, Robert Hersant was involved in La5. This TV channel did not attract enough viewers and advertising revenues remained insufficient. Hersant left La5 after having lost millions of francs. In Germany, Bertelsmann and WAZ are shareholders of RTL, Bauer and Burda of RTL2. Axel Springer Verlag is the second most important shareholder of SAT1 and of Deutsches Sportfernsehen. In smaller countries like Belgium, the Netherlands and the Scandinavian countries, newspaper publishers also moved into audiovisual media. In Finland, Sanoma moved from newspapers into cable television. The Swedish newspaper and magazine giant Bonnier has moved into video distribution and television production. A similar trend can be found in the Danish multimedia group Egmont, which was originally based in comics and magazines. In Norway, Schibsted is the main newspaper shareholder in commercial television.

In Western Europe, legal measures have been adopted to counter concentration. Anti-trust legislation has not been very efficient in stopping horizontal and diagonal forms of media concentration. In France, for instance, the anti-press trust law has legitimized Hersant's empire (30 per cent of the circulation can be owned by one group – this coincides with Hersant's position). Another example is Britain where the law provides exceptional circumstances that make exemptions possible. Murdoch was allowed to take over the *Sun*, *The Times*, *The Sunday Times* and *Today*. In the UK as well as in France, legal measures have not been applied because the government enjoyed the support of the newspaper publishers: Murdoch got support from the Thatcher government and Robert Hersant from Chirac. In other countries, such as Norway, the government has retreated under the pressure of the media and refrained from introducing restrictions on cross-ownership (diagonal concentration). In some instances, public authorities have even promoted cross-ownership. In Belgium, private commercial television was initially legally obliged to have at least 51 per cent shareholders of press enterprises in Flanders and 32 per cent in Wallonia.

In some countries with anti-trust and anti-cross-ownership laws, news-paper groups have expanded their activities in other countries in order to escape national restrictions. It must be said, however, that foreign par-ticipation in national daily newspapers is rather exceptional. In Belgium, Robert Hersant has a 40 per cent share in the leading newspaper group Rossel. In Austria as well as in the German-speaking part of Switzerland, the large German enterprises WAZ and Axel Springer Verlag are share-holders. In most European daily newspapers, however, foreign press holdings have been kept out. The only exception is Pearson, which tries to control the financial newspaper market in Europe. Pearson owns *Les Echos* in France, has a share of 39 per cent in *Expancion* and in *Actualidad Economica* in Spain, a share of 50 per cent in *The Australian Financial Review* and a share of 25 per cent in *The Financial Post* in Canada. Pearson also reached an agreement with the Russian *Isvestia* to launch *The Financial Isvestia* (1992). In Belgium and the Netherlands, Pearson negotiated with *De Financieel Economische Tijd* and *Het Financieele Dagblad*, but was not successful.

Transnational participations are much more common in the market of periodical publications (the so-called *Publikumszeitschriften*). Gruner and Jahr bought the French group Prisma Presse, the leading group in the French magazine market after Hachette/Filipacchi. Prisma Presse publishes the most read women's magazine *Femme Actuelle* and one of the most successful TV magazines *Télé Loisirs*. In 1994, the British company EMAP bought Editions Mondiales, the third group after Hachette and Prisma Presse. Editions Mondiales publishes *Télé Poche*, a TV magazine with a circulation of around 1.5 million, and many special interest periodicals. In Belgium, 70 per cent of the market share of periodical publications belongs to a Dutch holding, VNU.

Many authors consider increasing media concentration as a threat to pluralism. Newspapers are bought by the major press groups, they are amalgamated and their editorial identity disappears. Small independent newspapers are pushed out of the market. Other researchers argue that small newspapers can only survive when they are taken over by the large holdings. The crucial question is whether editorial autonomy is guaranteed. In most countries, we find evidence of both models.

Subsidizing the press

In order to counteract the trend towards concentration in the newspaper business, different kinds of state subsidies have been developed. So-called 'indirect' state subsidies, such as low postal and telecommunication rates, interest-free loans and a reduction of or exemption from VAT, are common in all European countries. These subsidies have been widely approved because all newspapers are involved.

Reduced VAT rates differ from country to country and the European Commission claims a harmonization of VAT rates at 6 per cent. Newspaper publishers aim at a general exemption rule for VAT in all European countries. Current VAT rates in EU countries are as follows:

	%		%
Belgium	0	Spain	3
Denmark	0	Greece	4
Finland	0	Italy	4
Norway	0	Portugal	5
Sweden	0	The Netherlands	6
UK	0	Germany	7
France	2.1	Austria	10
Luxembourg	3	Ireland	12.5

The research unit of Price Waterhouse studied the effects of the introduction of the 6 per cent VAT rule to the UK (where newspapers are currently zero-rated) and came to the conclusion that most regional dailies would disappear and that the circulation figures of the national dailies would drop by at least 10 per cent. Even if indirect subsidies do not help small newspapers to survive, they are of crucial importance today because of the many difficulties that most newspaper enterprises are confronted with, including a decline in readership and advertising revenue.

In order to counter concentration in the press, several countries (especially the Scandinavian countries, Austria, France, Belgium and the

Netherlands) have introduced direct subsidies to newspapers. The form and level of subsidies vary from country to country. In Sweden and Norway, the closing down of several newspapers and the fear of local newspaper monopolies triggered the introduction of the direct subsidy system in the 1960s. A comparison between the press structure in Denmark (no direct subsidies, relatively few papers) and that in Finland, Norway and Sweden (direct subsidies, many newspapers) gives some indication that the subsidies have at least some positive effects. In Norway and Sweden, the subsidies go to the smallest newspapers and particularly smaller newspapers in areas with local competition. There are formal rules for the allocation of subsidies, and there are no indications that the system has made the press less critical in its reporting of government. On the contrary, there are indications that some of the most persistent critics of the government would not be able to survive without the system of subsidies (for example, in Norway, the Marxist-Leninist daily *Klassekampen*). Other arguments against direct subsidies are that they prevent development in the press and that the market, not the government, should decide which newspapers should be allowed to survive.

In Holland, where the direct subsidy system was only applied to newspapers facing financial difficulties and to new initiatives, the concentration process was not stopped, but some newspapers were able to prolong their existence. In Belgium, the direct subsidy was given to all dailies, including the larger newspapers which already enjoyed a healthy financial status. Following a revision of policy, more selective criteria were applied and the total amount of the subsidy became so small that it is now hardly worth mentioning. Nevertheless, the direct subsidy system is still a contested topic in Belgium. In Flanders, the government has announced that it will be abolished in the near future because all newspapers have been taken over by major press groups. One could conclude that in Flanders the direct subsidy system was not well planned and failed to stop the process of concentration. More research should investigate the positive effects of the Norwegian and Swedish direct press subsidy system in order to draw meaningful conclusions.

The decline of the political opinion press

Newspapers with strong links to political parties have existed in most European countries. In the early 1970s, newspapers with party political content represented more than 80 per cent of the total circulation of the Norwegian and Swedish press (Hadenius and Weibull, 1978: 115; Hoyer, 1982: 161). Twenty-five years later, the newspapers – almost without exception – claim to be non-partisan and independent.

Depoliticization has taken place in most European countries. Partisan newspapers have broken their ties with their political parties. They often remain loyal to their former political ideology, but they are no longer owned and financed by the political parties.

Socialist newspapers were often the last dailies to belong to a political party or trade union: in the UK the *Daily Herald* until 1963; in France *Le Populaire* until 1970; in the Netherlands *Het Vrije Volk* until 1969; in Belgium *De Morgen* (Flanders) until 1986 and *Le Peuple/Journal de Charleroi* (Wallonia) until 1985. These Dutch and Belgian newspapers have survived because they have been taken over by newspaper groups; they are still left-wing papers because they have kept an autonomous editorial staff.

Most partisan newspapers have indeed dropped their party affiliations. This does not mean that they have become completely neutral. Very often they have a more general platform for editorial comments and investigative journalism. But in general news reporting, they are not very different from other newspapers and, when necessary, they voice criticism against the political party they are identified with. The tendency towards less partisanship has very often been an explicit decision to adapt to market considerations. By reducing their attacks on other parties and by tuning down the support for their own, these newspapers are able to attract readers from a broader range of the political spectrum.

Why has it become so difficult for the partisan newspapers to survive? Several explanations have been put forward. One is that political parties, and especially parties to the left, are bad newspaper managers. To some extent, this may be true. Strong political ideology may reduce the newspaper's ability to adapt to changes in the market. A second explanation is that the – in general non-socialist – business community prefers to place its advertising in non-socialist newspapers. Indications in this direction have been found in Norway even in the 1990s (Allern, 1996: 64–99), but this form of channelling resources to loyal newspapers was probably more important in earlier periods, and it may never have been the main driving force in the development. In many countries, differences in reading culture between the working class and the middle class may have been a major reason for the difficulties in establishing a strong working-class press. It is possible that the reading public has become less interested in politics, but it is more likely that the citizens have been more attracted by the more neutral – or 'objective' – news coverage on radio and television, and that they prefer this to the more one-sided and propagandist news reporting that used to characterize the strongly partisan newspapers.

Many small partisan newspapers have been forced to close down as a result of processes of concentration. Left-wing newspapers have had particular difficulties in surviving. Some left-wing newspapers like *Libération* (France), founded by Sartre in 1974, remained independent, but this situation is exceptional. Several times in the past *Libération* almost went bankrupt. In 1995, the transport company Chargeurs obtained two-thirds of the shares. Other less successful French independent left-wing dailies were *Le Combat* and *Le Matin*. *Le Combat* was launched after the Second World War by Albert Camus and closed down in 1974; *Le Matin*, launched in 1977, seemed to have more success, with a circulation of 170,000, but increasing financial problems made its closure inevitable in 1988. In Norway, the Marxist-Leninist newspaper *Klassekampen* was established as a weekly in 1973 and turned into a daily newspaper in 1977. It still exists as a small, respected, left-wing daily newspaper.

Effects of concentration on editorial content

There are two opposing views concerning the influence of concentration on newspaper quality. Some claim that because quality journalism requires resources, the general quality of the newspapers benefits from concentration in the newspaper market. Others claim that concentration stimulates commercialization and triggers a down-market trend: more human interest, more trivialization and more sensationalism. Crime, sex, disaster, celebrities, sports have become the core topics. It is very difficult to find clear evidence in either direction. One crucial question is how extra funds for the newspaper are spent. If the resources are ploughed back into improving editorial quality, the position is different from a situation where the surplus is paid out as increased dividends to the owners.

Concentration, however, is often a threat to ideological pluralism. Ben Bagdikian (1992: 6) has argued that concentration homogenizes newspaper content and that it is a myth that concentration can trigger diversity and pluralism. Ruotolo (1988: 124) does not consider concentration as a threat as long as it does not lead to editorial impoverishment. McQuail concludes that, despite the many studies of the positive and negative effects of press concentration, it remains difficult to pinpoint the effects because many other variables are involved (see also Chapters 4 and 13).

Newspapers have, however, important political functions. They contribute to the functioning of democracy in several ways. Broad, 'objective' newspapers may serve well as channels for general information and as arenas for public debate. They also serve the interests of the business community and the intellectuals, but they seldom represent the views of the underprivileged groups in society. The popular press may in some cases serve this task, but the lack of newspapers rooted in the labour movement may result in biased reporting. In Western Europe, in general, newspapers are still important agenda-setters for the big political issues and newspapers are still considered to be the watchdogs of democracy.

Newspaper consumption

In several European countries, circulation figures reached a peak during the 1950s and 1960s. Since then, in almost all European countries, the circulation figures have dropped. Only in some countries, such as the Netherlands and the Scandinavian countries, have sales figures continued to rise, or were at least stable well into the 1990s. There is a distinct north–south dimension in European newspaper reading. In northern Europe, people read a lot more than in the south. Daily newspaper circulation figures per 1,000 inhabitants were as follows in 1995:

Norway	606	Denmark	315
Sweden	479	The Netherlands	309
Finland	473	Belgium	150
Switzerland	411	France	155
Iceland	403	Italy	110
Austria	337	Greece	100
UK	330	Portugal	38
Germany	320		

As one copy of a newspaper may be read by several people, these figures are not an accurate description of newspaper reading. The number of readers per copy is probably higher in countries with relatively low circulation. The main explanation for the variation lies in the proportion of the population who are regular newspaper readers. In the north, newspaper reading is high in all sections of society, including the working class, and in rural areas as well as urban. There are several historical explanations for this pattern, including literacy in the labour class.

Linked to the distribution system is the question of how people order their newspaper. In Holland and the Scandinavian countries, people subscribe to their newspaper. Subscription seems to develop an attitude of loyalty towards the newspaper. In these countries, distribution systems also function well. High subscription rates always coincide with efficient distribution systems. The existence of popular newspapers or tabloids influences sales figures. In the UK, free sale of newspapers is dominant. The UK has a mass supply of tabloids, and the recent sensational news about the private lives of the royal family, politicians and actors has caused a rise in circulation. The fact that Rupert Murdoch halved the price of both the *Sun* and *The Times* also engaged other newspapers in a temporary 'price war'.

Cutting the price of the dailies made circulation figures rise, so that we can conclude that newspaper circulation is price elastic. The circulation of *The Times* doubled. This growth was not at the expense of the other quality papers (with the exception of the *Independent* whose circulation figures dropped by one-quarter (Sparks, 1995: 184ff.)). The price war, however, could have a temporary effect because once the prices rise again readers will probably quit. In 1995, the newspaper publishers were forced to raise the price of newspapers because the price of paper had increased, but it has fallen sharply since then (Tunstall, 1996). Gustafsson (1996: 100) has suggested another factor which influences the total circulation figure:

the balance between a national and a regional/local press. If there is a more or less even balance, readers will be tempted to buy more than one newspaper.

Portugal, Spain and Greece all experienced many years during the post-war period when human rights, including freedom of the press, were suppressed. This may have had long-term effects on newspaper circulation and readership patterns. In most countries (with the exception of the Netherlands and the Scandinavian countries), circulation figures have dropped, especially during the early 1990s. Commercial 'tabloid' television has often been blamed for this decline in readership. Many authors have some doubts about the exclusive 'doom' role of television. Other variables might be at stake: the rise of newspaper prices, bad distribution systems, unsuccessful promotion strategies which do not appeal to readers. In the 1960s and 1970s, newspapers entered the 'maturity' phase in the product lifecycle and expansion became difficult.

Newspaper publishers should conduct more research into readers' needs and uses. Readers' taste changes and publishers have to anticipate shifts in 'reading' culture. Recently, all over Europe, publishers have invested in product improvement and product differentiation. In the 1990s, most newspapers have had a face-lift, a new layout, and extra supplements and inserts have become trendy. Quality papers have increased the number of journalists (copy-setters have left the newspaper plants so more journalists can be employed) and invest in qualitative, investigative journalism.

Popular and tabloid newspapers have definitely chosen the down-market model and pay more attention than ever to human interest, sensation, crime and *faits divers*. As a result of strong competition and pressure from the commercial department, hunting for the ultimate 'scoop' becomes compulsive. Many authors claim that all dailies, quality as well as popular ones, have given in to the down-market model. The British quality papers, for example, paid considerable attention to the escapades of Hugh Grant and the royal family. The *Guardian* recently launched the term 'broadloids', an amalgamation of the words 'tabloids' and 'broadsheets' (synonym for quality papers). Although this assumption has become generally accepted, we must admit that empirical evidence for the 'pulp' trend is missing in communication research studies.

Advertising revenue trends

Newspapers operate in two markets: the market for advertisers and for readers. In most countries, revenues from advertising have become bigger over the years than revenues from sales. The growth of commercial television in all Western European countries means that the newspapers' share of advertising turnover has been reduced. In most countries, advertising contributes less to newspaper revenues than before. Despite this decline,

Table 2.3   *Media share of advertising in Western European countries,
1980/1995[a] (as % of total media advertising budget)*

	Newspapers	Magazines	Television	Radio	Cinema	Posters
Austria	36.6	12.9	30.3	12.1	1.0	7.0
	32.1	25.6	23.3	11.8	0.5	7.1
Belgium	42.7	32.4	8.1	0.2	1.7	14.7
	23.3	19.6	35.2	8.9	1.5	12.1
Denmark	49.6	31.9	10.1	3.6	0.9	3.8
	69.5	4.9	20.5	2.2	0.8	2.1
Finland	66.2	15.8	15.1	0	0.3	2.2
	56.8	14.1	22.0	3.8	0.1	3.2
France	27.0	33.0	14.3	10.3	1.4	14.0
	24.5	22.7	33.0	7.5	0.6	11.7
Germany	49.6	31.9	10.1	3.6	0.9	3.8
	47.0	25.6	20.4	3.7	1.0	3.2
Greece	26.0	18.5	48.1	7.4	0	0
	10.7	13.3	66.1	5.5	0.2	5.3
Ireland	48.3	8.0	28.7	9.2	0	4.6
	45.4	5.5	32.5	9.6	1.1	5.9
Italy	27.3	31.7	25.6	6.6	1.9	6.7
	22.0	17.2	53.3	3.9	0.4	3.2
The Netherlands	62.8	23.0	7.0	1.0	0.4	5.7
	47.9	24.4	18.6	4.6	0.4	4.1
Norway	82.3	15.4	0	0	0.9	1.3
	60.5	12.9	18.2	5.3	0.9	2.2
Portugal	26.7	–	53.3	13.3	0	6.7
	12.5	15.7	55.2	7.2	–	9.3
Spain	30.0	16.8	32.9	12.2	1.7	6.3
	34.2	13.2	37.4	9.8	0.8	4.5
Sweden	–	–	–	–	–	–
	62.1	13.8	17.1	0.3	0.7	5.9
Switzerland	62.0	23.0	8.0	0	0.9	6.0
	56.8	17.6	9.2	2.6	1.0	12.9
UK	44.8	21.1	27.1	2.2	0.7	4.1
	37.8	23.0	31.7	3.0	0.7	3.8
Europe	47.6	26.1	15.6	3.9	1.0	5.7
	38.2	20.9	29.9	4.8	0.7	5.4

[a] First figure given for each country = 1980; second figure = 1995.

Sources: Sánchez-Tabernero, 1993: 162–3; Zenith Media, 1997

advertising is still the main source of revenue for 'healthy' newspapers
(between 50 and 75 per cent). If advertising contributes less than 35 per cent
of revenue, it will be difficult for the newspaper to survive. Quality newspapers with rather low sales figures rely heavily on advertising income.

In most European countries, the bulk of advertising money is still spent
on newspapers and weeklies. But in Italy, Greece and Portugal particularly,
more advertising money goes to television (see Table 2.3). Classified advertising is an important source of revenue for newspapers. In this market, in
particular, they experience no competition from television. In most Western
European countries, classified advertising accounts for about 30 per cent of

advertising revenue. Statistics on advertising revenue of newspapers mainly refer to commercial advertising ('brand advertisements'), so we can conclude that the total advertising revenue of newspapers is higher than statistics reveal. In periods of economic recession, classified advertising drops (as in 1992–3, for example).

Newspapers use several strategies to retain a high share of the brand advertising market. Special pages and supplements (lifestyle, motor, house and gardening, entertainment) are often created more to attract specialized advertising than to interest readers. This means that the search for advertising money can influence editorial content. Improved printing quality and special colour supplements are developed in order to attract expensive advertisements. The increasing number of inserts is the response of publishers to the expansion of direct marketing.

Impact of new technologies on the newspaper

New technologies have diminished the number of print workers but increased the number of journalists. One could argue that new technologies (and the search for advertising revenues) has increased the editorial output of most newspapers (more special columns, more inserts). New technologies have also improved layout, colour printing and so on. The next step in the introduction of new technology is probably linked to new forms of distribution of information. Through Internet services and electronic printing, this process has already begun. Electronic publishing is strong in professional journals and some other forms of magazines. Most newspapers have a Website. Some authors, like Negroponte (1995), claim that the hard copy of the newspaper will be replaced by an electronic form. Readers, however, will not easily adapt themselves to the small computer screen on which the layout of the newspaper is completely lost. Readers want to turn the pages of 'their' familiar newspaper, feel and smell the paper and 'zap' through it at their own pace. Until now, pilot projects with electronic newspapers have failed (for example, the Knight Ridder electronic newspaper the 'Daily Me').

Direct access to news sources (news agencies, subsidy information and so on) could make newspapers superfluous. But the demand for edited material with the quality control that is normally provided by a newspaper will prolong the life of the editorial processes of newspapers. Journalists will be needed more than ever to make selections out of the endless, chaotic information flow as well as to comment and explain (Bardoel, 1996). In spite of the popularity of the audiovisual and electronic media, the power of the press seems likely to continue. According to Tunstall (1996: 427), the press will indeed continue 'to be extremely powerful both within the media and across the broad range of public policy and public life'.

Bibliography

Albert, P. (1994) *La presse*. Paris: PUF.

Allern, S. (1996) *Kildenes makt*. Oslo: Pax Forlag.

Bagdikian, B. (1992) *The Media Monopoly*. Boston: Beacon Press.

Bardoel, J. (1996) 'Beyond journalism: a profession between information society and civil society', *European Journal of Communication*, 3: 283–302.

Barile, P. and Rao, G. (1992) 'Trends in the Italian mass media and media law', *European Journal of Communication*, 2: 261–81.

Beninger, R. (1993) 'Les conditions économiques de la presse d'opinion', *Médiapouvoirs*, 31: 137–45.

Bertrand, C.J. (1969) *The British Press: An Historical Survey*. Paris: OCDL.

Bruck, P. (ed.) (1993) *Ökonomie und Zukunft der Printmedien*. Munich: Fischer.

Charon, J.M. (1991) *La presse en France de 1945 à nos jours*. Paris: Seuil.

Charon, J.M. (1992) 'Les Français et leurs médias: le doute toujours', *Médiapouvoirs*, 25: 24–35.

Charon, J.M. (1994) 'A propos des aides à la presse', *Médiapouvoirs*, 33: 110–14.

Curran, J. (1978) *The British Press: A Manifesto*. London: Macmillan.

Curran, J. and Smith, A. (1987) *Impacts and Influences: Essays on Media Power in the Twentieth Century*. London: Methuen.

De Bens, E. (1997) *De Pers in Belgie*. Tielt: Lannoo.

Euromedia Research Group (1997) *The Euromedia Handbook: The Media in Western Europe*. London: Sage.

Ferris, P. (1971) *The House of Northcliffe: The Harmsworths of Fleet Street*. London: Weidenfeld & Nicolson.

Frazer, T. (1992) *Monopoly, Competition and the Law*, 2nd edn. Hemel Hempstead: Harvester Wheatsheaf.

Greenslade, R.(1992) *Maxwell's Fall*. New York: Simon & Schuster.

Grisold, A. (1996) 'Press concentration and media policy in small countries', *European Journal of Communication*, 11 (4): 485–509.

Guillauma, Y. (1988) *La presse en France*. Paris: Maspero.

Guillou, B. (1984) *Les stratégies multimédias des groupes de communication*. Paris: La Documentation Française.

Gustafsson, K.E. (1996) *Dagspressen i Norden: Struktur och ekonomi*. Lund: Studentlitteratur.

Hadenius, S. and Weibull, L. (1978) *Massmedier: En bok om press, radio och tv*, 2nd edn. Stockholm: Bonniers.

Holtz-Bacha, C. (1994) 'Ungelöste Strukturprobleme: Krise der französischen Tagespresse und staatliche Förderungsmechanismen', *Media Perspektiven*, 10: 489–95.

Howard, P. (1964) *Beaverbrook: A Study of Max the Unknown*. London: Hutchinson.

Hoyer, S. (1982) 'Pressen – Økonomisk utvikling og politisk kontroll', in S. Høyer (ed.), *Maktutredningen: Rapporten om massemedier*. Oslo: Universitetforlaget.

Jenkins, S. (1979) *Newspapers: The Power and the Money*. London: Faber & Faber.

Junqua, D. (1995) *La presse écrite et audiovisuelle*. Paris: Le Centre de Formation et de Perfectionnement des Journalistes.

Koschnick, W. (1990) *Rupert Murdoch, der Medientycoon*. Dusseldorf: Econ.

Koss, S. (1984) *The Rise and Fall of the Political Press in Britain*. London: Hamilton.

Kuhn, R. (1995) *The Media in France*. London: Routledge.

Luyckx, T. (1978) *Evolutie van de communicatiemedia*. Brussels: Elsevier Sequoia.

McNair, B. (1994) *News and Journalism in the UK: A Textbook*. London: Routledge.

Mahle, W. (1990) *Medien in Deutschland: Nationale und internationale Perspektiven*. AKM-Studien, vol. 32. Munich: Verlag Ölschläger.

Mahle, W. (1991) *Medien im vereinten Deutschland: Nationale und internationale Perspektiven*. AKM-Studien, vol. 37. Munich: Verlag Ölschläger.

Media Trends (1995) *Nordic Media Trends 1*. Göteborg: Nordicom.

Negroponte, N. (1995) *Being Digital.* London: Hodder & Stoughton.

Østergaard, B.C. (ed.) (1993) *The Media in Western Europe: The Euromedia Handbook*, 2nd edn. London: Sage.

Picard, R. (ed.) (1988) *Press, Concentration and Monopoly: New Perspectives on Newspaper Ownership and Operation.* Norwood, NJ: Ablex.

Rauen, B. (1992) 'Der italienische Werbemarkt zwischen Wildwuchs und Regulierung', *Media Perspektiven*, 9: 569–79.

Röper, H. (1994) 'Formation deutscher Medienmultis 1993: Fortschreitende Differenzierung und Internationalisierung', *Media Perspektiven*, 3: 125–44.

Röper, H. (1995) 'Formation deutscher Medienmultis 1994/95: Veränderungen, Pläne und Strategien der größten Medienunternehmen', *Media Perspektiven*, 7: 310–30.

Ruotolo, C. (1988) 'Monopoly and socialization', in R. Picard (ed.), *Press, Concentration and Monopoly.* Norwood, NJ: Ablex.

Sánchez-Tabernero, A. (1993) *Media Concentration in Europe.* Dusseldorf: European Institute for the Media.

Sauer, U. (1991) 'Auswirkungen des neuen Mediengesetzes in Italien', *Media Perspektiven*, 3: 161–9.

Schütz, W.J. (1996) 'Deutsche Tagespresse 1995', *Media Perspektiven*, 6: 325.

Seymour-Ure, C. (1991) *The British Press and Broadcasting since 1945.* Oxford: Blackwell.

Sparks, C. (1995) 'Concentration and market entry in the UK national daily press', *European Journal of Communication*, 10 (2): 179–200.

Tunstall, J. (1996) *Newspaper Power.* Oxford: Oxford University Press.

Tunstall, J. and Palmer, M. (1991) *Mediamoguls.* London: Routledge.

Zenith Media (1997) *Worldwide for Figures 1995.*

3

Does Public Broadcasting Have a Future?

Karen Siune and Olof Hultén

The structure of European broadcasting is undergoing radical change. This chapter will examine how the structure of European television has developed since the beginning of the television era, and particularly how it has changed during the past decade. It also considers what is in store for television in the next few years.

In the beginning, there was one national television channel in each of the European countries. Television was believed to have great power and because the frequencies for television transmission were a scarce good, television was closely guarded and highly regulated. Public service responsibilities were attached to national television. As with radio, television was seen as an instrument of a unified national cultural project bringing the same high-quality programmes nationwide to everybody (Hultén, 1995a).

Today much is different: all Western European countries have access to more than one national television channel, some of them public and some of them private, and all have access to several television channels from other countries. These channels are received either by satellite dishes or via cable networks. The former strict and national regulation has been rewritten in every country. National terrestrial broadcasting is still regulated, but it has proved very difficult to regulate what is crossing the borders into each individual country.

In Western Europe, the EU member states have implemented the directive on transfrontier television from 1989, revised in 1997, to create common rules as to what can, must or may be accepted in satellite broadcasting. This directive supersedes national legislation. Broadcasting on a level below national coverage – local, regional and by cable – is often only lightly regulated or not at all.

What, then, about the public service responsibilities attached to the old national broadcasting monopolies? What are they and how are they applied? What role does public service responsibility play in European media structure today? The changes in the structure of television in Western Europe has been described as a combination of liberalization and commercialization of the public sector. Many new private channels have been granted licences to operate in a commercial mode, and in competition with existing public channels. Only one public channel has been privatized, TF1 of France. In Denmark, the government is mooting the sale of the public channel TV2 to private investors. Whether this means a full privatization or not still has to be decided by the Danish parliament.

Competition definitely sets its own rules according to commercial logic, which has led to revisions of laws and regulations for commercial operators. The changing business climate has gradually found its way into the public service television sector. Most public channels are partly financed by advertising, and earlier restrictions have often been eased. Sponsorship and merchandising is encouraged to help increase, or at least protect, the revenue sources for these channels. Commercial practices can also, more indirectly, exert an influence over public service television. New uses of audience research and scheduling techniques, more emphasis on personalities in programmes, as well as competition for programmes and co-productions influence the behaviour of public service broadcasters.

In *Dynamics of Media Politics* (Siune and Truetzschler, 1992) it was hypothesized that regulation would continue in Europe with respect to national broadcasting, and that new means of legislation would be applied side by side with old ones. Challenges from local media would play a smaller role than the challenges from national and transnational commercial channels. Four factors were identified as the pillars of national public broadcasting: the level of political support, a stable financial base, viewer support and loyalty, and the reactions of the public broadcasters themselves to the changes. Would they adapt, adopt or perish?

Brants and Siune (1992) raised these questions in *Dynamics of Media Politics* and Hultén and Brants (1992) elaborated on some of the reactions of public broadcasters in the same volume. The developments since 1990 with respect to these key issues will now be described.

The concept of public service

In the early days of television broadcasting there was much concern about the new medium's power which led to very strict regulations on access to broadcast via television. Broadcasting monopolies with public service responsibilities were established all over Western Europe. Over the years, the definition of public service has changed and become wider, in tune with changing political and social conditions in Europe. There have always, of course, been differences of opinion about the precise operationalization of the concept in different countries. The 'old order' of public broadcasting in Europe of the early 1990s embodied at least the following defining public service elements (Brants and Siune, 1992: 102):

• *Some form of accountability* to (political representatives of) the public, other than through market forces, and realized through some form of administrative organization.

- *Some element of public finance*: commercial revenues are not excluded but any profit made is used for programming or service-oriented purposes, not made for its own sake, as in the private commercial system.

- *(Close) regulation of content*, ranging from the more general rules of balance, impartiality and serving minority interests to banning certain kinds of advertising, violence and pornography.

- *Universal (in a territorial sense) service*, whereby the audience is addressed more as citizens (mixed and pluralistic schedules) than as consumers (schedules determined exclusively by ratings).

- *Regulated entrance*, i.e. limits to the number of competing channels: the state may not retain its broadcasting monopoly but may intervene to achieve what is regarded as the legitimate cultural and social goals of public service.

All Western European countries still have normative prescriptions for public broadcasting (Euromedia Research Group, 1997). All the long-established channels still exist, but as Table 3.1 shows, the number of national channels has grown overall, most of them in the private sector. Only a few general public service channels with a mixed programme output have been started since 1990. However, in many countries, public broadcasting organizations have themselves launched new specialty channels, some of them clearly defined as commercial activities, some of them with a public service remit.

The definition of which channels to include in Table 3.1 is simple as far as terrestrial national stations are concerned. Take for example the UK: there are two BBC channels and three commercial channels. In addition, however, there are a great number of satellite and cable channels offered to British viewers, but none of these can reach more than a quarter of the potential audience. Table 3.1 includes only channels intended for a national audience, reaching more than half the population, regardless of delivery mode: terrestrial, satellite or cable. In another example, Sweden: there are three commercial channels which meet this criterion, one terrestrial and two delivered by satellite/cable. Another three, intended for Swedish viewers, fail to reach half the population. In Germany, the total number of commercial channels offered to viewers exceeds the nine in Table 3.1, but they reach less than half the population. In Switzerland, Schweiz 4 is operated by public broadcaster SRG since 1995, but its transmission time is shared with private operators. In the table, the channel appears as a public channel.

Excluded from Table 3.1 are pay channels. Canal Plus in France is, however, available to all viewers during certain time slots and is included. A number of public broadcasters have launched (1997) subscriptions channels. Well known are the BBC pay channels operated outside the UK. In Belgium, Denmark, France and Switzerland, public broadcasters participate in such ventures.

Table 3.1 *Number of national TV channels in Europe (1980/1990/1997)
reaching more than 50 per cent of households*

	1980		1990		1997	
	Public	Commercial	Public	Commercial	Public	Commercial
Austria	2		2		2	
Belgium	4		4	2	4	4
Denmark	1		2		3[a]	2
Finland	2		2	1	2	2
France	3		3	3	3	3
Germany	3		4	4	5	9
Greece	2		3	4	3	5
Ireland	2		2	(1)[e]	2	
Italy	3		3	6	3	6
Luxembourg		4		2(4)[b]		3(4)[c]
The Netherlands	2		3	1	3	6
Norway	1		1		2	3
Portugal	2		2		2	2
Spain	2		3[d]	3	3[d]	3
Sweden	2		2		2	3
Switzerland	3		3		4	
UK	2		2	2	2	3

[a] DR TV2 started October 1996 with reference to DR's public responsibility.

[b] Two are based in Luxembourg but beamed to other countries.

[c] Two are aimed at local audiences (RTL TÉLÉ Lêtzebuerg, RTL9) and five are aimed at other countries. One of these, however, is also the most watched channel in Luxembourg (RTL Television, the German channel).

[d] Regional public channels together reach the whole country.

[e] One private channel approved, but designated operator was unable to raise the necessary capital.

Table 3.1 shows little growth in the number of public television channels (but see Denmark, Germany, Norway and Switzerland). There has, on the other hand, been a significant increase in the number of private channels in almost all the countries listed. Not included is a growing number of commercial channels at the regional and local level.

European television today

The picture we see today, as we approach the year 2000, is of a European television structure with a mix of elements. The current European scene can be summarized in terms of the following key points.

System change

National public service channels still exist in all Western European countries (see Euromedia Research Group, 1997, for further details of the

Table 3.2   *Typology of national systems (1980/1990/1997)*

System	1980	1990	1997
Public monopoly/ licence fee only	Belgium, Denmark, Norway, Sweden		
Public monopoly/ mixed revenue	Austria, Finland, France, Germany, Greece, Iceland, Ireland, The Netherlands, Portugal, Switzerland, Spain	Austria, Denmark, Iceland, Ireland, The Netherlands, Portugal, Switzerland	Austria, Ireland, Switzerland
Private monopoly/ advertising only	Luxembourg	Luxembourg	Luxembourg
Dual system	Italy, UK	Belgium, Finland, France, Germany, Greece, Italy, Norway, Spain, Sweden, UK	Belgium, Denmark, Finland, France, Germany, Greece, Iceland, Italy, The Netherlands, Norway, Portugal, Spain, Sweden, UK

situation in each country). The typology of national systems (Table 3.2) shows a new picture. Dual systems predominate, while 'pure' (licence fee only) public broadcasting systems have disappeared. A purely commercial national system is still only to be found in Luxembourg. Austria, Ireland and Switzerland are all preparing for, or have invited, commercial channels. In 1994 Austria was found to be in breach of the European Convention on Human Rights because the government only allowed ORF to broadcast. Laws regulating private radio and cable TV have changed so that, eventually, national terrestrial television can be opened to private channels. In Ireland and Switzerland, private operators have been invited, but the limited size of their television markets seem to render commercial stations uneconomical, at least for the time being. A licensed broadcaster in Ireland has for many years tried to secure the financial backing necessary for launch. In Switzerland, a private operator transmits part time on a public network.

Increased competition

Since 1990, a number of national channels have entered the market. Only a few of these have been launched by the former monopolies. Iceland (population of 0.3 million) is now the only country where the public service broadcaster RUV is still operating a single TV channel. The three remaining public service monopolies all face strong competition from foreign channels spilling over their borders or carried by cable and satellite.

Most countries in Europe are allocated frequencies for three to five terrestrial, analog, national channels. Cable and satellite distribution has made it possible and much less expensive to reach audiences across national frontiers, as well as to expand the number of channels beyond the capacity of terrestrial frequencies. Germany is a particularly complex example. Here, available terrestrial and cable frequencies are controlled by the 16 states. The only channels guaranteed transmission in all states are the two national public service channels, ARD and ZDF, by way of treaties signed by all states. Through a combination of regional terrestrial frequencies, cable re-transmission and direct reception from satellite, many new channels, public and private, can now reach a majority of the population in Germany.

The changes at the national level have been a great challenge to public service broadcasting principles. The number of people who watch the former monopoly channels has been drastically reduced, from at best half of total viewing time to sometimes a small proportion (see Euromedia Research Group, 1997, for further details). At the bottom of the list is Greece, where the three ERT channels get less than 10 per cent of total viewing time. At the top is Denmark and Austria, with shares of 69 per cent and 62 per cent respectively. On average, public service channels in Europe account for around 40 per cent of total viewing (1996 figures).

Response by public broadcasting

There is no common picture or consensus of how commercial competition has affected public service broadcasting in Europe. Critics of public service claim that the strategy chosen by most of these channels is 'adaptation': they imitate commercial television in an effort to try to beat the com-petition. This has been the case of RTVE in Spain, RAI in Italy, and for a while Antenne 2 in France. As a result, RTVE has accumulated huge deficits, covered by the government. Antenne 2 was heading for big losses when the French government intervened to change the direction of policy. The strategy of keeping the public service flag flying high, which Hultén and Brants labelled 'purification', has only been used in a very limited way (see Hultén and Brants, 1992, for strategies public broadcasters could use to fight back). France and Germany have introduced more thematic public channels, such as Arte for culture, documentaries and current affairs, and 3SAT, Phoenix and Kindernet for culture, information and documentation, and children's programmes respectively.

The majority of public service channels have chosen to adapt to the situation, retaining the traditional scope of their output with a broad mixture of programmes in varying combinations. In northern Europe, there is an emphasis on news, current affairs and domestic fiction and culture. Gradual shifts are made in the schedules. The result, according to the critics of public service, is that public service channels have come to resemble commercial channels anyway (see Chapter 7).

Convergence and divergence

There is a serious lack of systematic and comprehensive research to verify or reject such a general conclusion, however. According to long-range German research (Krüger, 1991), the so-called *convergence hypothesis* is not supported by empirical evidence. This hypothesis stipulates that competition will gradually make public and commercial channels more and more alike, since they will imitate the best from each other. Eventually, commercial television will offer the same output as public service channels, which as a result will be made superfluous. After a decade of mounting competition, the empirical evidence – at least from north-western Europe – is more in support of a *divergence hypothesis*: public service channels and commercial rivals emphasize different content segments (see Krüger, 1996). Research in the Nordic region shows much the same picture (cf. Hultén et al., 1996). Public service channels have, during the 1990s, increased the amount of news and current affairs, as well as (in the Nordic region) domestic fiction (see also Chapter 8).

A pattern of divergence does not, however, mean that public service channels are not affected by competition or that the pattern is identical in every country. Schedules have clearly become much more target group oriented. The tradition of aiming at the whole population with each and every programme is gone. Such a practice does not reflect today's heterogeneous audiences; perhaps it never did. Highbrow or traditional cultural programmes tend to be pushed outside prime time. New formats of 'infotainment' (talk shows, reality shows, magazine formats) have also been introduced on public channels, in response to changing viewing patterns, but also to save money.[1] Cost increases (for example, in sports, films, top performers) have to be met by cost reduction elsewhere.

According to some students of public service, the important changes are not to be found at the macro level of output but within different genres: news becomes sensational, current affairs becomes infotainment and talk shows, drama becomes soap operas. Public service broadcasters defend themselves with the argument that there can be no public service without a public. New social and cultural circumstances require new styles and formats. Drama and fiction, flagships for public service broadcasters, are still as important, but today single productions of the classics, opera and ballet are rarely found. There is more contemporary fiction, as a rule offered in serial productions.

Transnationalization

Viewers have access to an ever greater volume of not only more foreign channels, but also a growing output of domestic programmes. European viewers prefer to watch national channels be they public or private because they offer domestic programmes of different kinds (see Euromedia Research Group, 1997, for national details). News, sports, entertainment and fiction are today produced in much greater quantities then ever before. These programmes, then, tend to push the less interesting imported 'schedule fillers', primarily US fiction, out of prime time. Satellite distribution has increased enormously. There has been a heavy concentration on Astra and Eutelsat satellites so that these two organizations cover 60 per cent of all distribution via satellites, while Intelsat and a number of national European satellites account for the remaining 40 per cent. In the Nordic region, however, two regional satellite platforms have replaced both Astra and Eutelsat. Spain and Italy could be heading the same way. Astra and Eutelsat continue to be the dominant platforms for the British, French and German markets.

The number of pay TV channels continues to increase. Of about 125 channels launched in Western Europe between 1993 and 1996, no less than 30 were premium subscription channels. Of the current 250 to 275 channels (the number depends on definition) about 50 are premium channels and about 100 channels freely available (*Screen Digest*, 1997: 57–64). The rest, 100 or more channels, are broadcast encrypted and often available in packages of thematic services for a subscription fee.

The proliferation of channels has resulted in a sharp increase in the total volume of broadcast hours. The number of channels, according to the CSA (Counseil Supérieur de l'Audiovisual) study (CSA, 1995), increased by 30 per cent between 1993 and 1995, from 137 to 187. Despite the fact that the dominant national channels devote more time and resources to domestic productions than before, the number of new channels in distribution has meant a growing demand for US programme import, nevertheless. Many channels are thematic, some are for re-transmission of programmes and whole channels, and there is a large amount of redundancy in the satellite distribution system overall.

Implications of change

From a national point of view, informative and educational functions are still fulfilled to various degrees by public service channels because they have an obligation to do so, and to a much lesser degree by prestigious national commercial channels. There is definitely a fear among many public service broadcasters that their political and economic support will diminish if they fail to attract viewers. One thing is sure: as the number of channels available to viewers continues to grow, each channel will on average achieve a decreasing percentage of viewing time. The perception of what share of viewing is necessary to legitimate the licence fee cannot be expected to remain the same.

Having more and more channels to choose between has also meant that viewers' expectations have changed, if not necessarily their preferences. Viewers today know that they can select programmes of their choice much more readily than 10 years ago. As a consequence, watching something that is not on one's list of preferences is less likely and does not have to be accepted by viewers. The downside of this is that the opportunity to be exposed to something unusual or unexpected diminishes. In order not to discourage large numbers of viewers, public service channels must learn how to attract viewers without abandoning the core public service values. Adoption of new programme and scheduling styles has come to dominate their adjustment to competition. There is a growing demand for more domestic fiction and entertainment which has influenced their schedules. There are, at the same time, large numbers of viewers who want and prefer quality news and information and more demanding varieties of fiction and entertainment found primarily on public service channels.

Journalists and producers are, of course, influenced by changes in media structure (see Tunstall, 1993). Some have accepted new goals such as defining a narrow part of the population as target audience versus an earlier orientation towards a mass audience. Others are still unwilling to drop the concept of 'broadcasting for the masses'. More and more directors of radio and television say that they are on air to satisfy the wishes of the public as measured in audience ratings. The logic behind their behaviour has changed over the years. Their social prestige has been reduced drastically according to opinion polls. The legitimacy of their services has been challenged by a diminishing shares of the audience.

It seems that European and national political actors still, in principle and verbally, support the public broadcasting ideals and the designated organizations economically by keeping up the flow of licence fee money (see below on the decision of the Amsterdam EU summit meeting). At least one of the necessary preconditions for public service broadcasting mentioned at the start of this chapter is still in place (see Chapter 12).

In summary, it can be said that challenges to public service channels come from the growing number of private national and transnational channels. Those challenges have influenced programme schedules, the mix and style of programme production and, according to many, also the quality of programmes, although this is more difficult to define and measure. The proliferation of channels, the fragmentation of audiences and the increased orientation towards fiction and entertainment in total output and viewers' diets have reduced the role of television in that part of the public sphere we attach to democratic functions, such as participation in public debate (see Chapter 9).

Television structure in the future

How much are we able to predict about the evolution of television? It depends on how far in the future one cares to look. In the near future, say to the year 2005, we might expect the following structural trends:

- Continued growth of the number of distribution channels to the home, by satellites foremost, but also by cable and in some countries by terrestrial networks. Satellite systems are busy expanding. In 1998, Astra and Eutelsat, the two satellite systems serving all of Europe, will together have approximately 220 TV transponders in operation, of which the majority can transmit digital and thus carry up to 1,000–1,500 TV programmes simultaneously. National/regional satellite systems will add even more, for example in the Nordic region. Two systems there have about 40 and plan to expand to as many as 75–100 transponders before the end of the century. Cable operators will offer digital services as well, which will add to their present capacity of up to 30–35 analog channels. In the UK, as many as 30 digital terrestrial channels will be available to households investing in digital decoders when services begin in 1998. There will be no shortage of transmission channels and scarcity of frequencies will be a problem of the past (see Chapter 5).
- There will be a steadily growing international integration of programme production and distribution. Big multinational actors will expand through their own subsidiaries in different countries or by alliances with other companies. This will lead to more concentration, horizontally, vertically and diagonally by a limited number of dominating corporations (see Chapter 4 for further discussion of these concepts).
- Pay television will expand greatly. During 1996, Canal Plus, Nethold and DF1 introduced bouquets of digital pay channels in France, Italy and Germany. BSkyB has announced plans to go digital with up to 200 channels from 1998. Currently controversial are the plans to divert the most attractive sporting events to pay channels, which in 1997 prompted the EU to protect some of these from encryption. Each EU country now has the right to exclude some of the most attractive events from pay TV distribution, thus circumventing free-market forces.
- Diversification of pay channels will be greater. Fragmented audiences will break up into ever-shrinking shares. After a period with more and more mass entertainment on channels financed by advertising, the trend towards more profiled thematic channels might also lead to a greater number of channels with more demanding, serious content. The analogy to this trend is the magazine market.

How public service broadcasters will relate to this last trend is a matter of political strategy and available resources. Two examples of different policies will illustrate this. In Germany, public broadcasters have not been allowed to start new thematic channels financed by subscription. ARD and ZDF have launched some specialty channels by cable and satellite for free, financed by licence fee revenues. Even this move is challenged by their commercial rivals. In the UK, the BBC is rather encouraged by the government to become more commercially innovative, as long as the BBC provides its basic public service requirement. This will be offered on the BBC digital network; the commercial offering will be available elsewhere (satellite and via commercial digital terrestrial networks). Financed by advertising, they will not carry the BBC brand name; financed by subscriptions, they will. In smaller countries, the limited market potential will make either avenue more problematic. Fixed licence fee revenues cannot be stretched to finance new channels. The number of paying subscribers to thematic channels is soon exhausted, especially if their themes become more narrowly defined.

For public service channels as well as commercial channels financed by advertising, audience fragmentation is a common problem: pay channels eat into their existing audiences. The better that new thematic channels perform, the greater the danger to existing channels. A successful migration of public service broadcasting from today's analog, mixed national channels to the multi-channel, digital, mixed/thematic and free/subscription channel environment of the future will depend on a carefully planned strategy and good timing of actions.

Is there a future for public service television?

'Public service channels are necessary for Europe's future', said Patrick Imhaus, the president of the French TV5 in an interview in the Danish newspaper *Politiken* in August 1996. TV5, broadcast by satellite to European cable households for the first time in 1984, is an element of French cultural policy. TV5, however, now broadcasts French-speaking public service programmes from four French-speaking countries to five continents so in his vision public service channels are not necessarily bound to national functions. On the contrary, public channels are bound to be international, according to Imhaus, and he refers to the so-called 'Brügge Group', a cooperation consisting of public television channels from 14 different European countries. The Franco-German Arte channel and the German-language satellite channel 3SAT are further examples of international cooperation.

Imhaus's perception is that the stability and integration of Europe depend on a plurality of TV offers which can transmit information and a better understanding of what goes on in Europe. The old functions of public service will still be the same, but the area of coverage will be much larger. In *Dynamics of Media Politics* (Siune and Truetzschler, 1992), it was argued that public service television could survive in Western Europe if the necessary economic and political will to sustain it were present. Gradually we see the challenges at the national level, but also a growing awareness of what is at stake. Intensified cooperation at the European level or at the multinational level in Europe could be one way to support the public service ideal and its praxis. Television as a mass medium in Europe is, however, so embedded in national cultures and contexts that most important for the future of public service broadcasting is support at the national level. In order for this to be possible, political actions taken at the European level must not destroy the ecosystems of television in the member states, whether through directives or interpretations exclusively favouring a free-market, commercial logic.

Discussions leading up to the first TV directive in 1989 showed great differences of opinions regarding the nature of television. On the one hand, it was seen as part of the cultural sphere of individual countries and thus in the domain of national sovereignty and, on the other hand, as just another sector of the free and common market of goods and services. The latter perspective became the dominant one. National governments have few options to deviate. Some consequences of such a perspective suffice to illustrate this.

If the cooperation between public service broadcasters in the European Broadcasting Union (EBU), which the Commission in 1993 defined as an unlawful cartel according to the Treaty of Rome, is denied the (temporary) exception granted until 1998, the implications will be great. The Commission noted in its decision that the EBU practices of purchasing certain sports rights for its members have such cultural and economic benefits for people, especially in smaller countries, that an immediate and drastic change was then not appropriate. Only if and when commercial channels, like public channels, serve all the viewers of member states will there be an effective alternative to the EBU. And only then would the cooperation to acquire exclusive rights for EBU members constitute an effective cartel.

If the European Commission finds today's practice in most member states of using advertising revenues to finance part of public broadcasting to represent unlawful state intervention in the free market as defined by the Treaty of the Community, then public service broadcasting in many countries will be seriously affected. If the Commission finds the use of subscription revenues to finance thematic specialty pay channels operated by public broadcasters to be in breach of the Treaty, this would of course apply to all member states. And if the use of mandatory licence fees from all TV households to finance publicly owned TV and radio enterprises were to be interpreted as an unlawful state subsidy, as defined by the same Treaty, then the whole basis on which public service broadcasting rests in Europe is threatened.

The last three examples have all been brought to the Commission as complaints from different commercial actors in member states in the past few years. It is not clear when the Commission, or eventually the EU Court, will be ready to make a final decision. Most crucial is, of course, the principle of the licence fee. On the initiative of the Dutch government, with support from Belgium, Ireland, Sweden, the EBU and the EU parliament, a proposal was made to the EU Council of Ministers that the licence fee for financing public service broadcasting be excluded from the definition of state subsidy as stated in Article 92 of the Treaty of Rome.

At the Amsterdam summit meeting, 16–17 June 1997, the member states' heads of government unanimously accepted a so-called protocol on public service broadcasting. In the protocol, funding for public service is recognized within the legal framework of the European Union, whereby Article 92 is pre-empted as it were. At the same time, the protocol requires that the specific requirements conferred upon public service broadcasting organizations in each member country (in accordance with the subsidiarity principle) be clearly defined. The protocol thus strengthens the position of public service in the dual broadcasting system of Europe.[2]

There is a need for a continous reappraisal of the role and function of public service broadcasting. In Europe, it has indeed a long tradition and its contribution to European democracy and culture cannot be denied. In the wake of new information technologies and in view of the enormous consequences for established mass media and the social order of new forms of information services and markets, many see the principles of public service broadcasting as highly relevant for the future. It is a service available to all, as autonomous of vested interests as possible, reasonably well financed and accountable to an open set of criteria.

In the total ecology of the broadcasting system, it seems more important to implement the criteria for good public service than to try to define what high quality is. Quality is always related to the beholder and the purpose. To achieve optimal pluralism, openess and variety, many models of broadcasting and practices are needed.

The turn of the century

As we approach the year 2000, media structure has changed drastically from the old broadcasting structure in ways summarized in Table 3.3. The former broadcasting monopolies are now everywhere under heavy competition; goals have turned into success needed for survival. Selection of material, produced and bought on a commercial market, has increasingly become the means to fill broadcasting schedules. Market orientation dominates the logic of responsibility. Reference groups for broadcasters consist more of consumers than of citizens. The focus for content has turned to dynamic processes full of sensations and new conflict dimension instead of decisions taken by the elite established in a well-known power structure. Finally, the perspective of activities is either on a more global or more individual level, instead of the national system which used to predominate.

Different ideals regarding the role national television has to play in future society come into conflict. The liberal view that no public service television is needed in societies with perfect market mechanisms is poised against concern about the role and use of television in future democracies.

Can policy save public service broadcasting?

The argument in this chapter has been that the future of public service broadcasting can be discussed as a special form of adaptation to the new

Table 3.3 *Old and new media structures*

	Old media structure	New media structure
Broadcasting	Monopoly	Competition
Goals	Democracy	Survival/success/profit
Means	Programme production/ selection of material	Selection of material/ programme mix
Logic	Responsibility	Market/economic
Criteria for selection	Political relevance	Sale
Reference group	Citizens	Consumers
Focus on	Decisions taken/power structure	Processes of policy-making/ new conflict dimension
Perspective	Nation/system	Individual and global

media structure dominated by private corporations, commercialization and internationalization.

If the main reason for changes in different types of broadcasting organization and in other types of media is increased competition at the national level from private and transnational interests, we can argue for greater protection of public service-oriented mass media. We shall do so if it matters to the functioning of the political system, if it is a challenge to democracy. In the context of this book, the key issue is that these changes have consequences for the role television can play in Western European democracies.

Public service broadcasting will continue as long as there is a dual system at the national or European level with enough support from the political system as well as the audience for its services. In the future, public service broadcasting will exist in the spirit of its traditional concept but not equal in practice to what it was during the monopolistic era (Søndergaard, 1996). A continous discussion and review of the qualities of public service broadcasting is necessary if it is to be kept alive via media policy initiatives.

Notes

1 Detailed analyses show that on public channels in Germany talk shows are devoted more to 'serious' social information and on commercial channels more to human interest and sensational information (Krüger, 1996).

2 '[T]he system of public broadcasting in the Member States is directly related to the democratic, social and cultural needs of each society and the need to preserve media pluralism. . . . The provisions of this Treaty shall be without prejudice to the competence of Member States to provide for the funding of public service broadcasting in so far as such funding is granted to broadcasting organizations for the fulfilment of the public service remit as conferred, defined and organized by each Member State' (http://ue.eu.int/Amsterdam/en/treaty/citizen/main.htm#90).

Bibliography

Bakke, Marit (1986) 'Culture at stake', in D. McQuail and K. Siune (eds), *New Media Politics*. London: Sage. pp. 130–51.

Brants, Kees and Siune, Karen (1992) 'Public broadcasting in a state of flux', in K. Siune and W. Truetzschler (eds), *Dynamics of Media Politics*. London: Sage. pp. 101–15.

CSA (1995) 'Europe: le satellite à l'heure numérique', *La Lettre*, 73.

Euromedia Research Group (1997) *The Euromedia Handbook: The Media in Western Europe*. London: Sage.

Hillve, Peter and Rosengren, Karl-Erik (1994) 'Swedish public service television quality for sale?', *Studies of Broadcasting*, 30: 87–114. Tokyo, Broadcasting Culture Research Institute.

Hultén, Olof (1995a) 'Sweden: broadcasting and the social project', in Mark Raboy (ed.), *Public Broadcasting for the 21st Century*. Luton: John Libbey/University of Luton Press, Acamedia Monograph 17.

Hultén, Olof (1995b) 'Diversity or conformity? Television programming in competitive situations', *The Nordicom Review*, 1: 7–22.

Hultén, Olof and Brants, Kees (1992) 'Public service broadcasting: reactions to competition', in K. Siune and W. Truetzschler (eds), *Dynamics of Media Politics*. London: Sage. pp. 116–28.

Hultén, Olof, Søndergaard, Henrik and Carlsson, Ulla (1996) *Nordisk Forskning om Public Service*. Göteborg: Nordicom.

Krüger, Udo M. (1991) 'Zur Konvergens öffentlich-rechtlicher und privater Fernschpro-gramme: Entstehung und empirischer Gehalt einer Hypothese', *Rundfunk und Fernsehen*, 39 (1): 83–96.

Krüger, Udo M. (1996) 'Tendenzen in den Programmen der grossen Fernsehsender 1985 bis 1995', *Media Perspektiven*, 8: 418–40.

McQuail, Denis and Siune, Karen (eds) (1986) *New Media Politics*. London: Sage.

Siune, Karen and Truetzschler, Wolfgang (eds) (1992) *Dynamics of Media Politics*. London: Sage.

Smith, Anthony (1980) *The Geopolitics of Information: How Western Culture Dominates the World*. New York: Oxford University Press.

Søndergaard, Henrik (1996) 'Kvalitet og mangfoldighed i det nye medielandskab. Refleksioner over public service i multi-kanal systemet', in Olof Hultén, Henrik Søndergaard and Ulla Carlsson (eds), *Nordisk Forskning om Public Service*. Göteborg: Nordicom.

Syvertsen, Trine (1992) *Public Television in Transition*. Oslo: Norges allmennvitenskapeliga Forskningsråd, Levende Billeder, no. 5/92.

Tunstall, Jeremy (1993) *Television Producers*. London: Routledge.

Wilensky, Harold L. (1964) 'The professionalization of everyone?', *American Journal of Sociology*, 70 (2): 137–58.

Wright, Charles R. (1959) *Mass Communication*. New York: Random House.

Wright, Charles R. (1960) 'Functional analysis and mass communication', *Public Opinion Quarterly*, 24: 606–20.

Wright, Charles R. (1995) 'Functional analysis and mass communication revisited', in Jay G. Blumler and Elihu Katz (eds), *The Uses of Mass Communications*. London: Sage Annual Reviews and Communication Research, vol. III. pp. 197–212.

4

Media Concentration and the Public Interest

Werner A. Meier and Josef Trappel

An old problem with new dimensions

Why study the impact of media concentration? Media diversity is one of the main preconditions ensuring political and cultural pluralism and effective citizen participation in democratic decision-making processes. Media diversity and media pluralism are prerequisites for effective freedom of expression and information as laid down by Article 10 of the European Convention on Human Rights (Committee of Experts, 1997: 3). The potential risks to diversity of ideas, tastes and opinions caused by media concentration is certainly an old problem but with new dimensions and severe effects on society.

However, according to Bagdikian (1990: 4–5), some dominant media corporations exercise a disproportionate power in the public sphere:

> Market dominant corporations in the mass media have dominant influence over the public's news, information, public ideas, popular culture, and political attitudes. The same corporations exert considerable influence within government precisely because they influence their audiences' perceptions of public life, including perceptions of politics and politicians as they appear – or do not appear – in the media.

Indeed, the development of large private enterprises and the increasing internationalization and globalization of media activities and competition within and across the media industry during the past 10 years has made media concentration a fundamental economic, social and political pan-European phenomenon.

The deregulation of the audiovisual sector performed by governments and parliaments in Europe enabled publishers and investors from outside the media to enter the broadcast market, with substantial impact on media concentration. New communication technologies created new markets and possibilities for diversification. Furthermore, new trends within the advertising industry, in particular towards centralization regarding organizational structures and distribution, as well as the general advertising trend favouring the electronic media, have led towards increased concentration. Preferred business growth strategies, such as the formation of trusts and strategic alliances, and the search for economies of scale and scope, as well as attempts to spread risks and the search for new fields of operation, have likewise furthered the concentration process. Moreover, profitable companies have reached their national growth limit. National anti-trust legislation prevents them from further growth and suggests diversification into related business in other countries. In addition, restrictions upon foreign ownership reinforce concentration at the national level.

Contradictions in popular, political and scientific discourse

Daring to evaluate the impact of media concentration on media pluralism, media diversity and media quality, one can make at least six observations:

1 *Market power expands to political power.* As the economic strength of media conglomerates develops, their position in society at large increases. Media conglomerates develop from merely economic factors in public life into powerful institutions in society and eventually increase their political power.

2 *There is a lack of public debate on media concentration.* As a consequence of the increasing influence of media conglomerates on public opinion, facts about spectacular deals are prominently reported, but hardly any coverage is dedicated to the perceived or envisaged effects of these deals. Journalists are in most cases directly affected but do not (or probably cannot because of internal pressure) report their own concerns. Usually media owners are keen to advertise the advantages of horizontal, vertical, diagonal and international concentration and state agencies play down the potential risks and threats of media conglomeration to the public sphere in particular and to democracy in general.

3 *Media concentration policy operates in favour of big, highly integrated media corporations.* The common policy of privatization and deregulation all over Europe has aggravated the very problems they were intended to solve. In other words, state and administrative bodies in charge of media regulations have willingly stimulated – and not reduced – the concentration process. Knoche (1996, 1997) for Germany and Tunstall (1996) for Great Britain come to similar conclusions: 'In practice a monopoly law, intended to restrain concentration, was manipulated into a Newspaper Preservation Policy under which preservation in practice meant, not less, but more, concentration of ownership' (Tunstall, 1996: 378).

4 *There is a lack of empirical evidence from scientific research bodies.* The media concentration debate within the scientific community did not

present much empirical evidence, but is rather characterized by a confusing discourse. Denis McQuail (1992: 116) argues that 'despite the amount and ingenuity of research, it is hard to avoid the conclusion that it has failed to establish clear general effects from monopoly conditions on the balance of cost and benefits, in performance terms. Where there is evidence, the effects seem to be quite small.' Much of the confusion is caused by two fundamentally different approaches to the problem: on the one hand, the competition policy concept developed by economists and, on the other, the public policy concept (political and cultural concept) by social scientists.

5   *The competition policy concept of economists dominates discourse and policy.* Some national and international organizations refer to media concentration only and entirely under aspects of competition law. Within this concept, all measures in respect of media concentration are analysed from the point of view of possible distortion of competition. Take, for example, the following comment from an OECD document: 'The first issue for a competition policy analysis of media ownership concentration is whether a particular pattern of common ownership of control of media interests so reduces the substitutable alternatives available and increases horizontal concentration that it allows an increased exercise of market power' (OECD, 1993: 154). This competition-related concept has to some extent dominated the public debate on the media concentration policy of the European Union, as the European Commission declared a number of intended mergers to be incompatible with the internal market on grounds of alleged distortion of competition.

6   *The public policy concept (political and cultural concept) of social scientists is marginalized in media policy and public discourse.* Contrary to the competition policy concept, social scientists usually consider media concentration as an important factor influencing the fundamental functions of the media in pluralistic democracies. Moreover, this concept analyses the effects of ownership concentration on media freedom and on editorial independence. In other words, the public policy concept of media concentration research aims at describing potential effects of media concentration on the public interest, rather than on competition. Both concepts, however, are interrelated to some degree. Because the ruling principle of the print media in Western democracies – and more and more also of the broadcasting sector – is market competition, any analysis with respect to democratic rights and values performed by these media must necessarily take competition law issues into consideration. 'Democracy is best served by a situation in which many media operate on the market by offering a wide range of ideas, information and types of culture and that a viable marketplace of ideas depends in large measure upon a competitive economic marketplace in the media field' (Committee of Experts, 1997: 5). However, the public policy concept expands one step further by identifying media

policy objectives related to media functions and media performance: media pluralism within and between media, media diversity and media quality. Media policy, according to this approach, goes clearly beyond competition policy by involving considerations related to basic democratic rights.

Frequently used terms and definitions

Whenever the academic and public discourse touches upon media concentration issues, terms and notions are used in widely divergent meanings. *Pluralism, diversity, variety* are often used interchangeably and different types of concentration (*horizontal, vertical, diagonal*) are mixed up. The confusion is further promoted by the fact that notions evidently change meanings when translated into different languages. The word *pluralism* exists equally in English, French and German, but apparently stands for different ideas. Therefore, some of the most widely used notions are defined for the purpose of this book as follows (largely using the concepts outlined by Sánchez-Tabernero, 1993):

- *Media concentration or media integration* is defined as an increase in the presence of one (monopoly) or a few media companies (oligopoly) in any market as a result of acquisitions and mergers or the disappearance of competitors. Media *concentration* and media *integration* are often used as synonyms.
- *Horizontal (or monomedia) concentration* stands for concentration processes within one and the same media industry sector. The merger of two newspapers in the same geographical market is considered as typical horizontal concentration. A horizontal merger provides the firm with an alternative to the rigour of competition and can create a highly profitable dominant corporation because the control of a substantial share of the market usually leads to oligopolistic profits.
- *Vertical media concentration* stands for activities of a given media enterprise seeking or exercising control over all or some steps necessary for the production and distribution of a given media, such as preparing information, reproducing information, distribution, promotion, financing operations and so on. A vertical merger allows a greater market autonomy by simplifying long-range planning processes and legal contracting. At the end, the vertically integrated firm has the benefit of reduced competition and a market advantage over the others.
- *Cross-media concentration* stands for a situation whereby one media enterprise controls through cross-ownership different media products or outlets in different media markets and industries. This type of concentration enables the enterprise to take advantage of cross-marketing

(cross-promotion) and economies of production costs and leads to further dominant market power and positions.

- *Diagonal or conglomerate concentration* stands not only for cross-media concentration but also for activities of an enterprise from another economic sector outside the media industries taking certain control in media markets. This type of integration increases the size and the financial, political and market power of the corporation, but does not necessarily reduce competition.

This list of types of media concentration can be supplemented by the notion of *international concentration*, referring to a situation where one of the four different types of concentration takes place across national borders. There are a number of other frequently used terms:

- *Pluralism of media* refers to the traditional political concept that is opposed to any kind of authoritarian regime. In the context of the media, pluralism can take the form either of *internal pluralism* (within one media enterprise by means of legal obligations for democratic internal structures or aiming at 'objectivity', for example within public service broadcasting organizations) or *external pluralism* (competition between a variety of media enterprises which together provide for *pluralism*).
- *The benefits of media pluralism* are usually understood to be as follows: it serves democracy by providing the citizens with a broad range of information and views needed for the effective exercise of citizenship; it gives minorities the opportunity to maintain their separate existence in a larger society; it limits social conflict by increasing the chances of understanding between potentially opposed groups or interests; it adds generally to the richness and variety of cultural and social life; it opens the way for social and cultural change, especially where it takes the form of giving access to new, powerless or marginal voices (Committee of Experts, 1997: 6).
- *Variety of media* refers to the mere amount of different media entities (daily newspapers, magazines, television stations, radio stations) available in a given market.
- *Diversity of media* refers to the more complex notion of unrestricted access to information (freedom of reception) and unrestricted access to the means to impart information (freedom of expression). The concept of diversity of media supply can be measured by four elements: (a) the existence of a plurality of autonomous and independent media; (b) diversity of media types and content available to the public (diversity of choice); (c) segments of society capable of addressing the public by means of media owned by, or affiliated to, them; (d) diversity of media content in relation to media functions (information, entertainment), issues covered and audience group served (Committee of Experts, 1997: 7). Both aspects of diversity are cornerstones of Article 10 of the

European Convention on Human Rights, the fundamental piece of international media legislation for European states. While everyone agrees with the principle of the freedom of reception and expression, a difficulty with diversity immediately arises when, on the one hand, the amount of information necessary to inform the public at large has to be defined and, on the other hand, the variety of the media is restricted by economic mechanisms (market forces) or political decisions. Different political concepts have put into place different models to safeguard diversity. While some policy concepts favour market forces as those perfectly adjusting media diversity, others provide for political and financial assistance to correct imbalances following the allocation forces of the market.

• Finally, the notion of *quality* refers both to high professional quality of a given medium (high journalistic quality) and to the standard of the medium from the perspective of the public at large (what is considered as a 'high-quality' newspaper or programme). However, as the notion media *quality* is defined in line with specific needs, norms and values, it becomes instrumental to the power and professional elites dominating the political arena and it is constantly redefined accordingly.

Arguments for oligopolistic or monopolistic media markets

Much research on media freedom has been motivated by fears about the effects of concentration and monopoly, especially in relation to newspapers. A wave of concentration in several Western European countries in the 1950s and 1960s stimulated research activities. Such research into press concentration paid particular attention to the number of independent titles, the growth of newspaper groups and chains, especially where this led to local monopoly ownership in a single circulation area or to cross-media ownership. During the 1980s and early 1990s, the dimensions of media concentration have grown both in terms of geographical scope and media fields affected.

Much current concentration actually involves transnational media corporations (TNMC), regardless of the media in question. However, the business focus of media mergers has shifted from newspapers to television or, more generally, from locally or regionally based print media to nationally and internationally based audiovisual media. This trend has been supported by the accelerated speed of technological innovation, in particular as regards broadcasting distribution technology and digitalized on-line technology (data compression, personal computers becoming multimedia units and so on). Despite or because of the newest 'merger mania', the common arguments in favour of concentration processes within and across industry are more accepted than ever in society.

Monitoring the pros and cons of the debate on media concentration leads to a list of common arguments in favour of concentrated markets and in favour of competition. Arguments in favour of monopoly or oligopolistic competition suggest that:

- Monopoly or oligopolistic competition is a natural tendency of capitalistic economic systems or the result of commercial and market success.
- The consolidation of production in the hands of large corporations is one of the basic facts of modern economic life, taking advantage of economies of scale and scope and reducing the cost of goods and services to consumers.
- In the case of newspapers, the average production cost per copy of a newspaper declines as the number of sold copies increases and joint operations can cut the costs of preparing the first copy if news-sharing agreements are worked out or a central news bureau is created.
- The search for optimum size of the enterprise in a given market might suggest a need to join forces with others, as growth is accelerated when size and output in general fit the respective market.
- In most cases, only large media companies are able to overcome high barriers to market entry and establish new media products and services.
- Technological innovation pushes media concentration as well. As the high cost of sophisticated equipment both in print and electronic media are further increased, smaller competitors are forced into market niches. High barriers to entry prevent new competitors from establishing competition.
- Smaller media markets need to concentrate the economic forces so as to maintain a high media quality standard.
- As most of the main players in the global media system have emerged in the USA, European media groups have to become more integrated in order to be competitive in the global market.
- Inevitably, media conglomerates have to match the high costs of the implementation of a 'global information infrastructure' leading to the 'global information society'.
- Large media groups are more capable of protecting their independence and autonomy from political, cultural, economic and other vested interests groups in general.
- Media operating from within the haven of a group can take bolder editorial stands without being exposed to pressure from local authorities. Only large media backed by the strength of a group can systematically engage in the investigative journalism necessary for a healthy democracy.
- There is no empirical or scientific evidence that editorial quality has declined under monopoly conditions. Several studies have failed to find significant differences between competing and non-competing newspapers. The same might be true for other media, in particular television broadcasting.

Based on the arguments above, two conclusions can be drawn. First, monopoly or oligopolistic competition, as well as workable or perfect competition, can foster pluralism, content diversity and quality (see Table 4.1). And, secondly, there are many economic motives for entrepreneurs to strive for dominant market positions. These include:

1   To take over a company – friendly or unfriendly – is usually easier than to build up a new undertaking due to high start-up costs.
2   Only companies of a certain size can take advantage of economies of scale (advantage of size) and scope (advantage of diversified supply).
3   Larger companies generally enjoy preferential treatment in terms of low-interest bank loans and other financial benefits.
4   In a given region larger companies enjoy more political influence and are generally better placed for tenders in public procurement.
5   Actors in dominant market positions have easier access to loans of working capital.
6   Only a large company has sufficient borrowing power in order to upgrade technology or to buy very costly software rights to exploit.
7   Larger and diversified companies are usually better placed to survive economic recessions.

Arguments for competitive media markets

In political as well as in business circles, it is a common belief that media concentration, especially on an excessive level, distorts competition and gives existing media corporations the ability to deny market access to new independent entrants and leads ultimately to monopoly, which is undesirable on social and economic grounds. This argument can be studied during the market introduction of digital television. Control of viewers' access is essential there for market success. Further arguments against media concentration can be summarized as follows:

- Media concentration leads to a reduction in the number of different information sources and to greater uniformity of content.
- Competition between media increases the independence of editors and broadcasters from government and the political system in general.
- The quantity and quality of local and regional political news declines significantly when competition is eliminated.
- Competition increases the responsiveness and accountability of media companies.
- Competition between media improves their overall quality and the coverage of local and regional news improves after establishing competition.
- A significant loss of both quality and diversity in the news product results from cross-media monopolies.

Table 4.1   *Market structure and performance: positive effects*

Monopoly	Internal pluralism, content diversity and quality
Oligopolistic competition	External and internal pluralism, media and content diversity and quality
Perfect competition	External pluralism, media and content diversity and quality

- All transactions that increase concentration of ownership in the mass media are undesirable and contrary to the public interest unless shown to be otherwise.
- An 'iron law' in the media business suggests that the dominant market position always allows for disproportionately higher profits.
- Large media corporations with dominant market positions are easily capable of taking over or driving out smaller companies. The nature of most media as 'joint commodities' serving two economic markets – readers/spectators and advertising – with one physical product or service (Lacy and Simon, 1993: 18) leads to a spiral, forcing the smaller competitor out of the market. The spiral is fuelled by the market leader's investment in quality, leading to higher market penetration and circulation figures, which in turn attracts advertisers who strengthen the dominating position of the market leader. Simultaneously, the entry barriers for new competitors becomes higher. This mechanism has been shown for newspaper markets, but the same market logic equally applies for broadcasting.
- Studies have not shown that monopolistic conditions have produced any economic benefit for consumers; on the contrary, consumers have tended to pay higher prices for newspapers under monopoly conditions.
- Companies seek to establish higher degrees of market power (domination) by concentrating both the supply side and the demand side. This process leads finally to monopoly profits.
- Dominant actors in the market can use their financial power to cross-subsidize certain products in order to undercut the price of a competitor and foster their own performance.
- The accelerated concentration process remains in sharp contradiction to the ideology and theory of liberalism and leads therefore to increased legitimation problems for the economy as well as for society.

Tables 4.1 and 4.2 together suggest six different results of competition, some of which contradict each other.

Political influence and concentration

Besides economic and financial arguments, there are also the following of social and political motives for entrepreneurs to aim at increased company size and further growth:

Table 4.2   *Market structure and performance: negative effects*

Competition	⇨	Oligopolistic competition	⇨	Monopoly	⇨	Uniformity of content, reduction of sources and pluralism
Competition	⇨	Oligopolistic competition	⇨	Favouring mainstream positions		
Competition	⇨	Belligerent competition	⇨	Increase of sensational, marketing and chequebook journalism		

- Media ownership on a large scale allows an increase in social status, prestige and privilege.
- Mass media in dominant market positions allow owners, shareholders, managers and editors to use and abuse their programmes and titles as ideological vehicles.
- Media competition reduces the effects of direct and indirect relationships between ownership, control and ideological content.
- According to Humphreys (1996: 74–5), powerful media moguls and executives of big media firms have at times exercised pressure on politicians and political processes quite directly.

> In the first place, it is commonly accepted that press bias can affect the outcome of elections, although quite to what extent is a matter of fierce debate. . . . Secondly, media power can be deployed quite overtly to influence the direction of public policy on issues of public concern. Thirdly, media proprietors and top editors have exerted more subtle kinds of influence, playing upon the natural sensitivities of politicians about how they are represented in the media. Fourthly, they certainly act as 'gatekeepers' of media access. Fifthly, powerful media proprietors and leading editors may gain an influential voice in the innermost policy sanctums of individual parties and governments. . . . Certainly, it does not seem too polemical to suggest that the commercially organised press as a whole is naturally more likely to favour conservative political interests. . . . Press concentration . . . has tended to reduce the ideological pluralism of the press.

Media concentration in Europe: facts and figures

In order to obtain a preliminary, but reliable, picture, at least the following questions should be addressed and answered:

- Who are the main big players in and from Western Europe on the different media markets? Which media sectors are most concentrated at the national and European level?
- Which media companies dominate the various sectors of the European media industry?
- Is there any correlation between the dominance and position of the main players on a market and the degree of media pluralism?

• Is there any correlation between the dominance of large firms and the degree of homogenization (standardization) of content?

Table 4.3 shows three different rankings of the top European media corporations. Based on the figures, one can make several observations. According to Herman and McChesney (1997), Bertelsmann and Polygram, which was taken over by Seagram in 1998, are the only vertically integrated European media conglomerates in the global media market. Most of the top 10 dominant firms are based in the USA and operate in rather oligopolistic markets with substantial barriers to entry. Another 30–40 companies, 17 of which are Western European, round out important positions in the system. The first- and second-tier firms 'compete vigorously on a non-price basis, but their competition is softened not only by common interests as oligopolists, but also by a vast array of joint ventures, strategic alliances, and cross-ownership among the leading firms' (Herman and McChesney, 1997: 104).

According to Hachmeister and Rager (1997), half of the top 50 media corporations are based in Europe (eight in Germany, seven in Great Britain, four in France, three in Italy, two in the Netherlands and one in Luxembourg). In 1995, all 25 firms together could announce revenues of 135 billion DM. The top five companies of the 25 have a share of 42 per cent of total revenues.

According to statistics collected by the European Audiovisual Observatory (1997), the European firms in the audiovisual sector among the top 50 have a share of 38 per cent, followed by US companies with 36 per cent. Among the top 50 audiovisual firms from Europe, 11 are British, eight are German, seven are French, five are Turkish, three are Spanish and three are Dutch. Most of the firms are present in only one national market. Big European TV multinationals are only CLT and Canal Plus. CLT-Ufa, now under joint Bruxelles-Lambert/Bertelsmann control, is a major national player in each of the Benelux, German and French markets. Canal Plus, thanks to the acquisition of Nethold, is now the top pay TV operator in many Western European countries with the exception of Great Britain, Spain and Germany. In Germany, Bertelsmann and Kirch were constructing a dominant position in 1998 through the pay TV channel Premiere and the digital bouquet DF1. News Corporations, the archetype for the twenty-first century global media firm with sales of approximately 10 billion dollars in 1996, has still not joined any significant European ventures outside Great Britain, except the interests in the German TV channel Vox. None of the other big British media corporations, such as Carlton, Granada and Pearson, has ventured outside its home market. France TF1 has not taken any major steps abroad either. Berlusconi's Fininvest has only one major operation outside Italy, Spain's Tele 5. In short, it looks as if top European TV groups are rather unwilling or unable to globalize their activities on a large scale. On the other hand, there are no major general interest TV channels in Europe owned by American corporations either.

Table 4.3   *The largest European private media corporations*

European media firms (Herman and McChesney)		Sales (billion $)	Ranking of European firms on global scale (Hachmeister and Rager)		Revenues (billion DM) (1995)	Ranking top European enterprise in audiovisual sector (EAO)		AV revenues (million ECU) (1995)
First tier								
Bertelsmann	BRD	15 (1996)	2 Bertelsmann	D	20.6	ARD	D	5,170
Polygram (Seagram)	NL	6 (1997)	7 Havas	F	10.4	Polygram	NL	4,230
Second tier								
CEP	F	8.8 (1996)	8 ARD	D	9.5	Kirch	D	4,023
EMI	GB	5.4 (1996)	10 Lagardère Groupe	F	8.8	Bertelsmann	D	3,929
Reuters	GB	4.1 (1995)	11 Polygram	NL	7.9	Thorn EMI	GB	3,643
Granada Group	GB	3.6 (1996)	13 Reed Elsevier	GB	7.2	BBC	GB	2,520
BBC	GB	3.5 (1995)	17 Reuters	GB	6.1	CLT	LUX	2,446
Axel Springer	BRD	3.0 (1993)	20 KirchGruppe	D	5.4	RAI	I	1,917
CLT	LUX	3.0 (1996)	21 BBC	GB	5.0	Carlton	GB	1,903
Pearson	GB	2.9 (1996)	22 EMI	GB	5.0	Canal Plus	F	1,496
United News and Media	GB	2.9 (1996)	26 CLT Multi Media	LUX	4.5	TF1	F	1,407
Carlton Comm	GB	2.5 (1996)	27 United News and Media	GB	4.3	Fininvest	I	1,373
TF1	F	1.8 (1996)	28 Axel Springer	D	4.2	BSkyB	GB	1,215
Kinnevik	S	1.8 (1996)	29 Pearson	GB	4.1	ZDF	D	1,149
Bauer	BRD	1.7 (1993)	32 Carlton	GB	3.6	RTL	D	1,137
Wolters Kluwer	NL	1.7 (1994)	33 RAI	I	3.5	Rank	GB	920
RCS	I	1.6 (1993)	35 Fininvest	I	3.5	SAT1	D	868
VNU	NL	1.4 (1994)	41 WAZ	D	3.1	France 2	F	842
CEP	F	k.A.	42 Canal Plus	F	2.9	France 3	F	808
Prisa Group	E	k.A.	43 Bauer	D	2.9	Pro7	D	749
Antenna 3	E	k.A.	44 Holtzbrinck	D	2.8	ORF	A	743
			45 VNU	NL	2.7	SRG	CH	739
			46 TF1	F	2.6	Nethold	NL	733
			49 Rizzoli	I	2.3	Granada	GB	626
			50 ZDF	D	2.1	RTVE	E	624

Sources: European Audiovisual Observatory, 1997; Hachmeister and Rager, 1997; Herman and McChesney, 1997

The American presence is strong and expanding in the thematic cable and satellite sector, especially in children's channels, music video and TV documentaries.

Monomedia concentration in Western Europe

Contrary to the rather slow trend towards international concentration, relatively strong monomedia concentration can be observed in most countries. Usually, a dominant market position is assumed when (a) one supplier reaches a market share between 30 and 35 per cent; (b) two or three suppliers reach a market share of 50 per cent and more; (c) four or five suppliers reach a market share of 60 per cent and more. Based on this assumption, the following picture on the status of the monomedia concentration in Western Europe can be drawn (Table 4.4).

If one takes the accumulated market share in the newspaper sector, the concentration ratio is high in Luxembourg, the United Kingdom, the Netherlands and the French-speaking community of Belgium. Based on the share of the top five titles in total circulation, the phenomenon of press concentration appears widespread, despite missing figures in quite a number of cases.

In the TV sector, despite privatization and deregulation, the market share of the top two TV channels is still extremely high. Even in the German market, where six private and two public general interest channels are looking for sufficient ratings on a national level, the two market leaders have a share of 31 per cent (audience) and 52 per cent (advertising).

Of the origins of fictional TV programmes, almost two-thirds of all broadcast TV programmes in the top two channels are American. The domination is even higher if one takes not only the two leading channels but also the others in the market. In most cases, the share of fictional programmes takes a dominant position within a general interest TV channel. On average, 75 per cent of all movies shown in the countries given in Table 4.4 are of American origin.

Concentration on the national level

As Table 4.4 clearly shows, many important indices concerning horizontal, vertical and diagonal concentration are not available in many countries. Despite the missing transparency and data, the case of Germany can give some explanation of the status of media concentration. In Germany, five of six media markets (see Table 4.5) are controlled by companies with a dominant market position. With few exceptions daily newspapers operate on a regional market: 52 per cent of all cities above 100,000 inhabitants are

Table 4.4   *Monomedia concentration ratios in Western Europe*

Country	Circulation share of top 5 publishing companies	Circulation share of top 5 titles	Audience market share of top 2 TV channels	Share of US film (fiction) in top 2 TV channels	Share of top channel genre	Share of US film in movie theatres
Austria	45	69	68	61	46 (ORF)	–
Belgium (fr)	77	55	47	58	24 (RTBF)	–
Belgium (fl)	–	–	58	–	40 (BRTN)	70[a]
Denmark	50	49	78	65	41 (TV2)	81
Finland	42	39	71	69	31 (MTV3)	77
France	–	–	60	39	36 (TF1)	54
Germany	–	23	31	69	34 (RTL)	87
Ireland	–	–	60	–	42 (RTE)	91
Italy	–	–	47	63	38 (Canale 5)	63
Luxembourg	100	–	–	–	–	82
The Netherlands	95	–	39	72	24 (Ned 1,2,3)	82
Norway	53	38	80	–	23 (NRK)	74
Portugal	55	91	88	–	37 (RTP)	70
Spain	–	–	51	70	48 (TV3)	72
Sweden	49	33	55	–	28 (SVT)	66
Switzerland (d)	–	–	45	–	28 (SF DRS)	75[a]
Switzerland (fr)	–	–	49	–	36 (TSR)	–
UK	95	–	68	79	31 (ITV)	82

[a] All regions.

Sources: Committee of Experts, 1997; European Audiovisual Observatory, 1997

Table 4.5   *Monomedia – concentration in Germany (1994/1995)*

Media market	Year	Market share of top 3 (%)	Market share of top 5 (%)
Daily newspaper (circulation)	1995	34	42
Magazines (circulation)	1995	67	–
Magazines (revenue)	1994	45	60
Television: advertising revenue	1995	78	88
Television: audience	1995	48	72
Film distribution	1994	57	78

Source: Seufert, 1997

monopoly markets. Similarly, 56 per cent of all local and regional radio markets are dominated by monopoly radio stations.

Concerning the vertical and diagonal concentration (Röper, 1997; Seufert, 1997), the majority of newspaper publishers own their printing presses and most daily newspapers are distributed by an in-house company. All traditional publishers, such as Bertelsmann, Springer, Holtzbrinck, WAZ Group, Bauer and Burda, have invested in other media sectors, especially in radio and television. In addition, all media corporations are also transnationally integrated.

Concentration on the company level

Data on vertical and diagonal (cross-media ownership) concentration are difficult to obtain and less differentiated. However, most European media companies, with the exception of Reuters, operate in more than one media industry.

Since monomedia concentration has reached its legal limit in national markets, one could argue that a strategy for achieving synergies may be one of the most promising means of growth for large media companies. Therefore, mergers, acquisitions, joint ventures and strategic alliances play a role in cross-media concentration. Although cross-industry concentration seems to be a rather invisible form of concentration, Albarran and Dimmick (1996) have observed three different corporate strategies in order to get control of business in different media industries:

1   *Diversification*: the movement of a corporation into an industry in which it has not previously operated (see Table 4.6).
2   *Repurposing*: the use of an already existing media content in a new mode.
3   *Talent contracting*: contracting successful talent or transplanting existing content for different media owned by the same entity (Albarran and Dimmick, 1996: 43). Here, synergies result from control of the content

Table 4.6 *Diversification strategies by top European transnational media corporations*

	Newspapers	Magazines	Books	TV	Radio	Film	Music	Video	On-line	Multimedia	Other activities
Bertelsmann	X	X	X	X	X	X	X	X	X	X	Book clubs, rights/licences
Havas	X	X	X	X	X				X	X	Advertising, tourism, rights
Lagardère Group	X	X	X	X	X	X			X	X	Advertising
Polygram			X	X		X	X	X			Rights/licences
Reed Elsevier	X	X	X						X	X	Fairs and exhibitions
Kirch	X			X		X					Rights/licences
EMI							X				
CLT Multi Media		X		X	X	X		X	X		Rights/licences
United News and Media	X	X	X	X					X		Fairs and exhibitions, research
Axel Springer	X	X	X	X	X	X					
Pearson	X	X	X	X						X	Museums and leisure parks
Carlton			X	X				X			Post-production
Fininvest	X	X	X	X		X		X			Advertising
WAZ	X	X		X	X						
Canal Plus				X		X	X				Sports clubs
Bauer		X	X	X							
Holtzbrinck	X	X	X	X	X				X		Research
VNU	X	X	X	X	X					X	
Rizzoli	X	X	X	X		X		X			

Source: Hachmeister and Rager, 1997

or the performer's fame, and the capability of spreading the costs of the contract or content over multiple outlets, while at the same time deriving revenues from multiple sources.

The three top companies, Bertelsmann, Lagardère Group and Havas, are almost wholly integrated in all important media industries. Table 4.6 also shows that the concentration of forces has changed from traditional print media to the booming TV industry. Almost every top company has interest in this sector.

In general, cross-media ownership through vertical and cross-media integration allows for a variety of expanded efficiencies, including:

- Sharing and recycling of programme software (especially news, economic data, films, soaps, events).
- Cross-marketing and cross-promotion among the different media outlets and platforms.
- Bulk order or group discount for raw material and software.
- Sharing of costly resources in the form of manpower and know-how (journalists, market research, management skills).
- Offering clients package discounts, for instance in advertising. Transnational media corporations such as Bertelsmann routinely offer clients package discounts in advertising that cut across several of the company's own print and audiovisual media.
- Sharing of printing and distribution efficiencies.

Effects on economic competition

If media markets are concentrated and horizontally and vertically integrated, it is assumed that the conduct of the media company, especially pricing behaviour, changes with the final aim of raising profits. There are at least four areas in which media companies operating as monopolies can dictate their conditions to the market (Akhavan-Majid et al., 1991: 59–66).

First, media monopolies can adjust the price per copy upward. There are only a few studies comparing prices of monopoly newspapers to prices of competing newspapers. 'Competition lowers the prices of products, according to classical theory. One would thus assume that consumers benefit from papers operating in competition with other papers. The literature of newspaper economics, however, does not bear out this contention fully' (Picard, 1988: 62). 'In terms of circulation pricing, competition has also been shown not to be fully beneficial.' Competing 'papers have marginally significant higher rates for subscriptions than do monopoly newspapers' (Picard, 1988: 63).

Secondly, media monopolies can adjust the price of advertising upward. If the rate does not increase excessively there will be, *ceteris paribus*, no significant change to other media like television, radio or magazine. 'The literature strongly supports the view that monopoly papers have higher advertising rates than other papers' (Picard, 1988: 64).

Thirdly, media monopolies can adjust the price of labour downward. In limited markets, such as French-speaking Switzerland where one publishing house controls the four largest daily newspapers and together with the Société de radiodiffusion et de télévision de la Suisse romande approximately 80 per cent of the journalistic labour force, journalists remain with few options for mobility and change.

Fourthly, according to Entman (1985), competition – and not monopoly – enhances the quality of newspapers (meaning more cosmopolitan, indepth news and editorials); provides more diversity of views on public issues; encourages more fairness and balance in presenting political controversies (less one-sided, propaganda or biased news); stimulates greater responsiveness to the interests of citizens and provides stories and editorials that help encourage enlightened and rationally participant citizens. He concludes that his findings and analysis may apply to the electronic media too. 'Market pressure may not strongly and consistently promote diversity, fairness, or any other journalistic trait' (Entman, 1985: 164).

Effects on pluralism, diversity and quality

Since media – newspapers and electronic media – perform key functions for the development and reproduction of a democratic public sphere, a greater emphasis has to be placed on product performance. This must be especially underlined, since ambivalent results are common in research about media concentration effects: a 'majority of studies indicate no effect – or a balancing of advantages and disadvantages' (Hale, 1991: 35).

In a Canadian research project the news coverage of different newspapers in competitive and monopolistic situations have been analysed. The results of the study clearly indicate that there is no immediate link between content quality and the competitive situation of the market. 'Professional perspectives on journalism, not the presence or absence of competition, determine the content of the daily newspaper. Competition does not insure diversity' (McCombs, 1988: 137). Actually, the assumption that demise of a competitor will be followed by diminished quality is rebutted by the evidence. 'Only a few changes from before to after the end of competition were found, and all of these were positive changes in the quality of the editorial product' (McCombs, 1988: 136). Finally, the authors of the study conclude that these 'empirical findings undermine the notion that vigorous use of the antitrust statutes can insure a diversity of information in the marketplace' (McCombs, 1988: 136).

Further evidence from journalism research suggests that factors other than monopolistic competition are prominently threatening content diversity. In particular, homogeneity of media content is furthered by:

- A common news delivery system. International and national news is delivered by a few dominant global news agencies. National and local news is delivered by only one national news agency. Overall, journalistic sources of news coverage are limited in scope.
- A rather limited structure of news sections focusing journalists' attention, and thus media content, on simple structured dimensions of geography (local versus national versus global) and subject (politics versus economics versus culture and sports).
- The fact that journalists are dependent on the same public-relations oriented sources of powerful institutions and interest groups in society.
- The fact that news selection criteria focus journalists' attention, and thus media content, on the decisions and activities of the most powerful political actors, such as the president, the government and the parliament on different levels of a national political system.
- The fact that news selection criteria focus journalists' attention, and thus media content, on subjects like madness and love, power and powerlessness, death, drama, harm, passion and glory.
- The fact that most media organizations cover markets with a wide variety of different publics which are diversified and stratified. Thus *omnibus media*, transporting everything for everybody, often reduce diversity of opinions and commentary to the lowest common denominator.

All these findings suggest after all that economic competition cannot guarantee the highest degree of content diversity. Monopolistic media and media in a competitive market are not to be distinguished in accordance with their content. As shown above, competition does not automatically mean content diversity. There is evidence that even the contrary is true as regards quality. So-called competitive newspapers and television stations are often re-writes and re-broadcasts of the same material. A given medium in a monopolistic market will normally generate more profits, reflected in even greater editorial expenditures and journalistic quality. But this investment in quality is subject to the owner of the medium who might have different (economic) interests. In particular, *diagonal concentration* might convert profitable media in monopolistic markets into cash-cows to the detriment of further enhancement of journalistic and programme quality.

The decisive criterion for these media is the purpose of the owner and publisher. If investments in quality do not promise increased profits (saturated markets) and the purpose of the media is to generate profits, monopolistic media will hardly further improve quality. Generally, monopolies might focus on high profits rather than on social responsibility. Furthermore, monopolies in the media field are created and defended by a particular socioeconomic group, described by Candussi and Winter (1988: 140), who suggest that 'concentration and monopoly heighten the homogeneity of owners – essentially a small group of economies elites – and reinforce and legitimate the status quo with respect to ideology and consciousness'.

Another aspect of the effects which media concentration has on quality concerns the professional performance of journalists. The more media become exposed to profit-generating objectives (a serious concern in the cases of diagonal and multimedia concentration), the more *normative journalism* will be replaced by *market journalism*. Advertisers do not pay for high-level quality journalism, but for the requested 'quality' of the sector of society to be reached. Market journalism, however, provides for a different construction of reality in the media and for a substantially different media reality. Its first and foremost objective is not to inform but to satisfy the targeted sector of society.

Conclusions and perspectives

In a discourse on media concentration all traditional opinions must be re-examined thoroughly with regard to their empirical validity. In particular, we need to ask to what extent does economic variety also mean content diversity? To what extent does a reduction in the variety of broadcasters also mean a reduction in the diversity of opinions? To what extent can single interventions achieve all the objectives? To what extent are the national authorities and administrations interested in the implementation of restrictions on concentration? To what extent can academic media research postulate a meaningful connection between capital/ownership structures and editorial independence, content diversity and editorial quality?

The complex matter of media concentration needs careful distinctions between different types of concentration (horizontal, vertical, diagonal) and different markets. Furthermore, effects can only be assessed by different actors and societal levels affected (public at large and individual recipient, public interest, national and international media policy, media enterprises, media content). For the *individual recipient*, concentration processes reduce the diversity of information since pluralism becomes potentially limited by an increase in distribution channels under the control of very few owners or by barriers limiting access to the media. The *public interest* is affected by diagonal and horizontal media concentrations as overriding interests of profit generation for shareholders strictly limit the genuine social responsibility of the media.

For *media enterprises*, however, horizontal and vertical concentration is largely favoured as an important element of modern economy, generating new and interesting jobs, better education, learning on the job facilities, greater job security and higher wages. Usually the conclusions drawn by enterprises look overwhelmingly positive: power, influence and prestige increase, predominant market position can be achieved, new innovative possibilities are created, synergies between different products pay off, risks are dispersed, economies of scale and scope raise efficiency, profitability increases and, with regard to international competition, their own competitiveness is ensured. But the strengthened position of the enterprise in the concentrated markets could be 'abused' by lowering quality and diversity and by increased prices. Furthermore, economic power could transform itself into uncontrolled editorial and even political power, as can easily be studied in the case of the parliamentary election campaign of Silvio Berlusconi in early 1994.

Changes in the structure of the media business are envisaged by the mass market implementation of digital media. The early 1990s saw, at different speeds and to different degrees, the introduction of new digital media, fulfilling the classic criteria of mass media. By 1995, the Internet carried short sequences of moving image as well as sound, which must be considered as television and radio, according to the traditional definitions, since it is available to those who own or use reception equipment (in analog time called TV set and radio). Moreover, news agencies sell their content on the Net on the basis of subscription (Reuters). Other news media are in full or in part accessible on the Internet. These new forms of transmitting data wipe out or ignore the traditional borders of print and electronic media.

If the globalized media industrial complex is designed primarily to serve market ends and political goals, not citizenship needs, it is high time for responsive and accountable media researchers to face the complexity of the concentration process and to come up with detailed research findings in the true sense of the public interest.

Bibliography

Akhavan-Majid, Roya, Rife, Anita and Gopinath, Sheila (1991) 'Chain ownership and editorial independence: a case study of Gannett Newspapers', *Journalism Quarterly*, 68 (1/2): 59–66.

Albarran, Alan B. and Dimmick, John (1996) 'Concentration and economics of multiformity in the communication industries', *Journal of Media Economics*, 9 (4): 41–50.

Bagdikian, Ben (1990) *The Media Monopoly*. Boston: Beacon Press.

Candussi, Dores A. and Winter, James P. (1988) 'Monopoly and content in Winnipeg', in R.G. Picard, J.P Winter, M.E. McCombs and S. Lacy (eds), *Press Concentration and Monopoly: New Perspectives on Newspaper Ownership and Operation*. Norwood, NJ: Ablex. pp. 139–45.

Committee of Experts on Media Concentrations and Pluralism (MM-CM) (1997) *Report on Media Concentrations and Pluralism in Europe*, rev. edn. Strasbourg: Council of Europe. 20 January.

Eaman, Ross A. (1987) *The Media Society: Basic Issues and Controversies*. Toronto and Vancouver: Butterworths.

Entman, R.M. (1985) 'Newspaper competition and First Amendment ideals: does monopoly matter?', *Journal of Communication*, 35 (3): 147–65.

European Audiovisual Observatory (1997) *Statistical Yearbook 97*. Strasbourg: Council of Europe.

Gershon, Richard A. (1997) *The Transnational Media Corporation: Global Messages and Free Market Competition*. Mahwah, NJ: Lawrence Erlbaum.

Hachmeister, Lutz and Rager, Günther (1997) *Wer beherrscht die Medien? Die so grössten Medien Konzerne der Welt*. Munich: Verlag C.H. Beck.

Hale, Dennis F. (1991) 'The influence of chain ownership on news service subscribing', *Newspaper Research Journal*, 12 (3): 34–46.

Herman, Edward S. and McChesney, Robert W. (1997) *The Global Media: The New Missionaries of Global Capitalism*. London and Washington: Cassell.

Humphreys, Peter, J. (1996) *Mass Media and Media Policy in Western Europe*. Manchester: Manchester University Press.

Knoche, Manfred (1996) 'Konzentrationsförderung statt Konzentrationskontrolle', in Claudia Mast (ed.), *Markt – Macht – Medien*. Konstanz: UVK Medien.

Knoche, Manfred (1997) 'Medienpolitik als Konzentrationsförderungspolitik', *Medien Journal*, 2: 14–25.

Kohlstedt, Alexander et al. (1996–7) 'Medienkonzentration und strategische Allianzen im internationalen Medienmarkt', in Bernd-Peter Lange and Peter Seeger (eds), *Technisierung der Medien*. Baden-Baden: Nomos Verlagsgesellschaft. pp. 165–91.

Lacy, Stephen and Simon, Todd (1993) *The Economics and Regulation of United States Newspapers*. Norwood, NJ: Ablex.

Lorimer, Rowland (1994) *Mass Communications*. Manchester: Manchester University Press.

McCombs, Maxwell E. (1988) 'Concentration, monopoly and content', in R.G. Picard, J.P. Winter, M.E. McCombs and S. Lacy (eds), *Press Concentration and Monopoly: New Perspectives on Newspaper Ownership and Operation*. Norwood, NJ: Ablex. pp. 129–37.

McQuail, Denis (1992) *Media Performance: Mass Communication and the Public Interest*. London: Sage.

McQuail, Denis (1994) *Mass Communication Theory: An Introduction*, 3rd edn. London: Sage.

OECD (1993) *Competition Policy and a Changing Broadcast Industry*. Paris: OECD.

Picard, Robert G. (1988) 'Pricing behavior of newspapers', in R.G. Picard, J.P. Winter, M.E. McCombs and S. Lacy (eds), *Press Concentration and Monopoly: New Perspectives on Newspaper Ownership and Operation*. Norwood, NJ: Ablex. pp. 55–69.

Röper, Horst (1997) 'Formationen deutscher Medienmultis 1996', *Media Perspektiven*, 5: 226–55.

Sánchez-Tabernero, Alfonso (1993) *Media Concentration in Europe: Commercial Enterprise and the Public Interest*. Dusseldorf: European Institute for the Media.

Seufert, Wolfgang (1997) 'Medienübergreifende Unternehmenskonzentration – Mittel zur Kostensenkung oder zur Erhöhung der Marktmacht?', in Heribert Schatz et al. (eds), *Machtkonzentration in der Multimediagesellschaft?* Opladen: Westdeutscher Verlag. pp. 258–73.

Tunstall, Jeremy (1996) *Newspaper Power*. London: Oxford University Press.

PART II TECHNOLOGICAL CHANGES

5

The Digital Future

Hans J. Kleinsteuber

This chapter looks at the latest developments in Europe in the field of digital television. Digital television refers to a new technology that allows the transmission of TV images in a digitally compressed mode via satellite, cable or terrestrial transmission to the viewer (digital video broadcasting, DVB) (Lindberg, 1995; Proakis, 1995). To decode the picture on the site of the receiver, a set-top box is required that translates the digital signal into the analog 'language' of the conventional TV set. At present, the central transmission line passes through direct broadcasting satellites (DBS), mostly by Astra, but also by Eutelsat. Therefore digital TV cannot be understood without knowledge of the current state of DBS in Europe. The digital signal may also be fed into the head stations of cable systems via satellite or be transmitted terrestrially from a conventional antenna (DVB-T). Most activities take place in the field of digital television via DBS, but the feeding of digital TV signals line into coaxial cable systems is easy to manage and is in use as well. Due to a general lack of available frequencies in the electromagnetic spectrum, the introduction of DVB-T is planned in a few European countries only, mainly the UK and Sweden.

With digital TV we may experience the advent of another 'media revolution'. The Astra company SES forecasts that (in the year 2006) 35 million households will be equipped with units to receive packaged digital TV, another 10 million are expected to stay analog, either by direct-to-home (DTH) or through cable television (Baker, 1996). This chapter describes the major developments in Europe and also looks into the 'logic' of digital TV.

Cable and satellite

Twenty years ago nearly all TV transmission in Europe was terrestrial and usually limited to a small number of public service channels. In the 1980s, the picture was changed, not only by new commercial stations but also by

Table 5.1　*Penetration of new media in Western Europe, 1996 (selected indicators)*

Country	TV households (millions)	Cable connections (1,000s)	Cable penetration (%)	Satellite TV receivers (no.)
Austria	2.99	1.092	36.5	3–500,000
Belgium	4.08	3.843	94.0	40,000
Denmark	2.29	516	22.5	300,000
Finland	2.05	831	40.4	65,000
France	20.89	1.358	6.5	1,500,000
Germany	33.10	15.987	48.3	10,000,000
Greece	3.16	min	min	10,000
Ireland	1.04	489	47.1	75,000
Italy	20.20	min	min	6–800,000
Luxembourg	0.16	140	87.5	4,000
The Netherlands	6.28	5.84	93.0	300,000
Norway	1.76	610	34.7	270,000
Portugal	3.10	min	min	300,000
Spain	11.71	410	3.5	260,000
Sweden	3.98	1.850	46.5	530,000
Switzerland	2.88	2.390	83.0	200,000
United Kingdom	22.60	1.63	7.2	3,790,000

Source: *Cable and Satellite Europe* (1997), 1: 42–9

the introduction of cable and satellite in many European countries. Today, in some regions of Europe up to 90 per cent of all households receive their TV images via cable and/or satellite (see Table 5.1). The present situation is very diverse. Some countries (like Belgium) are nearly totally cabled; others have no cable at all (Italy). In some countries cabling was steered by the state as part of an active media policy (as in Germany, to create new distribution possibilities for the commercial TV industry); in other countries it was market driven (in the smaller countries to offer viewers access to programming in neighbouring countries). Digital TV may be transmitted terrestrially (and this will be done in Great Britain), but in most countries no frequencies are available for DVB-T. Digital TV therefore has to utilize the transmission lines provided by satellite and/or cable.

In the same way as cable, the market for DBS reception appears to be rather fragmented. The largest ones are those in Germany and Britain. In Britain, the attraction for DTH TV stems mainly from the offering of the BSkyB package, a bouquet of analog pay programmes. In Germany, DBS supplements the cable system and delivers, like cable, more than two dozen German-language programmes into the home.

What, then, did the European situation look like before the advent of digital TV? It seems appropriate to group Western European markets into three categories (Shepherd, 1996):

Group 1　This group consists of states with rather high cable and DTH satellite penetration and includes Scandinavia, Benelux and Germany

Table 5.2   *Expenditure on audiovisual media:*
international comparison, 1994 (per capita
expenditure in US dollars)

	Total (audio, cinema, video)	Pay TV only
France	97.66	25.03
Germany	97.93	4.29
Great Britain	103.22	15.77
Italy	31.55	2.94
Spain	40.81	7.03
USA	161.89	18.20

Source: *Screen Digest* 3, 1996, cited in Zimmer, 1996: 393

(Benelux, cable penetration more than 90 per cent; Germany, cable and satellite together more than 75 per cent). As a broad selection of generalist channels is available, pay TV services meet strong competition and have only limited success. The pay TV providers are going digital now, but are facing uncertainties.

Group 2   Countries in this group are latecomers in satellite and cable television, and penetration remains low. Terrestrial TV provides for a limited number of channels (around 4–6). This applies to countries like the United Kingdom, France and Spain, in which pay TV companies meet only limited competition and are very successful. Canal Plus in France (transmitted terrestrially) and BSkyB in the UK (transmitted via satellite and cable) are prominent and highly profitable. These actors have gone digital or will do so in the near future.

Group 3   This group includes states with little or no cable and DTH. Typical are southern states like Italy and Greece with a relatively good choice of free (i.e. non-pay) TV channels. New services have to be introduced via satellite, but DBS penetration is low. Pay services have a difficult start and the market outlook for digital television is not very clear.

The general rule might be that countries offering a wide selection of free TV channels like Germany or Italy make it hard for pay TV to conquer the market. If only a limited number of free channels are available, as in France and the United Kingdom, the stimulus to buy additional programming for extra cost is much higher (see Table 5.2).

Digital television: the technology

Digital television mainly refers to the digital compression of TV images, based on the standard of the Moving Picture Expert Group (MPEG 2) for DVB. In the digital version, each transponder, cable channel or terrestrial TV frequency may transmit between five and 10 TV channels. Content will be packaged and sold in 'bouquets'. The costs of transmission of each channel go down drastically, making multi-channel television fast a reality. Digital packages may consist of commercial channels that are not otherwise available (like MTV, Cartoon Network and so on) or topical channels (programmes for comedy, Western films and so on), sports events (including top events and specialized programmes for golfers); erotic programming may also play a role. Technology makes it easy to offer different packages, suited to the interests and purses of the individual subscriber. Advertising as the financial basis for programmes has reached its limit in many European countries; therefore, future digital services have to be paid for on a monthly basis. Certain channels are usually reserved for premium programmes, mainly new films and special sports events that are individually accessed on the basis of pay-per-view. Time-shifted programmes make near video-on-demand possible. Digital television can also be free and some public service broadcasters are experimenting with it (in Germany and Italy) but this is the exception. Interactive services, such as home shopping, telebanking, downloading of computer software (for video games), and other services may be possible, but development is still in its initial stages (Prognos, 1995).

The specification of the decoder, the set-top box, is of highest importance for the nature of digital television. It is equipped as a multimedia terminal. The TV signal is encoded on the sender side and it has to be decoded by this box. An electronic programme guide (EPG) manages the decoder and communicates with the viewer. A conditional access system opens the gate to the kind of programming that the viewer has subscribed to. A number of different designs are on the market today. Some will allow the use of a valid chip card, the 'smart card', to deduct payment for pay-per-view. The set-top box may stand separately or be connected to the telephone system for simple return signals to central computers, mainly for payment purposes. In this case, a low-capacity modem has to be installed in the box. One question that has not been solved is that of a common interface that allows equal access to all service providers. Competing types of box are currently on the market that only serve as a platform for their specific programmes.

This is not only a technical problem: the interests of the actors are dominant. The EPG shows the programmes that are available. Which ones are placed first, which ones are especially advertised? Whoever controls the set-top boxes has direct access to the participating TV households and may, if they choose to do so, discriminate against other content providers. The controller may also be able to monitor the consumption patterns of digital TV households in detail. If programmes are paid for via the telephone back channel, serious problems of data protection arise.

Digital television, as it appears today, is basically a technology to increase the number of programmes that may be transmitted to the viewer and to collect payment if appropriate. It follows mainly a one-directional pattern. But to make the set-top box interactive via a return channel through the telephone line is possible and in some systems provided for.

(Britain's BIB project for 1998 is promised to be interactive and should offer access to the Internet.) The decoder is a sophisticated piece of technology which does not come cheaply. The price of a standard box that includes pay TV should be at least 500 ecu, possibly more. Decoders for free digital TV (no pay options) could be delivered for perhaps half that price. Convincing households to invest in such a decoder is crucial for the introduction of digital TV. Broadcasters follow different introduction strategies, some lease the box, others sell them for a full or a subsidized price. Several options might be available to the consumer.

Major actors: Astra and DBS in Europe

Central to the introduction of digital television in Europe is the Astra system of direct broadcasting satellites (DBS) that delivers programmes direct-to-home (DTH) or via their head stations into cable systems. The first Astra 1A-satellite was launched in 1988. Astra began as an American business initiative in Europe, but – due mainly to the resistance of the European telecom companies – European investors took over. A Société Européenne des Satellites S.A. (SES) was established in 1985 for this purpose, based in Luxembourg. All Astra satellites are able to offer a high number of TV transponders and they provide a footprint that covers the entire European continent. With this capacity, Astra was able to push DBS initiatives out of the market that originated in Europe (TV-Sat in Germany and TDF in France) with a low number of transponders (maximum of five) and a small footprint. Astra was also able to marginalize the satellite services offered by its only European competitor, the European organization of the national telecoms Eutelsat. Today Astra maintains a kind of hegemony in Europe by controlling about or more than 90 per cent of the European DBS market. At the start of 1995, SES managed four satellites with analog technology (Astra 1A–1D) which are able to offer more than 60 different TV channels that go DTH and via cable to about 64 million households in Europe (data for 1996, see Table 5.3).

In October 1995, the SES company launched the first digitally equipped satellite Astra 1E into orbit, with Astra 1F and Astra 1G following in 1996 and 1997. When Astra 1H is launched in 1998, the Astra system alone may be able to offer between 500 and 1,000 additional digital TV channels for Europe. In addition, Eutelsat is active in DBS, mainly with its Hot Bird satellites. Its collection of five Hot Bird satellites is planned to offer up to 98 digital transponders in 1998, which provides capacities similar to Astra (Eutelsat, 1996). The Eutelsat system was first in digital TV and shows a performance as strong as Astra. Eutelsat mainly provides the southern European markets with digital programming because its satellite footprint is better suited for this region.

Table 5.3 *Astra satellites in Europe*

Name	Year of launch	No. of transponders	
1A	1988	16	analog
1B	1991	16	
1C	1993	18	
1D	1994	18	
1E	1995	18	digital
1F	1996	22	
1G	1997	32	
1H	1998	32	

Source: Astra

National case studies

To support the hypothesis of an extremely diverse situation in Europe's response to digital TV, some countries are analysed in more detail.

Germany

Among the larger European states Germany stands out because of a high penetration of cable and DBS television. More than 75 per cent of all households already receive their images this way. A multi-channel system has therefore already been established, resulting in a situation in which most Germans can see up to 30 free German-language channels. In such an environment, pay TV has no easy task. The only pay TV company, Premiere, served about 1.5 million subscribers (of about 33 million households) in 1997, offering one channel with premium films and top sports events. Premiere was founded by Bertelsmann and Canal Plus (with 37.5 per cent shares) and Kirch (with 25 per cent). As Bertelsmann and Canal Plus acted in a European alliance, Bertelsmann was in effective control of Premiere. After a difficult start Premiere now makes a profit.

In general the German commercial TV market is controlled by two large 'sender families' that each offer a number of general and special interest programmes. One 'family' is made up of Bertelsmann/UFA and CLT (both merged in 1996); the other is in the hands of the Kirch Group. Both 'families' have competed fiercely against each other during recent years. Kirch very much pushed ahead and introduced Digitales Fernsehen 1 (DF1) in July 1996. In 1997 DF1 offered roughly 30 TV channels in different packages; pay-audio was also available. As decoder, the d-box was chosen, developed by the Nokia company. Satellite transponders are leased from Astra. Most of the films and series shown on DF1 come from Kirch's huge film library, providing whole channels with topical films (Cine Comedy, Heart & Co. and so on). Kirch, as the largest film-trader in Europe, is ideally suited for this business. The set-top box is also provided for pay-per-view; that is, showing a premium film for a set amount of money (about three ecu). Popular demand for DF1 was unexpectedly low, however, and at the end of 1996 Kirch had hardly sold 20,000 subscriptions (projections were 200,000). In the spring of 1998 the number was just above 100,000.

Bertelsmann and CLT also announced a move into digital TV, based on the competing decoder Mediabox. Their venture, Club RTL, promised to offer a similar package to DF1. But Kirch systematically bought up all available international film and sports rights to keep the Club RTL competition away from the market. Kirch took most Hollywood studios under contract for the coming years and bought all rights for the world soccer championships (beginning in 2002). It is estimated that Kirch invested up to 10 billion ecu in the preparations for digital TV. The result was that Bertelsmann and CLT dropped out of the race and abandoned their digital activities.

German Telekom, the largest telecom business in Europe, announced in 1995 several pilot projects with multimedia services including video-on-demand. Telekom later withdrew, giving technical problems as a reason. At the same time Telekom came under pressure to make additional channels available for digital TV in the hyperband part of its cable systems. But Telekom, controlling access to most cable systems, had plans of its own to move into the selling of TV programmes.

In the summer of 1997 it became clear that Kirch's DF1 policy had failed. The company had accumulated huge losses that began to endanger the economic well-being of the whole Kirch Group. Also the conflict with Bertelsmann over Premiere had escalated and the pay TV company had trouble buying new films outside the Kirch empire. The result of the mutual stalemate was that the three large actors Kirch, Bertelsmann (acting for the CLT/UFA consortium) and Telekom started negotiations at so-called 'cable summits'. They were moderated by two politicians, the Ministers of Economics of the two largest *Länder* of North-Rhine-Westphalia (seat of the Bertelsmann Company) and Bavaria (the home of Kirch).

These actors, the three largest communication companies in Germany, decided to go together into the digital future. As part of the deal, Canal Plus will leave Premiere and Bertelsmann and Kirch will each take 50 per cent in this company that will be crucial for the introduction of digital TV. Telekom will join the deal and invest in its cable systems (it already increased the subscription fee for its systems) to provide for additional digital channels. The platform for all digital TV will be Kirch's d-box. The consortium promised to guarantee non-discriminative access for other broadcasters, but complaints abound. The public service broadcasters ARD and ZDF work on an alternative system of free digital TV that uses a simple decoder without pay installations. Their demand for equal participation in the company that provides d-box technology has been denied and they fear being put on the backbench of the digital age.

The Kirch-CLT/UFA-Telekom alliance was submitted to the European Union that declared it to be unacceptable because of its monopolistic character. If the EU rejects the scheme altogether, CLT/UFA might leave the alliance and go its own way. Segments of the Bertelsmann company were always opposed to the coalition with Kirch. One option is to increase cooperation with Canal Plus.

France

Pay TV has proved to be most successful in France: in 1997 up to 6 million French households received either analog or digital pay TV. The basic difference from Germany is that most households have access to only six over-the-air channels, and the effect of cable and satellite is low (reaching less than 15 per cent of all households) (Decker, 1996; Meise, 1996). The leading provider for pay TV is Canal Plus which was established in the years of the socialist government under President François Mitterrand and began to operate in 1984. As it could utilize a terrestrial network it reaches about 80 per cent of all households. Canal Plus served about 4.2 million subscribers with analog pay TV in 1997 and is highly profitable. In 1992 it started CanalSatellite as a multi-channel package, mainly for satellite and cable distribution. CanalSatellite has about half a million subscribers.

In April 1996 CanalSatellite started its first digital package CanalSatellite Numerique with about 30 channels, including theme channels and pay-per-view. The decoder technology had been jointly developed by Canal Plus and Bertelsmann and sold under the brand name Mediabox. By the middle of 1997 about 400,000 Canal Plus decoders were in use in French households. Two competitors entered the French market for digital TV late in 1996. Télévision par Satellite (TPS) is mainly owned by the free TV industry (TF1 has a 25 per cent share; M6 20 per cent; CLT/UFA 20 per cent) and offers programming similar to Canal Plus to about 150,000 customers. Another competitor is AB Sat, a daughter company of the largest film production and trading company in France Groupe AB, but its multi-channel package has found very few subscribers so far.

Central to the French situation is the very successful company Canal Plus which has extended its reach to a number of other European countries (see below), but retreated from the German market. By 1997 Canal Plus had gathered much experience in pay TV and is well prepared to enter the digital age. Clearly, the French TV market offers much less competition in free TV, therefore making it much easier to convince households to invest in pay TV, compared with the multi-channel markets for free TV as in Germany.

Great Britain

Pay TV so far is controlled by one company in the UK: British Sky Broadcasting (BSkyB) which is financially very successful. BSkyB was the result of a fusion of two competing satellite companies Sky Television and BSB in 1990. The main owner of BSkyB is Rupert Murdoch's News

International (40 per cent); other shareholders include the French group Chargeurs and the English Granada Group. At the end of 1996 BSkyB provided about six million subscribers (including some in Ireland), either via satellite or via cable, with packaged pay TV, which adds up to about one-fifth of all British households. BSkyB offers around 30 channels, all trans-mitted by analog technology. The price differs according to the number of programmes bought. Most successful are film and sports channels, especially since Murdoch began to buy up the rights to the Premier Football League in 1992 and other top events in rugby, cricket and golf.

As packaged pay TV is already available in the UK, the priority to introduce digital TV via satellite is relatively low compared to other Euro-pean countries. But the British Isles still have over-the-air frequencies available that can be utilized for digital terrestrial television (DTT) based on DVB-T. The UK Independent Television Commission (ITC) decided in 1997 to award licences for DTT to the newly established company British Digital Broadcasting (BDB) owned by Carlton Communications and the Granada Group. BSkyB originally participated in BDB, but under pressure from the ITC decided to sell out to its partners. BDB has signed an accord with the public service broadcaster the BBC and it is expected that BSkyB will remain an important content provider. Several channels may be reserved for pay-per-view. Based on BDB's platform, a maximum of about 30 channels may be distributed in different packages and for different monthly subscription fees.

BSkyB revealed details of a new venture for packaged digital TV to be launched in 1998, named British Interactive Broadcasting (BIB). Besides BSkyB, British Telecom, the Midland Bank and Matsushita are also involved in BIB. The plans are to distribute up to 200 channels of digital TV based on Astra satellite transmission. BSkyB has placed orders for a million set-top boxes, among the producers being Matsushita. To make digital TV more attractive, BIB plans to subsidize the price of every decoder. BIB promises other broadcasters access to its system, but they all have to pass through BIB's conditional access system. By 'interactive', BIB refers to pay-per-view, home banking, on-line games and related services. BDB and BIB are in active discussion about possible collaboration; for example, using the same set-top box.

Spain

The situation in Spain mainly reflects the French experience: the country is not cabled and the number of terrestrial TV channels is limited. Besides two public service channels (RTVE), since 1990 two commercial stations have been offered. Furthermore, Canal Plus España serves pay TV to about 1.4 million homes, which is more than one in 10 households. As in France, Canal Plus is distributed via terrestrial frequencies to most parts of the country (80 per cent). Even more than in France, media developments are politicized in Spain. The public broadcaster RTVE is effectively controlled by the government and in a financially difficult situation.

Digital television has become a central topic of political conflict in a complex web of interests and actors. Early in 1997 Canal Satélite Digital started a package of two dozen digital channels via satellite. Canal Satélite is owned by the same company Sogecable that runs the successful Canal Plus service. Shareholders are, in addition to Spanish banks, the French Canal Plus mother company and the Spanish media company Prisa. Prisa controls the largest chain of radio stations and publishes the most prestigious newspaper *El País*. This newspaper is politically close to the socialist party.

Since the spring of 1996 the conservative government of Premier José María Aznar has been in power. One of its first moves was to put its own representatives into the leadership of RTVE. In February 1997 (immediately after Canal Satélite started its digital service) the Spanish government decreed that any platform should be open to competing systems, something Canal Satélite could not guarantee. This measure was interpreted as a strategy of the conservative government against the left-leaning Prisa. Canal Satélite fought back by calling in the Spanish and European courts.

At the same time the government supported the establishment of a second consortium for digital TV under the leadership of the recently privatized telecom company Telefonica, including RTVE, TV stations and publications close to the government and the Mexican TV empire Televisa. Their digital service Via Digital was scheduled for late 1997. Several political moves by the government demonstrated that it was attempting to support Via Digital over Canal Satélite Digital, including legal investigations against Canal Plus España. Another conflict arose over the exclusive rights for the Spanish soccer league which are being kept by the TV company Antena 3. Originally Antena 3 cooperated with Canal Satélite but Telefonica and Spanish banks bought into this company to secure its soccer rights for Via Digital.

The general impression is that the government still claims the right to control the major media, a tradition left over from the times of the Franco dictatorship. But the fact remains that the introduction of digital TV is so risky and requires so much capital that only a small number of national (and international) actors are able to participate. This fact invites governments to intervene and play their political game – not just in Spain.

Italy

Italy started early in commercial TV but is a latecomer to pay TV. The country is virtually uncabled. The public service broadcaster RAI offers three channels, Berlusconi's Mediaset company controls another three commercial channels. Smaller broadcasters (like TMC) are also active. Berlusconi's media holding began analog pay TV with Telepiú in 1991; in

1993 three pay channels (films, sports, culture) were distributed via terrestrial transmission. Because of legal restraints, Berlusconi had to divest of Telepiú; in 1996 it was controlled by Leo Kirch and Johann Rupert's Nethold (Muscará and Zamparutti, 1996). In 1997 Canal Plus took effective control of Telepiú. This was possible because Nethold took his share into the merger with Canal Plus and in addition Kirch and Canal Plus exchanged ownerships. As was described above, Canal Plus sold its shares in the German Premiere venture to Kirch (and CLT/UFA) and in turn took over Kirch's shares in Telepiú. In 1997 Canal Plus held 90 per cent of Telepiú and Berlusconi's Mediaset the remaining 10 per cent. By 1997 Telepiú served about 900,000 subscribers.

In 1996 Telepiú started digital TV with a first package of programmes (Telepiú Digital); a little later TeleCalcio offered broadcasts of soccer games. Satellite transmission is via Eutelsat's Hot Bird (Eutelsat satellite's footprint is better positioned for Italy than Astra's). Telepiú Digital offers the three Telepiú channels and additional programming with mainly international services (for example, CNN, MTV and Discovery). An important part of this scheme included live broadcasts of the highest Italian soccer league introduced in September 1996 as pay TV on TeleCalcio. Telepiú Digital and TeleCalcio are not doing well: by mid-1997 they had less than 100,000 subscribers.

In 1997 the broadcaster RAI and the STET-Telecom Italia company cooperated to introduce another variation of digital TV. Market studies had shown, though, that there was no room for more than one actor and STET and Canal Plus began working together. But the Italian anti-trust authority banned their cooperation. RAI/STET started to offer undecoded digital TV in the autumn of 1997 (programmes for schools, children, culture). To support the introduction of digital TV, parliament passed a new media law that regulates its introduction. The government also lowered taxes to make digital decoders and satellite antennae cheaper and thus more attractive to the consumer. Clearly Canal Plus has become the leading force in Italian digital TV, but the market, flooded by many free TV programmes, turns out to be reluctant concerning pay TV.

Smaller countries

The leading company to provide smaller European markets with pay TV was Nethold, formally owned by Johann Rupert, which merged into Canal Plus in September 1996. Nethold is active in Belgium, the Netherlands, Denmark, Sweden, Norway and Finland. In Scandinavia, Kinnevik's TV 1000 is Nethold's main competitor, in French-speaking Belgium Canal Plus cooperates with the Wallonic broadcaster RTBF to offer a version of France's Canal Plus programme. By pooling the resources of Nethold, Canal Plus turns out to be the leading force in European pay TV as well as in digital TV.

European alliances and digital television

In 1994 the technological opportunities for digital television became clear to the large media players. After years of delay, the three largest communication actors in Germany, Telekom, Bertelsmann and Kirch founded a joint venture, the Media Service GmbH (MSG) to provide for digital services as outlined above. MSG was devised as a monopoly company, but promised to offer services to all other interested parties on an equal basis. The establishment of MSG met very strong resistance from all other European media companies; they accused the MSG shareholders of trying to construct a virtual monopoly that would effectively keep competitors out. As MSG was based in Germany and received support from influential power centres inside the country, anti-trust opposition could only come from outside. It centred around the EU and its newly gained anti-cartel policy. The MSG was banned late in 1994 by Brussels. This also meant the end of the rather precarious coalition that had shaped it, as Kirch and Bertelsmann became bold competitors. After that the European alliances were rearranged.

In the summer of 1996 the major European media companies formed two large alliances and rallied behind one of the two technologies for digital TV, as represented by their respective digital decoders (Mediabox v. d-box). When it became clear that Europe could be divided again because of incompatible decoder standards, the EU stepped in, trying to negotiate a 'truce' between both sides. In June 1996 Commissioner Martin Bangemann of the EU invited top representatives of the European broadcasting industry to discuss the matter again, but without results.

The shaping of European alliances was accompanied by frequent dealing by the major actors behind closed doors. As a result, made public in April 1996, Bertelsmann/UFA and CLT decided to pool their European TV activities and merge them. This CLT/UFA venture is now the largest TV company in Europe and controls TV channels in a number of countries including the Netherlands, Belgium, France, the UK and Germany. This fusion of two major European actors was quickly accepted by the EU. As CLT and Bertelsmann were allies before, this seemed not to change the European balance of media actors. But in fact it started a rearrangement of alliances, as former allies of Bertelsmann turned away. Bertelsmann's partner Canal Plus and RTL are fierce competitors on the French market and Canal Plus felt negatively affected by the announced 'mega-merger'.

Another rather dramatic shift in alliances took place: Murdoch announced his intention to change sides, cooperate with Kirch and leave his loose cooperation with Bertelsmann (which had started with common ventures, especially the German Vox TV channel). But as Kirch's DF1 turned out to be unsuccessful, Murdoch withdrew and left Kirch to himself (Underhill and Waldrop, 1996). The negotiations between CLT/UFA and Kirch, as described above, had estranged Canal Plus as the latter had not been properly informed. Another important event took place in September 1996. Johann Rupert, owner of Nethold, the third largest pay TV company in Europe, announced his intention to sell to Canal Plus. Nethold merged into Canal Plus and in return Rupert took about 15 per cent stock in Canal Plus, being now one of the largest stockholders in that company.

The most important consequence was that, by the autumn of 1997, a small number of large media actors controlled the European market for digital TV. Clearly best suited for the future is Canal Plus with activities in France, Italy and Spain and (through Nethold) in many of the smaller countries of Europe. Murdoch is in a strong position in Britain, Bertelsmann (CLT/UFA) and Kirch will jointly develop the German market but may split up because of European opposition. In a number of countries these media actors work in close cooperation with the respective governments. Additional actors attempt to move into the emerging market for digital TV, but they will have a hard time. Among them are some public service broadcasters (for example, ARD, RTVE, RAI) and some telecom companies (for example, Deutsche Telekom, STET, Telefonica), but they are having a dificult start. As national strategies and rivalries accompany the introduction of digital TV in Europe, the decoders, which are employed in different countries, are only partly compatible: new technological borders are being erected on the European television market.

Conclusion

It seems certain that the introduction of digital TV marks a third phase in the development of European television, which began with a first period of public service monopolies, followed by a second period shaped by a dual system of public and commercial broadcasters. Crucial to the successful launching of digital TV will be a handful of the largest media companies of Europe, with public service broadcasters and telecom companies following far behind. Digital TV implies that scarcity of frequencies will be a problem of the past. Digital transponders on satellites are already available that allow for the transportation of many hundred channels. For the year 2000 forecasts project the capacity to make between 3,000 and 4,000 digital TV channels available for all of Europe. These programmes will come in packages, which by themselves are no innovation as they have existed before in analog technology, especially in the UK. But the employment of digital decoders in participating households will provide the viewer with very specific services, including pay TV, pay-per-view, pay-audio, loading of computer software, a simple back channel and so on.

Pay TV as such is not new to Europe. Developments still centre around national or language markets and the situation in Europe is extremely diversified. Pay TV is successful in some markets (mainly France, UK, Spain); it is available but not booming in other markets (Germany, Italy).

In most cases only one national actor provides pay TV; competition is the exception. Pay TV seems to be most successful where terrestrial TV provides only a small number of free channels, cable and satellite reception is not prominent and where it is transmitted terrestrially. In a free multi-channel environment its attraction seems to be much lower.

Digital TV is identified with pay TV for two main reasons. First, the market for commercial TV, financed solely by advertisements, is drawing to a close. Most forecasts see only a modest increase in advertisement money that may flow into television in the near future. Expansion therefore has to be financed by new sources of income. Secondly, the set-top box is ideally suited for different forms of pay TV, including pay-per-view, payment for home shopping and so on. Different forms of accounting are available, including using a chip-card, loaded with money or a simple back channel via telephone for the central management of accounts. Connecting the decoder to the Internet via a modem is easily possible (and is planned in the UK by BIB), but may not be pushed ahead. Broadcasting companies are in the traditional business of providing programmes and feel uncomfortable about possible competition from the Internet, a market that is controlled by quite different companies. Also, US experiences show that Internet households tend to watch less TV. In any case, the packages for viewers can be designed, starting with a basic bouquet and going on to all kinds of added features, all with an extra price tag on them.

Additional channels create demand for additional programme software: movies, sports events, special interest programming and also erotic film material. With the advent of digital TV, the large media companies of Europe bought up all available film material, mainly from the large American producers for ever-increasing prices. TV companies are also trying to buy attractive live sports on an exclusive basis, especially games of national soccer leagues and world championships. The exclusive rights to the soccer world championships of 2002 and 2006 have been bought up by Kirch. To recover the heavy investment in exclusive rights, attractive content will increasingly move from free television to pay TV. The conventional free programmes may be 'cannibalized' to provide the necessary material for the new pay packages. It seems that television will never be as cheap as it was for the consumer in the old days.

In spite of all the conflicts between the major European actors, they seem to depend on – more or less – the same technological logic. Looking strictly at the technology, the strategies represent the idea of channel multiplication with very rudimentary (or no) interactivity. In technical terms, DBS works like a filter that commands communication only in one direction. The utilization of a large-scale technology like a satellite guarantees that this one-directional stream of information will stay under the control of a few technical (Astra, Eutelsat) and economic (Canal Plus, Murdoch) 'centres', ensuring central control of European markets. Digital television very much reflects the intention of the leading media players to provide for multi-channel TV. The interactive potential of digitalization, as reflected by the

Internet and visions of 'information highways', is only partially used: digitalization appears to be 'crippled' in Europe (Kleinsteuber, 1997). Other options are possible though. The Steering Board of the Europe DVB-project is working to develop a Multimedia Home Platform (MHP) with an open architecture (open to all actors) that might offer many kinds of media and interactive services (TV, PC, telephone, Internet).

Most forecasts see a polarization of the use of audiovisual media in the future between 'information rich' and 'information poor'. In this 'two-class information society' one group of users develops a high competence in working with new digital media including computers, has the buying power to use pay TV selectively and knows ways to apply the potential of the new technology for individual and interactive usage. Another group will remain in the passive mode of viewing, will stay outside the cyberspace community, will not have the purchasing power to buy much of the pay programmes and might even be worse off than at present.

Bibliography

Astra (1995) *Astra aktuell*, no. 21, August. Eschborn: Astra-marketing GmbH.

Baker, Paul (1996) 'Double illumination', *Cable and Satellite Europe*, 7: 25–6.

Decker, Arnaud (1996) 'La Télévision Numérique – L'Heure de l'alliance?', *Mediapouvoirs*, 1: 88–106.

Digitales TV (1995) 'Wettlauf um das Fernsehen der Zukunft, *Tendenz*, 3 ('Digitales TV', topical issue).

Eutelsat (1996) *Das Hot Bird Satellitensystem für Europa*. Paris: European Telecommunications Satellite Organization.

Hamann, Kai (1996) 'Settop-Boxen – TV total', *PC Professionell*, 4: 18–19.

Kaiser, Lothar (1996) 'Rivalen an der Box', *Journalist*, 1: 28–30.

Kleinsteuber, Hans J. (1997) 'Crippled digitalization: superhighways or one-way streets?', in Herbert Kubicek et al. (eds), *The Social Shaping of Information Highways: European and American Roads to the Information Society*. Frankfurt/New York: Campus. pp. 79–96.

Lindberg, Bertil C. (1995) *Digital Broadband Networks and Services*. New York: McGraw Hill.

MediaGruppe (1995) *Interaktives TV: Tests, Projekte, Systeme – Ein Überblick*. Munich: MediaGruppe.

Meise, Martin (1996) 'Mit digitalen Bouquets zum Erfolg?', *Media Perspektiven*, 3: 153–63.

Muscará, Piero and Zamparutti, Eleonora (1996) 'Cinquecento Canali', *Cable and Satellite Europe*, 10: 22–5.

Proakis, John G. (1995) *Digital Communications*. New York: McGraw Hill.

Prognos, A.G. (1995) *Digitales Fernsehen: Marktchancen und ordnungspolitischer Bedarf*. Munich: Verlag Reinhard Fischer.

Scott, Toby (1996) 'UK preps for terrestrial digital', *Broadcasting and Cable International*, 10: 24–5.

Shepherd, Lloyd (1996) 'Annus mirabilis for digital DTH', *Broadcasting and Cable International*, 10: 38.

Underhill, William and Waldrop, Theresa (1996) 'Cut to the case – Murdoch and Kirch do a digital deal', *Newsweek*, 22 July, p. 41.

Zimmer, Jochen (1996) 'Pay TV: Durchbruch im digitalen Fernsehen?', *Media Perspektiven*, 7: 386–401.

6

The Internet: A New Mass Medium?

Wolfgang Truetzschler

The rapid development of the Internet, particularly over the past two or three years, was not foreseen in the early 1980s, certainly not in the social sciences. Even communication scholars have only fairly recently begun to make the Internet, the main constituent of the 'information superhighway', the object of their studies, although computer-mediated communication (CMC) is not a new field of study (see, for example, Kling, 1996). A discussion of the Internet is fraught with difficulties due to its vastness and its very rapid development, expansion and spread among the more affluent population of the developed world.

This chapter discusses some of the more noteworthy features of the Internet and outlines some of the characteristics that can be seen as distinguishing it from traditional mass media. The extent to which traditional European mass media have 'embraced' the Internet is also briefly examined. This discussion does not include an outline of all the different forms of interactive communication: the different types of 'shared user environments' available on the Internet, namely the various types of Internet relay chats (IRC), 'multi-user dungeons' (MUD), 'multi-user shared hallucinations' (MUSH) and so on. (For a description of these, see Griffin, 1996; for a discussion of how computers are making us re-evaluate our identities in the age of the Internet, see Turkle, 1995.) Instead, the chapter endeavours to comment on some international and European developments that seem to be a direct result of the spread of the Net, including some comments on the major policy issues that have arisen over the past two years. This includes a discussion of what is widely perceived as the more negative side of the Net.

Reach of the Internet

The Internet is a global communication system, available in virtually all countries of the world with the exception of some smaller African and Asian states (*On the Internet*, May/June 1997: 46–7). By June 1997, 171 countries were connected, with 195 countries of a world total of 207 able to send or receive e-mail. The levels of Internet connectivity vary from access to the Internet from a network that is really not part of the Internet (for example, on-line services such as Compuserve, AOL, Microsoft Network and so on), use of a modem from a personal computer in order to access a 'host' computer which is actually 'on' the Internet, to direct Internet access, i.e. a computer is directly wired to the Internet. This level of connectivity includes the services provided by the Internet service providers (ISPs) that are now found in most European countries (Crispen, 1996). In several African countries (and for undergraduate courses in some European third-level educational institutions) the sole form of Internet connectivity is via e-mail only. But even e-mail connectivity enables access to all the other elements of the Internet (Rankin, 1997).

Although the Net is available in so many countries, nothing very definite is known about the exact numbers of people using it. There are myriad Internet surveys (see, for example, http://www.asiresearch.com/surveys/oresults.htm), but very few of these are based on the results of accepted scientific sampling techniques. The biggest and most recent global survey, the Graphic, Visualization and Usability Center's eighth WWW User Survey (conducted in October/November 1997) with over 19,000 participants, is based on a questionnaire study of the World Wide Web (WWW or Web, the graphical or hypermedia system for accessing Internet sites) usage of a self-selected group of Internet users. Most 'surveys' come up with broadly similar results for North America, namely that 38.49 per cent of Web users are women (an increase of 7 per cent since the Center's seventh WWW User Survey), the average age of Web users is 36.5 years, and 35.2 per cent of respondents claim that they use the Web instead of watching television, etc. Currently there are fewer and probably even less reliable results for Europe.

In Europe there are two companies providing regular information on Internet surveys in Europe and elsewhere, namely http://www.nua.ie and http://www.internet-sales.com/hot. In April 1998 Nua estimated that there are approximately 117 million people worldwide using the Internet, an increase of 50 to 100 per cent over 1996. Survey data suggest that there are 70 million users in North America, 23 million in Europe and 7.25 million in Australia and Japan. Europe is generally viewed as lagging behind the USA in terms of Internet usage. It seems that Germany has the largest Internet access market (with roughly 30 per cent of the European market, followed by the UK, the Netherlands and Sweden). But it should be pointed out that none of these figures is necessarily accurate; at best they can give a reasonable 'guesstimate'.

The Internet as information resource

The Internet is an extremely powerful research tool enabling any person to gather information on any conceivable topic. Some commentators (for example, Sternberg, 1996) claim that 'the Internet contains 30,000 times more material than the information found in the world's biggest library, the [US] Library of Congress'. In fact, to use the phrase coined by Postman (1990), we can 'inform ourselves to death' using the Internet. One of the main problems here is not only finding the relevant information, but also sifting the useless from the useful information. In order to help people to achieve both there are around 6,000 'search engines' (computer programmes that search for documents containing keywords or phrases specified by the user) on the Net which search all or only some Internet sites (see Peterson, 1997), 'directories' (subject catalogues to organize information, see for example http://www.thecodex.com/search.html) and 'meta search engines' which allow for keyword searches on multiple engines and directories at once (for example, MetaCrawler (http://www.metacrawler.com, or 'ifind' at http://www.inference.com/ifind/). Useful in this context is a knowledge of searching skills, which, as so many other matters, can be acquired over the Net (see, for example, Solock, 1996; Tyner, 1996; Peterson, 1997), and/or special software that enables the simultaneous quizzing of several search engines, for example Symantec's 'Internet FastFind' (http://symantec.com), 'morelikethis' (http://morelikethis.com) and Webseeker (http://www.ffg.com) and so on. An excellent overview of search engines and searching skills can be found in the regularly updated electronic publication 'SearchMania' (http://www.mirage.co.uk/delta/search.html). Additionally, there is increasing development of 'intelligent agents', such as 'Agentware' (http://www.agentware.com), software which incorporates artificial intelligence, enabling the user to 'train' such agents in order intelligently to seek out information on the World Wide Web desired by the user.

New search engines and similar tools designed to find the desired information without the user being 'swamped' with masses of undesired information are being developed constantly. Early 1997, for example, saw the introduction of WWW sites (http:www.powerpub.com/search.htm and http://www.zigzag.co.uk) that enable the choice of 250 search engines (for WWW pages and for pages classified into certain categories such as references, computers, books, music and so on) on one page.

The Internet and democracy

It is now possible to receive information electronically from elected representatives, parliaments and governments throughout Europe. There are great variations across Europe in terms of parliamentarians who are 'online', and the kind and amount of information that can be accessed over the Net. Some countries such as Sweden provide their 'netizens' with free information about all parliamentary events; others such as Britain only provide information that has to be ordered and paid for; others like Ireland provide little or no on-line information at all. But, overall, the on-line citizens are probably provided with easier access to government information. Most Western European governments and parliaments have established Web pages in which an ever-increasing amount of information is available to everyone (for an overview see, for example, http://europa. eu.int/en/gonline.html). In fact, the G7 Government On-Line Project is one of the eleven G7 (group of seven large industrialized nations) large-scale pilot projects agreed upon at the 1995 Brussels meeting of the G7 Ministerial Conference on the Global Information Society. Several non-G7 administrations from around the world are now participating in this project (see http://www.open.gov.uk/govoline.golintro.htm).

Not only does the Net provide near instant information from governments and parliaments to those who are 'on-line', it can also be used as a medium for discussion and debate during parliamentary election times as was and is the case with the Minnesota E-Democracy (see Aikens, 1994). On the assumption that improvements can be made in governments in all countries, in the quality of decision-making and in the design of policy, an electronic network such as the Internet can (at least in theory) lead to an enhancement of the democratic process by improving citizen participation and public discourse, creating awareness about elections, election candidates and policy issues that occur outside regular elections (see Kurland and Egan, 1996). This is the aim of the Minnesota project mentioned above and a similar project recently started in the UK, 'UK Citizens Online Democracy' (http://www.democracy.org.uk). Clift (1997) gives a concise outline of steps that must be taken in the establishment and carrying out of such citizen-based on-line political participation efforts such as the UK one. The UK project attempts to provide a new interface between the public and politicians giving citizens the opportunity to become better informed about and discuss the political and social issues that affect them. This is achieved by providing on the World Wide Web a library of information resources and a number of forums: a public forum in which members of the public can express their own visions for a better society, discuss their proposed solutions to political issues and put questions to politicians; a civic forum to enable civic organizations to make a direct input into government decision-making; a politicians forum designed (among other things) to answer questions raised in the other forums.

On-line democracy projects such as the ones sketched above (in the USA, Canada, the Netherlands and in Brazil) are outlined by Macpherson (1997) in a very informative paper on citizen participation in politics and electronic communication. Even if more such on-line democracy projects are implemented (and leaving aside the objections and barriers to direct democracy mentioned in Macpherson's paper), such projects will probably take several years to establish and may necessitate a greater spread of computer literacy and/or the development of more user-friendly and less sophisticated technology such as, for example, Internet (television) set-top boxes like Web TV (outlined below). Current surveys suggest that the average Internet user tends to be a well-educated, high-income earner who is computer literate and probably somebody who already has more avenues for participation in the political process open to him or her than the average citizen.

Official political information (information produced by governments and other state bodies rather than ordinary citizens) that is of particular relevance to Europeans can be found on the WWW pages of the European Union, namely http://www.echo.lu, http://www.ispo.cec.be and http://europa.eu.int. These WWW sites increasingly provide the texts of EU directives, the latest press releases by the EU Commission and reports drawn up for the EU Commission by various groups and consultancy firms. Most noteworthy here is the Information Society Project Office (ISPO) (http://www.ispo.cec.be). ISPO publishes an informative newsletter *Information Society Trends* every two weeks which summarizes world developments in the information society. The term 'information society' is rarely defined in EU documents, but a recent definition is given in the final policy report of the high-level expert group of the European Commission:

> The information society is the society currently being put into place, where low-cost information and data storage and transmission technologies are in general use. This generalization of information and data use is being accompanied by organizational, commercial, social and legal innovations that will profoundly change life both in the world of work and in society generally. . . . (European Union, 1997a: 9)

Education

The Internet is above all a vast educational resource both in terms of lifelong learning and formal education as it exists in all countries. Information on any conceivable topic can be found on the Net in the form of WWW pages, the numbers of which seem to be increasing by several hundred a day. There are several electronic newsletters announcing new WWW pages on a daily/weekly/monthly basis such as 'NetHappenings' (http://scout.cs.wisc.edu/scout/net-help/index.html), 'The Scout Report' (http://scout.cs.wisc.edu/scout/report), 'The Weekly Bookmark Standard' (http://www.weeklyb.com). Other sources of information include Usenet newsgroups (which require access to a news server) of which there are currently more than 28,000 and mailing lists of which there are currently more than 89,000 and which necessitate e-mail access to the Internet only. One of the difficulties of using the Net is to find the appropriate mailing list or newsgroup, but there are WWW pages such as http://www.liszt.com which enable a keyword search to find the relevant list or newsgroup. There is also a mailing list (new list) which provides information on new mailing lists that have been established.

Formal education in several countries is witnessing the (albeit slow) integration of the Internet in the classroom and in the lecture hall. A brief summary of such recent national and European public initiatives in schools can be found in the 'Action Plan for a European Education Initiative 1996–1998 *Learning in the Information Society* (http://www.ispo.cec.be), a plan to accelerate primary and secondary educational establishments' entry into the information society. (In this context see also http://www.un.org/Pubs/CyberSchoolBus). Such initiatives are appropriate in light of the wealth of educational information available on the Net. This information is already so vast that a few examples only can be mentioned here such as the Global SchoolNet Foundation (http://www.gsn.org/) and its various newsletters/mailing lists for secondary education; for third-level education the world lecture hall at http://www.utexas.edu/world/lecture which includes academic syllabuses in all sciences from various universities from around the world. Furthermore, there are countless academic and other electronic journals available on the Net, both new ones and electronic versions of printed journals, consumer and other interest magazines. An excellent source of information about new journals available on the Net is the mailing list New-jour-digest (available at http://www.gort.ucsd.edu/newjour/).

The utilization of computer-mediated communications in educational establishments is not without problems. Aside from the illegal and possibly harmful content of the Internet discussed below, there is a substantial cost factor involved in giving students access to the Net. Not only does it necessitate investment costs for computer equipment (which is sometimes partially offset by sponsorship from the computer industry), it also requires training of teaching staff, not only in terms of computer literacy but also in possibly devising forms of teaching or lecturing that are different from the centuries-old 'chalk and talk' way of teaching (Negroponte, 1995). Schools and colleges are also faced with constantly increasing running costs in the form of telephone charges. As the number of people using the Net increases, the bandwidth requirements for telephone lines also increase. Although European telecommunications charges are still higher than those of the USA, and despite increases in bandwidth in the developed world, it is unlikely that bandwidth will increase while simultaneously costs will decrease (see Meyer, 1996). Some of the problems faced by US universities, which can probably be generalized to most other Western industrialized countries, can be found in Black (1996). What is certainly required in all educational establishments is increased access to computing resources. 'If you don't have access to [these] computing resources they're damn near useless. Imagine that you'd just invented pencils and paper and there aren't very many of them around so you have paper-and-pencil training 15 minutes a week . . .' (interview with Vincent Cerf often described as the 'Father of the Internet', in Tebbit, 1996). It is by no means certain that projects designed to provide Internet access to schools, currently underway in several countries, will be sufficient to ensure that everybody in society will have equal access to the Internet (see also http://www.bbar.dtu.dk/~itsig/wwwboard/).

A new form of communication or mass media?

As the preceding paragraphs may suggest, the Internet is a new form of communication which is different from most forms of communication that we are used to, whether interpersonal or mass-mediated communication, in the sense that people can use the Net for both. In the words of the US Supreme Court in its judgment on the constitutionality of the US Communications Decency Act 1996: 'The Internet is "a unique and wholly new medium of worldwide communication"' (Supreme Court of the United States, 1997). Communication scholars have attempted to 'get to grips' with this new, very rapidly spreading form of communication. Most noteworthy in this regard is a 1995 joint edition of the *Journal of Communications* and *Journal of Computer-mediated Communication* (http://jcmc.huji.ax.il/). In this edition, one of the editors (Newhagen and Rafaeli, 1995) points to five defining qualities of communication on the Net: (a) multimedia (text, voice, pictures, animation, video); (b) hypertextuality instead of linear texts determined by the text author; (c) packet switching (the Net is designed to be route oblivious); (d) synchronicity (Net communication can be synchronous or asynchronous); and (e) interactivity ('the extent to which communication reflects back on itself, feeds on and responds to the past': Newhagen and Rafaeli, 1995). Of course, the Net is still very new and may evolve in an as yet unforeseen manner over the next decade or so and it may ultimately constitute a new mass medium. Some scholars (for example, Morris and Ogan, 1996) already conceptualize the Net as a mass medium or at least as showing some characteristics of mass media. Or as Perrone et al. (1997) in an article on the use of computers in the classroom put it: 'Surfing the Net is still largely a passive consumption activity. . . . Students and adults alike are subject to getting "hypertracked" – moving from Web page to Web page until they forget what they were looking for in the first place, and merely responding to whatever sparks an immediate reaction.'

A consideration of the policy issues discussed below and the various attempts at regulating the Internet around the world also show that the Internet is not necessarily viewed as a (new) mass medium. Policy-makers in North America and Europe seem to view the Internet as something fundamentally different from existing mass media in that they have begun to enact new regulations concerning on-line communication. On the other hand, countries in south-east Asia such as Singapore and Australia seem to be more likely to entrust broadcasting authorities with the regulation of on-line communication (see, for example, http://www.dca.gov.au/).

One way in which the Internet could evolve as a mass medium is as an 'integrator' of all existing media as we know them; that is, as a network to which a person who is connected to it by means of a computer can access digitized information which is currently available as newspapers, as sound or as video, perhaps more in the form of personal newspapers and personal radio and video programmes. This is already happening to the extent that several newspapers are available on-line, some radio stations broadcast some of their programmes over the Internet and some television stations make their television broadcasts available on the Net, as outlined below. It is difficult to predict the development of the Internet: on the one hand, even if the Net evolves into a mass medium in the sense that the audience of Internet messages is mainly a passive rather than an active one, the amount of information provided on the Net currently exceeds that provided by any existing form of mass media. On the other hand, as Schiller (1996, 1997) argues in discussion of the convergence between television and the Internet (or the 'televisionization' of the Internet), the practices of (US) commercial networked television can increasingly be found on the Internet (for example, through the 'push' services outlined below) so that the Internet prevails as a variant of commercial networks. Similarly, Seiter (1998) discusses the many cultural aspects of the Internet's seeming convergence with television.

As outlined by Schiller (1996) and illustrated in the following section, there is an 'ongoing initiative to transform the Web into a "push" rather than "pull" medium'. Push refers to the concept of delivering content to Internet users rather than expecting the user to visit Web sites in order to view the content. This is akin to broadcasting in that users sign up to receive certain content such as news which is then automatically down-loaded to their computers as soon as they are on-line and without having to specifically look for the desired content.

Relation between the Internet and traditional mass media

A large number of national and regional dailies and magazines in Europe make available their daily or weekly editions or at least excerpts from these over the Net. A directory of these with hypertext links to the individual papers can be found at http://www.newslink.org (more than 4,000 global media links) and http://www.pressoftheworld.com, a database service which contains every on-line newspaper in the world. Most of these newspapers provide an on-line version of their printed edition, in most cases free of charge, either the complete version of their printed counterpart, such as *The Times* (http://www.The-times.co.uk), or excerpts from it, such as *Der Spiegel* (http://www.spiegel.de). A few newspapers levy a charge in order to be able to read the on-line version, such as the *Wall Street Journal* (http://www.wsj.com/) or for the delivery of an e-mail version of the printed edition; for example, the *Irish Times* (http://www.irish-times.ie). Several on-line newspapers include advertising in their on-line editions. However, as of mid-1997, it seems likely that very few if any of the electronic newspapers are at this stage profitable. Different economic and revenue-generating models have been tried since 1995 (see Mings and White, 1997), but the economic viability of on-line newspapers is unclear. Perhaps the existence of on-line newspapers is a transitional phase to a different type of system to provide news and information.

One such system is the provision of news in the form of a personalized 'on-line newspaper' or a 'Daily Me'. According to Brackman (1996) there are six types of personalized newspapers available on the Net: first, personalized news services such as those provided by Netscape (http://www.netscape.com) and Yahoo (http://my.yahoo.com), which provide daily abstracts of headlines from various news sources chosen by the user to the user's e-mail box. Secondly, there are personalized news services using information push technology such as that provided at http://www. pointcast.com (which provides its own software that enables the computer user to receive news provided by Reuters news agency, technology news, a number of on-line newspapers, weather maps and satellite images, as well as advertising.) Currently, there are at least six such services including one by MSNBC the company jointly owned by the computer company Microsoft and the US television network NBC. Thirdly, there are personalized news services using publish and subscribe technology (Brackmann, 1996) such as Intermind (http://www.intermind.com) which enables a user to be informed about changes in the information provided on certain Internet sites. The fourth category consists of traditional newspapers that provide personalized news such as those mentioned above. Others, mainly US companies such as Individual (http://www.individual.com), charge for the provision of personalized news from different sectors of industry. The remaining two personalized news services include 'clipping services', which allow the user to build personalized electronic newspapers that follow certain industries, companies and products, and 'Surf Assistants or Net Agents' which are artificial intelligence programmes that perform tasks on behalf of a user and are capable of reasoning, communicating and learning and which can automate a number of 'Internet surfing tasks' (see Brackmann, 1996).

If at this early stage in the development of the global information infrastructure (GII) it is very difficult or impossible to predict the future of electronic newspapers, the future of radio and television on the Net seems even more difficult to forecast. For radio, the computer user of mid-1997 was able to receive 334 radio stations (see http://ontheair.com) or 'Internet broadcasts', i.e. live radio and other audio programmes 'transmitted' over the Net, using software such as that of the company Realaudio (http://www.realaudio.com). Most of these programmes are currently of North American origin, such as the hourly news bulletins of ABC or CBC (Canadian Broadcasting Corporation). Similarly with video or television over the Net, both the software which enables the viewing of 'video' and the 'programmes' are primarily of North American origin. Thus the necessary software, such as that available from http://www.vdo.net or from www.real.com, enables the viewing of a few US public broadcasting service programmes (http://www.pbs.org), the televised CBC news and a few other 'videos'. By mid-1997 a number of European television programmes were available in the VDO or realvideo formats, including the traditional 'flagship' of German television news *Die Tagesschau* available daily over the Net, the UK ITN news and the Austrian *Zeit im Blick* current affairs programme. The number of such television programmes available on the Internet is increasing on a monthly basis.

Even though the technology of audio and video streaming over the Net is constantly improving, the quality of the 'broadcasts' over the Net is such that, once the novelty of being able to watch or listen to programmes from other parts of the world wears off, it is a relief to watch television programmes or listen to a radio programme on traditional television and radio sets. But it does point to the possible future availability of traditional broadcasting over the Net if problems of bandwidth availability are resolved. Of course, it is as yet unclear whether this type of 'broadcasting' would still be known as such and whether it would be comparable to traditional broadcasting.

Policy issues

This section attempts to give an overview of the major issues of concern to policy-makers, especially in light of the rapid increase in the number of Internet users in the mid-1990s. The Internet is a means of communication that is fundamentally decentralized (no person or group or nation has control); it transcends national boundaries and has literally hundreds of thousands of publishers and authors. Each user has equal power to access, collect, copy and publish information. The Internet can be viewed in terms of the democratic-participant theory of the media as outlined by McQuail (1994), a theory that favours the absence of centralized political or state bureaucratic control of the organization and content of the media, an interchange of sender–receiver roles and a deinstitutionalization of the media. Currently, the Internet is such a libertarian system that it is subject to very little state or political control. Existing laws apply to the Internet, although the enforcement of these on a global basis is certainly unfamiliar. Canada seems to be one of very few countries where research has been undertaken to show the applicability of Canadian law to the Internet (see Racicot et al., 1997).

However, there are increasing attempts all over the world to introduce some sort of state control of the Internet in order to deal with those aspects of Internet use that are considered to be offensive and/or illegal both by Internet users and those who are not so familiar with the Net and who are horrified by the more sensationalist newspaper reports of illegal conduct over the Net. The Internet uses that are most objectionable are summarized by Sansom (1995) and, from a more journalistic perspective, by Boyle (1996) and Farrell (1997).

Obscenity

Obscenity and child pornography form one type of offensive communication that is probably the issue most frequently addressed in the mass media and the one which is of concern to regulators around the world who seek explicit limits on Internet use. On the other hand, libertarian Net-activists such as the EFF (Electronic Frontier Foundation – http://www.eff.org) argue that there is little need for regulations specifically written for the Internet as offences committed on the Net are already covered by existing legislation. Net libertarians are of the view that the Internet is adequately self-regulated by the adherence of 'netizens' (citizens of the Internet) to 'netiquette' (the rules of etiquette that guide on-line interaction on the Internet; see Crispen, 1996) and that any serious digression from these rules of conduct are adequately dealt with by the Internet community. Although existing legislation has been used to 'censor' certain activities occurring on the Internet (see, for example, the Computer Underground Digest available at www.soci.niu.edu/~cudigest), governments seem to be of the opinion that existing legislation is inadequate or insufficient in dealing with this form of illegal/offensive activity on the Internet.

The latter point is well illustrated by ever-increasing legislative attempts to deal with obscene sexually explicit material, especially child pornography (banned by existing laws) available on the Internet. As is the case with many other Internet developments in which the USA 'leads' the rest of the world, the USA was the first country that attempted to regulate the content of the Internet when in February 1996 the US Congress approved by overwhelming majorities the Communications Decency Act (CDA) which makes it an offence punishable by law for anybody to knowingly use a computer service to send to persons under the age of 18 'a message that depicts or describes, in terms patently offensive as measured by contemporary community standards, sexual or excretory activities or organs'. Civil liberties groups challenged the constitutionality of this Act in two US federal courts (in Washington and Pennsylvania) both of which held the Act to be unconstitutional. These judgments were appealed to the US Supreme Court which (in June 1997) also found the CDA unconstitutional on the grounds that the statute 'abridges the "freedom of speech" protected by the First Amendment'. However, this judgment does not necessarily help pornographers to open their doors to children on the Internet – there are other statutes in US law which prevent such worrying scenarios (Black, 1997). The judgment also leaves open the possibility of introducing software screening filters as outlined below.

The European Union followed the US example in publishing, in September/October 1996, two documents on short- and long-term measures to tackle the harmful and illegal content disseminated on the Net. The former is contained in the Communication 'Illegal and harmful content on the Interenet'; the latter in a Green Paper (European Union, 1996a). Both documents advocate a closer cooperation between member states; the use of blocking/filtering software (designed to prevent access to certain material on the Net) and rating systems such as PICS (Platform for Internet Content Selection) by the end user (see Resnick, 1997) and the encouragement of industry self-regulation and a 'code of conduct' among Internet access providers. Responses to the Green Paper were to be made by the end of February 1997, with possible new legislation on industry self-regulation (in terms of not providing access to certain Internet sites) following around mid-1997. Most EU countries had responded to the Green Paper by early June 1997 along the lines outlined in the Green Paper (see European Union, 1997b). However, the measures designed to combat illegal and harmful content are not necessarily uncontroversial: for example, the (mainly US) software filters are apparently easily circumvented (see Black, 1997) and tend to block WWW sites containing specific words such as 'girl' which results in the blocking of innocuous pages such as ones containing information for girl scouts or pages containing useful health information. Examples of sites that have been blocked by popular commercial filtering software products include ones on breast cancer, AIDS, women's rights, and animal rights (see http://peacefire.org/censorware/). Software filters therefore raise the question as to who decides which WWW sites should be blocked (see Campbell, 1997).

In the first part of this century, the debate over offensive communications was conducted with respect to paintings, books, sound recordings and films; subsequently, it evolved around the video cassette, videotex, such as France's Minitel, and pay-per-view television (Kendrick, 1996). It seems that many of the main innovations in communications are tried out first and developed by the 'adult entertainment' business, a multi-billion dollar industry – the Internet seems to fit into this mould. Communication on the Net is cheap to use over long distances, it is global and therefore hard to regulate. This is probably one of the reasons for the increasing efforts of regulators to control the Internet by means of legislation designed speci-fically for electronic communications such as the multimedia law passed by the German parliament (*Informations- und Kommunikationsdienste-Gesetz*) in July 1997. The law extends existing German law to the dominion of 'cyberspace' (the digital world constructed by computer networks, in par-ticular the Internet cyberspace) and took effect from August 1997 prior to the 1998 deregulation of the European telecommunications market. Under the law, on-line services could be held responsible for illegal material if they have the technology to block transmission of such content and, after notification, still disseminate the objectionable material. Several other European countries have also introduced new legislation or amendments to existing legislation.

Other offensive content

Apart from obscenity and child pornography, there are a number of other types of offensive communication on the Internet that enter the realm of illegality in all or in most countries of the world, namely sexual harassment in the form of obscene e-mail; 'net-stalking' which can raise the fear of real-world abduction; hate propaganda such as Nazi or white supremacist Web sites that distribute hate propaganda; defamation and libel. Existing laws in most countries cover these instances of illegal communication and enable prosecution of offenders. However, the global nature of the Internet enables an offender to move to another country where the offensive communication is not illegal, thereby circumventing prosecution at home and enabling access to the offensive communication in the home country. Thus successful prosecution of offenders may necessitate multilateral or bilateral agreements between nation states.

A number of other Internet communications are considered to be illegal in some countries. These include cultural nonconformity: matters such as satanism, drug, abortion and gambling information may be subject to Net regulations in various countries; terrorism in the form of on-line archives providing instructions for making bombs (which is of concern to governments in all countries); and subversion, i.e. transmission of criticism of governments around the world which is seen in some countries as a breach of national security. Boyle (1996) gives a more detailed account of these instances of illegal communication on the Internet.

Economic aspects

What is arguably even more significant for the global community than illegal and harmful content is the increasing use of the Internet for commercial purposes. Electronic commerce has brought other policy issues to the forefront of policy-makers' concern. Various surveys estimate the value of global electronic commerce to be in the region of 40–200 billion US dollars by the year 2000, up from its present level of 15 billion US dollars in 1996. Advertising revenue from the World Wide Web is also expected to increase at a phenomenal rate: from 80 million US dollars in 1996 to four billion US dollars by the year 2000 (see http://www.nua.ie). Governments around the world are keenly aware of the Internet's potential for electronic commerce (see, for example, the ministerial declaration made at the July 1997 European Ministèrial Conference entitled 'Global Information Networks: Realizing the Potential' – http://www.echo.lu) and the US administration's Framework for Electronic Commerce (http://www.whitehouse.gov/). The main issues of concern in the area of electronic commerce include computer fraud and 'hacking', electronic banking over the Internet, privacy, encryption and copyright.

'Hacking' refers to the illegal entry into other people's computers, keeping information confidential, integrity (providing assurance that information has not been altered during transmission), authentication (i.e. providing proof of the identity of the originator of information) and non-repudiation (preventing a sender from denying having sent information). For a discussion of the subculture of 'hackers', who believe that information-sharing and cracking computer systems is ethically acceptable, see, for example, 'The Hackers' Dictionary' at http://www.tpconsultants. com/tnhd/index.htm). The 'Codex Surveillance and Privacy News' (http:// www.thecodex.com/codexof.html) shows the relative simplicity with which computers and cordless and mobile telephones can be cracked, thus enabling 'spying' or computer fraud to take place.

Privacy

Not only can confidential and private information be illegally tapped, but information in general from individuals can be gleaned over the Internet. Most browsers (software enabling access to the World Wide Web) leave a user's trace on the accessed computer (contained in the browser's 'cookie' file). It is also possible to access the lists containing the Internet addresses of subscribers to mailing lists provided the appropriate software is used. This may result, for example, in the Internet user's 'e-mail box' being flooded with 'spam' or unwanted 'junk' e-mail messages. There are relatively simple ways to circumvent this by, for example, deleting the cookie files, setting the browser software not to accept cookie files, adding an extra letter to one's e-mail address and so on, but it does necessitate some familiarity with computers. (Some detailed information pertaining to various issues relevant to computer crime and security can be found at http://www.ovnet.com/ ~dckinder/crime.htm).

Encryption

One way in which regulators can try to prevent fraudulent use in order to ensure the safety of electronic communication is by means of providing the infrastructure necessary for the encryption of messages and for the provision of digital signatures. A digital signature is a string of coded information that would clearly identify the origin of messages, files and images shipped via the Internet. Such signatures would use a central authority to prevent fraudulent commercial transactions on the computer network by matching a publicly accessible data string with a confidential string of numbers also called a 'key'. Several countries have already introduced or are in the process of enacting 'digital signature' legislation aimed at the development of a public key infrastructure.

At the end of March 1997 the OECD, after an intensive year-long negotiation, published a set of guidelines for cryptography for the effective protection of data which are transmitted and stored in information and communication systems such as the Internet. The guidelines emphasize the commercial importance of cryptography for ensuring confidentiality, integrity and availability of data; reject the US demand for key escrow encryption which would allow government access to private keys; and endorse trade and commerce in new cryptographic products (see http:// www.oecd.org for the guidelines and http://epic.org for an analysis). However, as Froomkin (1996) and Biddle (1997) point out, it is not quite clear yet to what extent policy-makers have fully considered the long-term consequences of such legislation such as the jurisdictional level (national or international) at which such legislation should occur, who issues the digital certificates (private or state companies), liability issues in the case of fraudulent use of digital signatures and so on. Furthermore, the deployment of key-recovery-based encryption infrastructures that provide government access to encryption keys involve 'risks and costs . . . which may ultimately prove unacceptable' (Abelson et al., 1997). (Details of the current EU policy on digital signatures and encryption can be found at http://www.ispo.cec.be/ef/policy/.)

The creation of digital signatures for every Internet user will further accelerate the use of Internet banking which began in earnest in 1996. Early 1997 saw several US banks providing an extensive range of on-line banking facilities such as bill payments, loan applications and investment transactions (see Goldfinger, 1996). In the same period, banks in several European countries (for example, the Deutsche Bank, the Royal Bank of Scotland, the Bank of Ireland) began offering on-line banking services on a trial or pilot basis. These services became operational during 1997. Additionally, 1996–7 saw an increase in the number of 'micro-payments' or 'pay-per-view' or 'pay-per-transaction', i.e. small spontaneous, incremental sales, which are expected to dominate the Internet digital goods market with an 80–90 per cent share of the market. Secure or encrypted credit-card payments are also on the increase.

With micro-system payments being installed in order to support pay-per-use purchasing systems and the amount of material available on the Net, as well as the fear that existing copyright laws may not fully extend to the digital domain, a greater value has been placed on intellectual property and creative works available on the Internet. Thus in December 1996 the World Intellectual Property Organization (WIPO) (http://www.wipo.org) passed two treaties which reform the present copyright policies and laws established at the Paris Berne Convention. The two treaties address digital creative works: the WIPO Copyright Treaty, a supplement to the 1971 Paris Berne Conventions on Literary and Artistic Works, allows for the digital transmission and distribution of a literary or artistic work under standing copyright laws and reconciles the inconsistent copyright laws used by the USA and European countries (for example, the USA has not historically recognized some of the rights covered by European copyright laws).

The second WIPO agreement, the Treaty on Performance and Phonograms, will protect on a global basis the exploitation of sound recordings by means other than simple physical reproduction. This treaty addresses the issues of digitally received music and recordings such as those widely available on the Internet (for example, midi files which can be downloaded, digitally manipulated and incorporated into other music – a not uncommon practice). A third WIPO treaty (the Database Treaty, which sought to extend copyright laws to protect facts and statistical data found in databases) was not passed. This treaty would have extended copyright protection to information and data found in databases and public domain directories. This controversial treaty is likely to be discussed again, as the European Union has approved a directive which is similar to this treaty and which will become law in the EU member states by the end of 1998. The directive allows for a certain level of protection for substantial investment in databases. (An overview of EU policy on copyright can be found in European Union, 1996b.)

Access

Relevant to the policy issues sketched above is the fact that only a small section of society actively use the Net. The existing Internet surveys mentioned above show that the vast majority of Internet users come from the more affluent and well-educated sections of society. There is, therefore, the danger of the creation of information 'have-nots', i.e. sections of society who through no fault of their own lack the economic means or the educational wherewithal to share in the benefits of the Internet. Defining access as not only 'the physical entree that the technology provides but access to the culture that comprises the Net', Kurland and Egan (1996: 391) suggest that 'barriers to access come in at least three forms: educational, economic and cultural'. Negotiating the Internet requires a certain amount of familiarity with computer hardware and software, a knowledge that cannot as yet be obtained in all educational establishments. Governments and industry in some countries are quite aware of this, judging by official publications as, for example, the Final Report of the (Canadian) Information Highway Advisory Council, 1995 (see also Anderson et al., 1995). Two recent EU studies would suggest an awareness of this danger: the 1996 Action Plan 'Learning in the Information Society, which calls for, *inter alia*, an acceleration of the entry of primary and secondary schools into the information society, and the ongoing study on Libraries and the Information Age (http://www.echo.lu).

Economic barriers refer to the costs involved in obtaining the hardware and software necessary to access the Internet, as well as paying variable costs for the service to connect to the Internet, i.e. telephone charges and account charges for an on-line service or Internet service provider. Telephone charges are currently higher in Europe than in North America, but in the long run it can be expected that the differences between the two continents will disappear due to the introduction of competition in the European telecommunications sector and the likely introduction of local call charges in North America. The hardware costs may decrease as has happened over the past few years, but not substantially as any decrease in price tends to be 'compensated for' by additional computer peripherals so that it is likely that prices will stay at their current levels. Notwithstanding the numerous plans to provide Internet access in schools and public libraries in different countries, it seems likely that existing social inequalities in society will continue to be reflected in cyberspace as is documented by the various surveys of Internet use mentioned above. Current cultural barriers to Net access include those that can be seen in society in general, namely a predominance of male values in several electronic forums (see Kurland and Egan, 1996) and a corresponding lack of female presence in the overall number of Internet users (see Seiter, 1998), for a detailed analysis of the gendered use of computers), a dominance of US culture and of the English language.

One way in which Internet use may spread to everybody in society is by means of developing more user-friendly platforms designed to access the Net. Four such devices began their development stage in 1996 (see http:// www.web-vantage.com/wv/webster/10250.cfm): small hand-held 'gadgets', which have yet to hit the market, that permit users to access the Net from wherever they are (provided they can tap into a telephone line); network computers, inexpensive stand-alone 'dumb' terminals (i.e. stripped-down computers) which are connected to a network that holds most of their software and data and that takes the user straight to the Net (also in development); telephones that offer limitless long-distance calls for the cost of an Internet connection (see for example http://vocaltech.com); Web TV (http://webtv.net), a set-top box that enables the viewing of World Wide Web pages and the use of other Internet resources such as e-mail on a television set – the only alternative that has made any sort of impact. This set-top box came to the market in the USA towards the end of 1996; a similar device called NetStation was launched in the UK in July 1997. This type of Internet set-top box simply plugs into any television set and necessitates a telephone line coming into the home. On first use, the set-top box automatically dials the nearest Internet service provider (ISP) which is connected with the manufacturing company of the set-top box and gives the user the option of opening an account with the ISP. Once an account has been opened the user can then connect to the Internet for a monthly fee of just under 20 US dollars (in the case of Web TV). Use of the set-top box requires no computer skills and is operated by means of a remote control; the cost of the set-top box amounts to about 20 per cent of the average computer. An optional keyboard (for sending e-mail) can also be purchased. Survey figures from the USA differ as to how successful Web TV is, or will be in the future. Internet set-top boxes are likely to be introduced in Europe during 1998; BSkyB is expected to offer Internet satellite access on TV as part of its digital satellite service to be launched in 1997–8.

Conclusion

Overall it is difficult if not impossible to make any predictions concerning the development not only of regulations concerning the Internet but of the development of this global network of networks. It is something different from established media and may call for a different approach at regulation altogether. Perhaps the Internet should not be seen as akin to broadcasting, which is highly regulated, but more akin to other areas of society. For example, Van Camp (1996) suggests that the concept of 'indecency' could be viewed in terms of how it is defined in the art world. Or perhaps computer-mediated communication like that of the Internet could be seen more in terms of another instance of policy issues arising from telecommunications and audiovisual convergence (see KPMG, 1996). What can certainly be argued is that the Internet ('cyberspace') is getting too big for individual nations to handle (Boyle, 1996) and that regulation of it can only succeeed by multinational agreements made in international forums such as the OECD, the ITU or the UN. This happened in the matters of digital signatures in the OECD in March 1997 and of Internet content at the UN in November 1997.

Bibliography

Abelson, H., Anderson, R., Bellovin, S., Benaloh, J., Blaze, M., Diffie, W., Gilmore, J., Neumann, P., Rivest, R., Schiller, J. and Schneier, B. (1997) The risks of key recovery, key escrow, and trusted third-party encryption. (http://www.crypto.com/key_study)

Aikens, G. Scott (1994) 'A history of Minnesota electronic democracy', *First Monday*, 1 (5). (http://www.firstmonday.dk/issues/issue5/aikens/index.html)

Anderson, R.H., Bikson, T., Law, S. and Mitchell, B. (1995) Universal access to email. (http://www.rand.org)

Biddle, C.B. (1997) Public key infrastructure and 'digital signature' legislation: 10 public policy questions. Posting by the author (biddlecb@cooley.com) to the mailing list RRE, 5 February.

Black, Jane (1996) Universities face challenges. (http://www.news.com/Special Features/)

Black, L. (1997) 'Internet law heads-uP #6', *CU Digest*, 9: 55.

Boyle, Alan (1996) The wired curtain, an MSNBC special report. (http://www.msnbc.com/news/WIRED_CURTAIN.asp)

Brackmann, G. (1996) Personalized news: Web robots compiled. Posting by the author to the mailing list Dreamwave. (http://www.cybercom.net/~wmcguire/dreamwave/)

Campbell, K. (1997) 'Who's watching the watchers?', Net column in *The Toronto Star*, 30 January. (http://kkc.net/toronto-star/1997/ts0130.htm)

Clift, S. (1997) 'Building citizen-based electronic democracy efforts', draft paper presented at the Conference on the Modernization of Democracy through the Electronic Media, Munich, 19–21 February.

Crispen, P. (1996) Roadmap 96 (an Internet tracing course). (http://ua1vm.ua.edu/~crispen/roadmap.html)

December, J. (1997) *The World Wide Web Unleashed 1997*. Indianapolis: Sams.net Publishing.

European Union (1996a) Green Paper on the protection of minors and human dignity in audiovisual and information services. (http://www.echo.lu)

European Union (1996b) Follow-up to the Green Paper on copyright and related rights in the information society (communication from the Commission). (http://www.ispo.cec.be)

European Union (1997a) Building the European information society for us all: final policy report of the high-level expert group. (http://www.ispo.cec.be)

European Union (1997b) Illegal and harmful content in the Internet: interim report (version 7). (http://www.ipso.cec.be)

Farrell, K. (1997) Dark side of the Web. (http://www.cnet.com/Content/Features/Dlife/Dark/info.html)

Froomkin, M. (1996) The essential role of trusted third parties in electronic commerce. (http://law.miami.edu/~froomkin/articles/trusted.htm)

Goldfinger, C. (1996) Electronic money in the United States: current status, prospects and major issues. Report of the fact-finding commission for the Financial Issues Working Group of the European Commission. (http://www.ispo.cec.be/infosoc/elecmoney.html)

Graphic, Visualization, and Usability Center (1997) Seventh WWW user survey. (http://www.cc.gatech.edu/gvu/user surveys/)

Griffin, A. (1996) The Electric Frontier Foundation's (EFF) guide to the Internet, v. 3.20. (http://www.eff.org)

Information Highway Advisory Council (1995) Final Report of the Information Highway Advisory Council. (http://info.ic.gc.ca/info-gighway/ih.html)

Kendrick, W. (1996) *The Secret Museum: Pornography in Modern Culture.* Berkeley, CA: University of California Press.

Kling, R. (1996) *Computerization and Controversy.* London: Academic Press.

KPMG (1996) Public policy issues arising from telecommunications and audiovisual convergence: a report for the European Commission. (http://www.ispo.cec.be)

Kurland, N. and Egan, T. (1996) 'Engendering democratic participation via the Net: access, voice and dialogue', *The Information Society*, 12: 4.

Macpherson, M. (1997) Citizen participation in politics and the new systems of communication. (http://www.snafu.de~mjm/CP/cp.html)

McQuail, D. (1994) *Mass Communication Theory: An Introduction*, 3rd edn. London: Sage.

Meyer, Eric (1996) The 10 myths of online publishing. (http://www.ajr.org/emcol3.html)

Mings, S. and White, P. (1997) *Making Money from the Web? Business Models for Online News.* Bundoora, Australia: La Trobe University.

Morris, M. and Ogan, C. (1996) 'The Internet as a mass medium', *Journal of Communications*, 46 (1): 39–50.

Negroponte, Nicholas (1995) *Being Digital.* London: Hodder & Stoughton.

Newhagen, J. and Rafaeli, S. (1995) 'Why communication researchers should study the Internet: a dialogue', *Journal of Computer-Mediated Communcation*, 1 (4). (http://jcmc.huji.ac.il/vol1/issue4/vol1no4.html)

Perrone, C., Repenning, A., Spencer, S. and Ambach, J. (1997) 'Computers in the classroom: moving from tool to medium', *Journal of Computer-Mediated Communication*, 2 (3). (http://jcmc.mscc.huji.ac.il/vol2/perrone.html)

Peterson, R. (1997) 'Eight Internet search engines compared', *First Monday*, 2 (2). (http:www.firstmonday.dk/issues/issue2 2/peterson/index.html)

Postman, Neil (1990) Informing ourselves to death. (http://www.fh.muenchen.de/home/fb/fb13/projects/Chaos/DK/neil-postman.txt)

Racicot, M., Hayes, M., Szibbo, A. and Trudel, P. (1997) Cyberspace is not a 'no law land'. (http://strategis.ic.gc.ca/nme)

Rankin, Bob (1997) Accessing the Internet via email. (ftp://rtfm.mit.edu/pub/usenet/news-answers/internet-services/access-via-email)

Resnick, Paul (1997) PICS, censorship, and intellectual freedom FAQ. (http://www.si.umich.edu/~resnick/pics/intfree/FAQ.htm)

Sansom, G. (1995) Illegal and offensive conduct on the information highway. (http://ifo.ic.gc.ca/info-highway/ih.html)

Schiller, D. (1996) Internet television: net makeover? Posting to the mailing list 'dreamwave@cybercom.net', 18 December.

Schiller, D. (1997) Killer applications. Posting to the RRE News Service, 9 June.

Seiter, E. (1998) 'Television and the Internet', in C. Brunsdon and John Caughie (eds), *Television and New Media Audiences.* Oxford: Oxford University Press. (Posting to the RRE News Service, 17 July.)

Solock, Jack (1996) 'Searching the Internet: I', *InterNic News.* (http://rs. internic.net)

Sternberg, S. (1996) The Internet as a business resource. (http://www.nstn.ca/bizguide/a-toc.html)

Supreme Court of the United States (1997) *Janet Reno, Attorney General of the United States, et al. Appellants* v. *American Civil Liberties Union et al.* (http://supct.law.cornell.edu/supct/html/96-511.ZS.html)

Tebbit, D./Australian Consolidated Press (1996) Interview with the Father of the Internet, Vincent Cerf. (http://www.apcmag.com/profiles/213a_1ce.htm)

Turkle, S. (1995) *Life on the Screen: Identity in the Age of the Internet.* New York: Simon & Schuster.

Tyner, R. (1996) Connections '96 (1996) Sink or swim: Internet search tools and techniques. (http://www.sci,ouc.bc.ca/libr/connect96/search.htm)

Van Camp, J. (1996) 'Indecency on the Internet: lessons from the art world', in S. Breimer, R. Thorne and J. Viera (eds), *1996–97 Entertainment, Publishing and the Arts Handbook.* New York: Clark, Boardman & Callaghan. pp. 255–75. (http://www.csulb.edn/~jvancamp/bio.html)

7

Convergence: Legislative Dilemmas

Bernt Stubbe Østergaard

Technological developments are an important component in the structural change in the European media landscape. This change is driven by digitalization, which breaks down the barriers between electronic media services. Mass-media legislation has hitherto been closely tied to the specific transport mode used (radio and television over the air, film and music via physical distribution, newspaper via print). Digitalization allows any content to be freely transmitted in any electronic transport mode. This convergence has clear implications for mass-media legislation.

Convergence involves a shift from *legislation* based on the social functions of media towards *regulation* addressing technical and industry policy issues. Convergence is also changing the media sector organizations. Dominant actors are repositioning to control the whole media process from content inception to delivery to individual audience segments. In this respect, media convergence heralds media concentration. However, the new multimedia environments are also spawning new actors, notably using Internet technology. This chapter discusses their strategies and positioning as convergence between telecommunications, computing and electronic mass media gathers momentum. Convergence is throwing up new media services at a prodigious rate. This chapter looks at the ones likely to reach European households over the next five to ten years, and how the EU-backed standardization efforts may, over time, contribute to an integrated global information infrastructure. However, convergence creates fundamental differences of interest between users and converged industries. Political decision-making must define and ensure the openness of the national electronic infrastructure, as today's carriers move into content and broadcasting (Figure 7.1).

Media legislation

The fast pace of innovation far exceeds the ability of democratic legislative bodies to develop single media legislation. This has moved the political process away from traditional mass media legislation focusing on a given medium's social impact. Gathering momentum is US-type regulation where

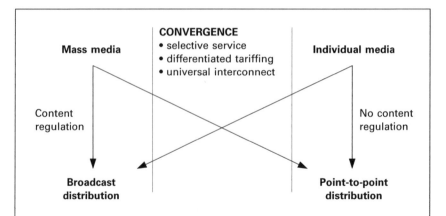

Figure 7.1   *Media crossing distribution boundaries*

general guidelines for a broad range of media are enshrined in law and a specialized authority assesses compliance in the marketplace.

Traditional legislation of networks and transmission systems that are affected by convergence in four key areas, according to Prosser (1996), are as follows:

1   *Universal service*: universal access to national public service channels via *common carrier obligations*.
2   *Regulation for diversity*: broad access to media via *non-discriminatory tariffing*.
3   *Regulation for competition*: forcing *de facto* monopolies to provide cost-based services to smaller competitors via *inter-connect agreements*.
4   *Regulation of content*: protection of national identity, minors and democratic processes via *language requirements, film censorship and must-carry rules*.

For broadcasting, both the distribution networks and the content have been regulated. This regulation was based upon political and cultural criteria. Access to scarce spectrum resources was controlled by licences and this power to license was, in its turn, used both to ensure universal signal coverage and as a basis for content regulation.

Table 7.1   *Examples of content–distribution regulatory mismatch*

Mass-medium content via point-to-point distribution medium
Multiplex broadcasting
Broadcasting over communication satellite
Music/information via phone (off-talk services)
Bulletin board services on a computer network
Broadcasting (radio, television) over the Internet

Point-to-point communication via mass medium
Telephone services over cable TV
Video-on-demand over cable TV
Paging services over FM radio

For the film industry, cinema ownership and film distribution have been regulated by competition legislation. Film content has been regulated by a system of censorship classification. Film production, distribution and showing have all benefited in different ways in each EU country from state aid based on unfair terms of trade legitimized by cultural heritage arguments. Regulation of individual media like telephone and computer communication initially emphasized universal access but has now moved to debates on 'basic service rights', allowing telecommunication carriers selectively to launch high-end telecom services in commercially viable locations.

Serious media convergence problems appeared in 1990 when the EU Commission abolished restrictions on the use of cable TV networks (amendment of directive 90/388/EEC), thereby opening for the supply of telecommunication services: initially voice telephony, followed later by subscriber and pay-per-view television as well as near video-on-demand. Convergence continued when point-to-point distribution systems were liberalized in the telecom deregulation drive (1993–8), while mass media remain content regulated (Table 7.1).

Any regulation tied to specific technologies or specific organizations, especially those that operate in a protected environment such as licensed services (carriers as well as public broadcasting services), needs to be reviewed. Legislation must accommodate the ongoing change as integration of existing media leads to new forms of multimedia environment wholly outside existing media organizations and any existing legal framework.

Media convergence is characterized by globalization of content, transport medium and by the type of actor involved. This raises the question of the need for a European supranational control body like the Federal Communication Commission (FCC) in the USA. Such a body should apply consistent regulations for all service providers to ensure content production, content distribution, user access and pricing in line with basic citizen rights and obligations. However, this is unlikely in the existing EU setting where media policy is not always determined on the national level. Specifically, the German *Länder* will resist any curtailing of their media powers.

End-to-end media control

Digitalizing transmission systems increases transmission capacity many fold and allows new forms of digitalized communication to take place. From a regulatory point of view, therefore, it will become harder to distinguish between broadcast services with an interactive component, and telecommunications services with a broadcast or video- based component. The business ramifications of this technological development indicate a horizontal expansion. This allows media players to control end-to-end content production and transmission, and thereby leverage content across a range of delivery vehicles. However, the investment muscle needed reduces the field to a select few players. National political regulators are thus faced with the need to review relevant regulation in several different fluid, semi-competitive markets. This may involve withdrawal of sector-specific horizontal regulation in some areas and replacing it with general competition laws. The inverse approach may be applied in other sectors.

However, European public policy-makers may in order to counter this blatant commercialism give priority to interactive communication between individual citizens. This requires a low-cost, but universal, infrastructure as opposed to the selectively rolled out broadband infrastructure essential to the commercialization of converged multimedia. Internet technology could provide a basis for such policy.

The commercial control of converged media

The heavy commercial players want to control the whole electronic distribution chain from the development of concepts (original content ideas), production of content, distribution and customer handling (creating consumer product options and billing individual usage). To do this they must control the set-top box decoder in the home. Existing technology allows many hundreds of channels to the home via cable and satellite. This allows the service provider to deliver customized services to individual house holds, such as telecom services and Internet access along with mass-media services like television and radio and the intermediate services given in Table 7.1. Control of the set-top box is crucial to control of the multimedia converged future. For this reason, set-top standard disputes are rampant among the interested parties, with no agreement in sight. Without such a standard users are locked into the content of specific providers due to the proprietary nature of their decoder.

Telecom carriers are changing into this type of full distribution chain organization based on their control of the household connections (cable as well as satellite), their economic strength and the liberalization and internationalization of telecom services. Competing hard with them are the media moguls who control commercial TV channels and film titles.

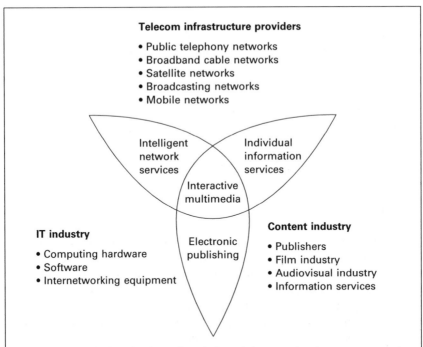

Telecom infrastructure providers

- Public telephony networks
- Broadband cable networks
- Satellite networks
- Broadcasting networks
- Mobile networks

Intelligent network services

Individual information services

Interactive multimedia

IT industry

- Computing hardware
- Software
- Internetworking equipment

Electronic publishing

Content industry

- Publishers
- Film industry
- Audiovisual industry
- Information services

As common digital technology foundations bring previously separate, analog technologies together, new hybrid services emerge. The inherent global nature of hybrid media make national legal systems obsolete.

Intelligent network services: create international virtual private networks across carriers' wide area networks.

Individual informatic services: allow content providers to tailor information services to specific customer needs.

Electronic publishing: gives any Internet-connected user global (at least European, North American and SE Asian) access to publish, advertise, sell any product. It also allows any recipient to reorganize any data received electronically.

Figure 7.2   *Convergence of computing, transmission and content industries*

Traditional broadcasters have a much harder time developing their business perspective due to lack of funds and stricter content and service provision regulations. However, no single player has it all, so complex and shifting alliances emerge and evaporate again in quickly changing patterns.

New media services force legislators either to develop 'holistic' legislation or to accept the *de facto* commoditization and commercialization of mass media. Holistic European mass-media legislators are looking to incorporate traits of telecom regulation by defining public standards for the interfaces between different parts of the communication system (see Figure 7.2) and combining this with universal access. This leaves scope for technological progress, innovation and competition in the future without disfranchising any social group. It does, however, entail acceptance of systematic social inequalities between the information 'haves' and 'have-nots'.

Published standards and designs for the global information infrastructure between applications suggest that a worldwide consensus on critical interfaces is feasible in the near term (1998–2002). Network-related standards are relatively well defined (TCP/IP communications and Web technology). Standards for applications and services are still fraught with proprietary specifications. Developing industry standards, however, is crucial for the multimedia aspects of the new services, where strongest growth is expected.

The new actors

The technology-based integration of previously separate production processes is challenging the social organization built around specific production types and organizations. The internationalization and decoupling of media and distribution systems gives rise to a new type of international 'broker', who buys programmes from independent producers, adds 20 per cent advertising time, and then leases up-link capacity in the most competitively priced up-link facility. With over 30 broadcasting satellites beaming programmes to a European-wide audience, the market is very competitive.

Ten years ago, 30 to 40 cable and satellite television channels became available to any European household able to afford a 500–600 dollar satellite receiver. Viewers have shown a considerable acceptance of high churn rates, cheap (fiction, non-art and non-moral) programming, heavily laced with commercials, to the chagrin of public broadcasters. These broadcasters emphasize reality, art and morality to use Denis McQuail's (1994) terminology.

Another group of new actors base their business on the growth of computers in households and national interconnect agreements forcing the dominant carriers to provide network access at prices approaching actual costs. By setting themselves up as independent service providers (ISPs), these new players enlist the help of sophisticated software boutiques to turn out innovative JAVA-based multimedia applications providing access to the whole range of Internet services (see Table 7.2).

The old actors

New media and novel ways to reach consumers, however, are a very costly business and few start-ups make it alone, aiming instead to be bought up by bigger players with the financial muscle to succeed. The huge investments needed come from the old media players, primarily carriers with cable and satellite distribution networks, PSBs going commercial, film rights owners, publishers, newspapers and individual financiers.

Table 7.2 *Internet cross-media and multimedia services*

Internet with its image-based services using JAVA scripts (multimedia computer programs that break the fixed links between an application (content) and the operating system, allowing any content on any user terminal via a common Internet interface, a so-called browser). Whereas JAVA is a very American concept, the Internet browser is a European development coming out of CERN (Centre Européene de Recherché Nuclear), a major powerhouse on the Internet. However, only the USA could provide a market environment to launch the concept commercially.

- Internet radio
- Internet telephone
- NetBot – the personalized news gatherer
- Video conferencing
- Networked video games with hundreds of participants
- MPEG – Internet television using digitally compressed video transmissions
- CNN video news fed to the desktop screen

From the content side of the media industry, programme producers are busy buying into the means of transmission. Their aim is to get the maximum leverage out of constantly more expensive media products, and as more channels open up, the churn rate increasingly becomes a problem. Owners of telecom infrastructure are buying into software and content industry. Content industries are also adapting to new transmission and user terminals (moving from paper to computer screen). As these three spheres converge, true multimedia services emerge.

Technological advances now allow integration of different media at mass consumer price levels, creating a new type of multimedia content and a new market for interactive multimedia products and services. Reduced legal barriers (lax cross-ownership legislation, dismantled public monopolies and freer access to international audiences) in an increasingly international market makes this a viable business proposition also in Europe.

Technological convergence: extent of the phenomenon

Digital technologies in telecommunications, broadcasting and computing are linking different terminals (telephone, television and PCs) to create intelligent user interfaces in fixed as well as mobile environments. A wide range of value-added multimedia products and services are targeted at the household market via set-top converters and decoders. Messaging services include telephony, data transfer, e-mail, voice mail, store-and-forward fax, on-line business information, Internet access and educational services. Transactional services comprise tele-shopping, home banking, electronic data interchange (EDI), electronic funds transfer (EFT) and interactive Internet games. On the business side, services include remote working, tele-business, business internets, advertising, database transactions, collaborative working, tele-medicine and so on.

Delivery vehicles being developed by telecom carriers are numerous: high-definition TV via direct broadcasting satellites (DBS), direct television broadcasting links, video-based services over existing telephone cable (high-speed digital subscriber link, HDSL) and cable TV as well as high-speed Internet access using cable modems over broadband cable. The markets for narrowcasting services are closed user groups and video-on-demand to individual households. Radio spectrum services provide mobile and personal communications.

Convergence is also combining the functionality of telephone and broadcast networks. This goes all the way from broadband multi-service (synchronous digital hierarchies, SDH; asynchronous transfer mode, ATM) networks to narrow band integrated services digital network (ISDN) and cable TV. There is also strong growth in bandwidth adaptive, leased private services, such as video circuits for the media industry.

Convergence is making fixed services mobile and personalizing the public communication networks. Interconnection in the context of the EU's open network provision (ONP) enables communication between traditional fixed operators and new entrants providing radio-based mobile communications, satellite mobile and personal communication services. This development is also driving the creation of hybrid cellular telephones. Out of the office, the hybrid functions as a normal GSM mobile telephone, but in the office it connects to the corporate internal telephone system using the DECT (digital European cordless telephony) standard. Digital radio connecting to corporate telephone systems will be commercially available by 1999 based on the TETRA (trans-European trunk radio) standard.

The intelligent network (IN) is paving the way for universal personal telecom (UPT) numbering, giving each individual a universal caller ID-number across any terminal on any network. This will give users the freedom to change service provider without having to change their 'address'. To facilitate new converged services across national boundaries in Europe a number of trans-European networks (TENs) initiatives focus on common Euro-ISDN definitions ensuring transborder access to bearer networks and generic services. This also requires the removal of special or exclusive rights over mobile services, removal of restrictions on self-provision or use of third-party infrastructure. Whether the success of GSM mobile telephony can be followed up by other genuine pan-European services like DECT, TETRA, paging and DCS-1800 is still an open question. North American and Japanese switch manufacturers are developing similar and, in many cases, more advanced functionality that are not compliant with the European standards.

Equipment disharmonization

Whether European-style standards succeed internationally also depends on the demonstrated ability to get new types of equipment quickly onto the

European market (indicating regulatory procedures rather than legislation). Europe still lacks mutual, fast recognition of equipment, as well as conformity and type examination procedures, standards, self-certification schemes (mutual recognition of networks and services licences) and common technical regulations. To develop these common standards for the new converging products and services will require strong political support for a coordinated European-level standard procedure. This is unlikely due to the large number of institutions involved. The main ones are ETSI (European Telecommunications Standards Institute), CEN (Comité Européen de Normalisation), CENELEC (the electronics industry section of CEN), and even IETF (the global Internet Engineering Task Force, which sets Internet standards).

As bandwidth requirements escalate high-end (2.4Gbps) SDH and SONET-based information superhighways will require setting up a global information infrastructure with defined interfaces for transborder flows of multimedia data, interactive communications, real-time cooperative communication, integrated film, sound and text. Every deregulated European telecom carrier wants to move into cable television and content production. However, some government regulators prohibit dominant carriers from doing so, in order to encourage competition. This has not deterred the involved carriers from experimenting with video-on-demand and pay-per-view services. The competition is coming from other national carriers, specialized high-speed carriers and cable television companies.

These companies are all building SDH networks (155Mpbs to 2.4Gbps backbones) offering customers E1 (2Mbps) to E3 (34Mbps) speeds with the ability to deliver voice services with video and broadcast television. The next step is to introduce intelligent network services like virtual private network services. Carriers are also going international, initially through alliances with other national carriers, but also through buy-ups of other carriers. Of the European carriers, BT is furthest along with globalization of its business, being the first European carrier to formulate a global strategy in a separate corporate entity. This has given the new company, Concert, 43 million customers in 70 countries. Similar developments are unfolding across Europe.

As market privileges are stripped away from traditional broadcasters, powerful entertainment and media conglomerates are focusing on media-in-the-home usage and programming-on-demand services in order to assemble mass-media supermarkets.

Consequences

As already noted, the contemporary approach to global information infrastructure standardization has been assigned high political priority. This is mainly due to the convergence of business interests among the principal mass media and the communications infrastructure. Otherwise, telecommunications and computing as well as audiovisual media, each with their own distinct existing structures and methodology, could remain apart for another half a century. Now the increasing overlap (and conflict) between the standards concerns of the EBU (European Broadcasting Union), ETSI and the Internet standards emphasize the merger of all digital media.

Differences in approach still exist between the principal international players in this field. The European penchant for standardization and emphasis on open systems before market forces have field-tested different approaches often clashes with American 'if it ain't broke don't fix it' attitudes. Typical European examples are ISDN, the digital telephony standard that took 10 years to get from specification to service launch. Another is GSM, the global mobile telephony standard that was implemented in 40 countries within six years of final specification. The American attitude dominates in high-speed data services like ATM (asynchronous transfer mode) which relegates full interoperability to later more mature stages of technology in the market. These differences are, however, less accentuated today than they were 10 years ago, and an international consensus is now developing fast. Standardization on the content side includes defining a common basket of services supplied through fully liberalized basic and alternative infrastructures.

Conclusion

In a converged digital environment, networks are increasingly neutral as to the nature of the service being carried over them. Thus, regulatory distinctions between different types of networks can no longer be mapped onto distinctive characteristics of the underlying electronic infrastructure. From the point of view of users, legislation should ensure that network owners and operators do not raise discriminatory barriers to access, or to any-to-any interconnectivity, or derive excess monopoly profits from non-standard network control. From the point of view of the network operators, media regulation should ensure that efficiency is maximized by the full exploitation of existing economies of scale.

These two regulatory perspectives may well be in conflict, and balancing them in a rapidly changing technological environment is not easy. Nevertheless, it seems likely that the eventual solution lies in separation of carrier network and content once carriers have been privatized and state owner interests are minimized (Figure 7.3). In a European context, this would involve a horizontal re-regulation of carriers. The US solution has been to create local loop companies solely responsible for ensuring as wide accessibility as possible. This will leave the carriers with their convergence strategies on the regional, national and international networks. Present

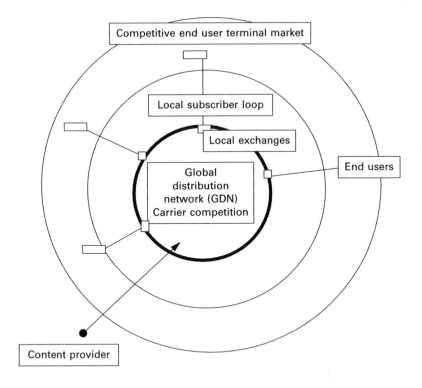

In the converged media world, content and services are provided via the GDN. By ensuring carrier-independent access to the GDN, users can access alternative carriers. However, carriers will resist any such initiative since it will remove their mainstay income – the monthly subscription fee from the end user.

Figure 7.3 *Creating layered competition in global telecoms*

attempts to regulate service provision and competition by means of network regulation are dysfunctional for network development. Placing limits on competition between telephone networks and cable TV networks or using broadcast transmission licensing as a tool of content regulation will be increasingly unworkable. A thorny issue is where to regulate the software required for service configuration, delivery and access (for example, signalling and encryption). Is it a part of the network or the service? If subscription TV encryption systems are left to the service providers, they can mount barriers to access via specific networks. If it is left with the carriers, they will have a good chance of dominating this market themselves. Today's proprietary consumer equipment in Europe limits cable and satellite distributed television to one-way transmission of TV channels. Multimedia is developing instead on the more open, US-dominated Internet.

Bibliography

Clements, Bernhard (1996) *Convergence between Telecommunications and Audiovisual: Consequences for the Rules Governing the Information Market – Background Note.* Brussels: European Commission, Legal Advisory Board.

EU Commission (1995) *Liberalization of Telecom Infrastructure and Cable TV Networks* (Green Paper). Brussels: EU Commission.

Garnham, Nicolas (1996) *Convergence between Telecommunications and Audiovisual: Consequences for the Rules Governing the Information Market – Regulatory Issues.* Brussels: European Commission, Legal Advisory Board.

Hamada, Junichi (1997) 'Advanced "public" and public broadcasting: toward a theory of "public broadcasting"', in *Studies of Broadcasting*, no. 33. Tokyo: Maruzen.

Knight, Julia and Weedon, Alexis (eds) (1996) *Convergence*, 2(2) (special issue), *Journal of Research into New Media Technologies.*

Kraemer, Joseph S. (1994) The realities of convergence. (http://www.eds.com/insights/ whitepap/err43000.shtml)

McQuail, Denis (1994) *Mass Communication Theory: An Introduction*, 3rd edn. London: Sage.

Negroponte, Nicholas (1995) *Being Digital.* New York: Alfred E. Knopf.

Prosser, Tony (1996) *Brighton Talk: Regulating the Changing Media.* Glasgow: University of Glasgow, School of Law.

PART III MEDIA AND SOCIOCULTURAL CHANGE

8

Commercialization and Beyond

Denis McQuail

Looking back to the dawn of the 'new media' age

As far as Europe is concerned, the age of new media can be said to have
begun at the start of the 1980s, prompted by two major innovations in
communication: the arrival of satellite broadcasting and the computer-based
text and image information services, known first as teletext and videotext.
Both of these prompted widespread speculation about the consequences for
established broadcasting systems and for the media as a whole. At that time,
the typical electronic media 'system' of each country consisted of nationally
exclusive radio and television broadcasting institutions, nearly all enjoying
monopoly status, and nearly all publicly financed, owned or controlled and
subject to close regulation. Supply was limited and it was unusual for
a country (in Europe) to have more than two or three television channels.
Here and there, the new electronic media were beginning to make their
appearance, but they were largely experimental or very restricted in reach.

The exceptions to this generalization about television and radio are easy
to identify. Britain was different in having a long-established dual public
and commercially financed system, but the latter was tightly regulated by
law to ensure performance close to that of the BBC. Italy was also different
in having a *de facto* dual system, the commercial wing of which was entirely
unregulated. A number of countries had significant elements of private
finance by way of television advertising. Spain was the leading example, but
the system was still state controlled. Luxembourg was quite unusual in
already making a national industry out of its commercial broadcasting
system, but with a restricted regional and language range. It does not go
too far to say that politics, exerted through governments and parties, was
everywhere in charge of the electronic media.

In this context, contemporary discussion of 'commercialism' and 'commercialization' followed well-worn and familiar paths. Numerous publications analysed media changes during the early years in terms of a framework

which continued to treat the status quo of national, public and non-commercial broadcasting as the norm, albeit one strongly challenged by the new developments (Ferguson, 1986, 1991; McQuail and Siune, 1986; Blumler, 1992; Siune and Truetszchler, 1992). In this chapter, it is recognized that this framework is no longer adequate to the task, and an alternative view of the electronic media order is considered which is more consistent with the present-day reality of the media industry and current trends of media policy.

Commercialism and the media

Commercialism and the process which leads to it – commercialization – are complex concepts with historical roots which are too deep to expose fully, but several specific connections with media policy need to be identified. In the first era of the printing press, private publishers came into conflict with state power which sought to maintain existing political or religious control. Market freedom for the early press was closely linked with individual freedom of expression and had a positive value in the broad movement towards greater democracy. A secondary meaning of commercialism, which developed during the nineteenth and early twentieth centuries gave a less positive connotation to the resulting 'free market place of ideas'.

'Commercialism' became identified with the pursuit of profit above all else and was associated with large-scale, low-cost, 'low-taste' production and distribution, especially aimed at the new industrial working class. Commercially free media also tended to develop into large-scale capitalist industries and earned the criticism often directed at monopoly capitalism. There was some extra opprobrium because of the implications for politics: control of the media gave the commercial ruling class differential access to the new propaganda power of the mass press. 'Commercialization' of the press often went hand in hand with 'depoliticization', in the sense of breaking the direct connection between a popular press and religious and politicial organizations to give rise to neutral, secular media forms.

Large private press monopolies were perceived in the first half of the twentieth century as posing a very real threat to democracy. This monopolizing tendency was especially marked in Britain and North America, since on much of the European continent the newspaper press retained closer ties with progressive political parties and movements. When the same commercial processes were associated with lower cultural standards and even morally dangerous publications, the circle of judgement around the new media industries (of press and film) seemed to be largely complete.

When radio broadcasting began in Europe during the 1920s, it was either sponsored by governments or very quickly brought within the scope of government control for a variety of reasons, but especially the wish to limit or direct its influence. Criticism of capitalism or commercialism was not the main driving force for regulation, but it helped to make political control more acceptable. Early attempts in Europe to exploit radio commercially were stillborn, and when television's turn came in the post-war era, the economic circumstances as well as the political climate were again unfavourable to commercial development.

It was a time of national economic and social reconstruction, a project to which broadcast media were harnessed under the banner of 'public service'. Although there soon developed active lobbies in several countries for opening television to the market, 'commercialization' was widely associated with social and cultural dangers attributed to the new medium (especially in the light of the American example, as perceived in Europe). Critics feared: loss of control over the national society and its culture, mores and standards of behaviour; increased power going to the business interests which already controlled most of the print media; cultural and educational debasement associated with catering for popular tastes and with the 'Americanization' of mass culture. Governments and parties of left, right and centre all shared some of the values which were embodied in public broadcasting.

Nothwithstanding significant inter-country variations, typical arrangements all conformed to the same basic model. The key features of the status quo were that the broadcasting system should be national in character, subject to a public monopoly and non-commercial (or non-profit) in character (see Chapter 3).

The values and virtues of 'non-commercialism'

The traditional 'non-commercialism' of European broadcasting is what concerns us here. As we have seen, it covers a wide range of meanings, drawing broad support as a result. A first meaning relates to structures of ownership and control. Before 1980, with the exceptions noted above, no radio or television service of any significance in Europe was funded by private capital or operated primarily for profit. Even the British exception was carefully regulated to ensure that many normal free-market mechanisms could not operate, especially those leading to true competition or conglomeration. This takes us to a separate aspect of 'commercialism': the logic and spirit of commerce, especially the pursuit of profit as a primary goal, which implicitly denies or subordinates other communication purposes. Depending on one's political beliefs and ideology, one could regard non-commercialism as a positive value in itself or just a condition which allows more idealistic, non-profit goals to be pursued.

Thirdly, national broadcasting systems were generally non-commercial in being deliberately organized to serve public rather then private interests. They were intended, in varying degrees, to help support what would now be widely called a 'public sphere' (Verstraeten, 1996). In practice this meant guaranteeing access to a range of representative political and social views and organizations and securing a flow of reliable information for the conduct of democratic public life. Other 'public interest' goals, such as maintaining overall media diversity and supporting various national and civic projects, were seen to call for a degree of public control that was inconsistent with a free-market system. In general, keeping broadcasting in public hands ensured a high degree of accountability for carrying out public tasks. This more direct accountability to the political system was also intended to ensure high standards of performance quality and of ethics.

Non-commercialism was also expressed in a positive discrimination for educational and cultural content, well beyond what could be justified on grounds of audience demand. The preferred cultural provision consisted especially of works belonging to the traditionally valued arts ('high' culture) or of works belonging to the national and linguistic cultural heritage. This feature of non-commercialism involved a widespread refusal to satisfy popular demand for television entertainment, as measured by normal audience market criteria.

Finally, the spirit of non-commercialism was reflected in the attitude and policy towards advertising and sponsorship, which at best were widely regarded as 'necessary evils' of commercial media. The typical attitude to advertising was negative, regarding it as insidious, manipulative and often mendacious. Even if innocent of these sins, it encouraged 'consumerism' and habits of waste and extravagance and victimized the less well-educated or more vulnerable by promoting unhealthy habits and products in an irresponsible way. Advertising in European broadcasting, if not banned altogether, was strictly regulated in respect of amount, placement and actual content.

The breakdown of consensus

In the early 1980s and beyond, most of the 'new media' and new technologies were either publicly sponsored experiments or rather futuristic fantasies which achieved little general success in the marketplace. Often the technologies available as well as the investment fell short of what was needed to break into the established media system. The early European transborder satellite ventures, whether commercial (like Sky) or public (like the EBU in 1985) turned out to have little or no success. The frequently heralded new media revolution was extremely slow in materializing, and where it made progress it was surprisingly similar to what had gone before.

The basic structures of the media (both press and broadcasting) were unchanged, even when broadcasting monopolies were ended and new commercial television services, based on cable and satellite, began to proliferate in the early 1990s. Public service broadcasting, after a decade of change, still seemed fairly secure in most Western European countries and the really new technologies had barely taken off. Even at the end of the 1990s, the diffusion of cable and satellite distribution is still rather slow in Europe and patchy in its effects on the media landscape.

A changed climate of opinion

It is notoriously easy to invent one's own version of the 'spirit of the age' or the 'climate of the times', since there is never any decisive evidence, only impressions and other opinions. Nevertheless, when we look today at the range of positions and projects taken up by the most significant categories of policy-relevant actors in Europe, it is hard to find much support for the main features of the old broadcasting order, which can be summarized as follows:

- monopoly
- public funding
- rationing of airtime
- elite-driven programming
- closed frontiers
- slow technical development

There are compelling reasons why these features cannot be sustained or brought back. The pressures for change include:

- moves towards European unity
- reductions in government spending
- new technologies
- unstoppable media globalization
- the changed labour market
- lack of popular support
- the 'treason' of politicians

Leaving politics aside, the various ideals which once sustained the pro-public broadcasting coalition are no longer held together by the cement of widespread anti-commercial beliefs and attitudes. What seems to have happened is that the unified paradigm which consolidated diverse anti-commercial ideas has been fragmented and there is no longer a single organized constellation of ideas guiding policy. The component parts of the old paradigm have been disassembled and if they are still pursued it is fragmentarily and by other means. The principle of 'non-commercialism' has lost recognition as well as adherents. It has been effectively transformed into one particular minority value (perhaps expressed as anti-consumerism, pro-ecologism) or expressed in terms of taste and convenience (more minority culture, fewer commercial breaks), things which the market itself can also provide at a price to the individual consumer.

Some of the elements of the old anti-commercial paradigm have almost disappeared. There is already little trace of any principled or effective resistance to broadcasting being run as a private business, as long as the public sector does not have to be sacrificed to this end. Operating rules and conditions can still be set by government and specific policy objectives for the national society can still be realized. Parties of the left show little sign of wanting to return to a non-commercial past and theorists of the left also seem more interested in finding accommodations to the new spirit of the age than fighting old battles against commercialism (see Collins and Murroni, 1996).

The fundamental critique of commercialism as such, as an agency of capitalism, seems largely to have been extinguished in mainstream politics. The fact that public broadcasting managements are also thinking more about surviving and perhaps even prospering in the new climate has made it less likely that they will be saved by social democracy and a return to the past.

The only countries in Western Europe where public monopolies for television remain are Austria and Switzerland, and in both cases there are plenty of German-language (and other) commercial alternatives available by cable and satellite. The motives for maintaining these arrangements are a mixture of the economic, nationalistic, cultural and political, but not anti-commercial as such. The examples illustrate the fact that smaller countries, much more than larger ones, experience difficulties in maintaining the integrity and autonomy of a national broadcasting system, which all states still want, whether it is in public or private ownership.

The admission of advertising as a major source of finance for public broadcasting is no longer a controversial political issue, except in so far as private broadcasters object to unfair competition. There seems no longer to be a principle involved, as long as the basic rules of the EU television directive, or better, are generally adhered to. The BBC in Britain remains almost the last bastion of resistance to advertising and this is more the choice of the organization for strategic reasons, of the commercial competition out of self-interest and of the political establishment for its own reasons than a conviction that advertising would destroy the character of the service. Commercial modes of management and programming strategies are certainly not foreign to the BBC and it has its own ambitions to become a global media player in due course. The ongoing privatization of major public telecommunications bodies in Europe gives a powerful impetus to the commercializing trend.

At the moment it seems that profit-seeking and consumerism have been widely and largely de-demonized in Europe and have acquired respectability. This transformation has been helped by a public perception of immediate benefits for large sections of the audience in the form of more choice of channels and more popular programming at little extra cost. The public has seemed to gain without obvious loss (since a public sector remains) and, at least in the early stages of entry, commercial channels have tended to behave themselves.

Whatever the mixture of expectations and motives behind the deliberate commercialization of broadcasting during and beyond the 1980s, the calculation that the change would be popular has turned out to be correct. However much the process now seems in retrospect to have been inevitable, it was certainly a political project in the countries that made the running, especially Germany, France and Britain. Despite the historical reverse correlation between commercialization and politicization noted above, the project of commercialization was initially intended to assist parties of the right by increasing the influence of their friends and by reducing the role and influence of public sector media. However, the results have not all turned out according to this logic. The left in power also acquired some novel ways of making friends for itself, and a general result has probably been a reduction of political power over electronic media across the board.

Continuity in the new order

To acknowledge a receptive popular opinion and a somewhat muted opposition on the part of the main public interest groups and informed elites does not mean that the issue is closed or that nothing remains of principled and effective policy action in response to commercialization. It is more that maintaining the original goals of the public sector are not seen to require a position which is anti-commercial as such.

Four key features of the original paradigm which have survived in a more or less healthy form in Europe are:

1 The aspiration to protect a 'public sphere' for debate and information, with rights of access and protection for diversity.
2 Positive discrimination for the national language and culture in respect of audiovisual production and distribution.
3 Maintaining and enforcing public accountability for a wide range of media ethical and performance issues on which there is public concern.
4 Limits are set to excessive private monopoly growth, especially by restricting cross-media ownership and conglomeration of audience reach.

In addition, the wish to protect cultural and educational values more generally, and support for the idea that national broadcasting is a resource for social objectives, have survived the rise of private television and are influential in modifying strictly business decisions.

Any revised model of the new semi-commercial order of electronic media in Europe has consequently to take account of a good deal of continuity of values and public expectations. New commercial television services have managed to avoid expensive programming for minority tastes, but have not escaped obligations in relation to news, information and conventional values about matters such as violence and sex. When it comes down to it, the means of finance as such ceases to be a very burning issue, but many of the other issues once connected with it have not been extinguished.

Commercialism as an engine of change

Current developments in television and audiovisual services in Europe are now spurred on almost exclusively by commercial motives and private investment. This applies to cable, satellite, digital television, multimedia and interactive media of all kinds including the Internet. Nearly everywhere it has become easier to enter the different markets, sometimes with positive encouragement from governments. It is now almost unthinkable that a government ministry would take an active role in developing any of the new technologies, except by deregulation or very indirect encouragement.

The gradual privatization of former telecommunication monopolies has begun and will give an enormous push to commercial expansion based on potential demand. The new corporations are potentially very large and multinational, with enormous and more or less guaranteed cash flows and often with limited competition within national boundaries. They are actively looking for investment opportunities in media developments which will increase their own revenues as well as having a potential for growth in value. They want to see more cable in the ground and more traffic for the telephone lines. The former ethos of public service and non-commercialism of these bodies and their older administrative logic have presumably been transformed or are being so.

While the actual shape of demand for electronic media goods and services is still very unclear and hard to predict far into the future, few doubt that there will be room for large expansion, continual replacement and innovation and an increased share of the media sector generally in the national economic balance sheet. There is also no doubt of the demand for media software products, especially to fill the appetites of expanding television channels. Television production companies such as Endemol in Holland are becoming major industrial players. Their success in turn stimulates more growth in the market.

The valuation of big media groups is steadily rising and units are increasing in size as a result of business alliances, increasingly crossing national frontiers as a result of national limitations on cross-media ownership. Most of the larger American media firms, including Disney, Time Warner, Turner Broadcasting, News Corporation and NBC, already have some footholds in the expanding European media scene. In some countries, public broadcasting bodies are well financed and are expected to behave according to a commercial logic in everything but fulfilling their minimal public service programming obligations (which are sometimes open to redefinition). They are also expected to compete in the market for valuable media products like rights to sporting events. The result is an industrial-commercial climate, in which nearly all 'news' about the media (and there is a lot) is dominated by themes of success or failure in the cut and thrust of the marketplace.

The general implication of these remarks is to support the argument that commercial operation and commercial logic are now the norm rather than the exception for the world of European broadcasting and that this becomes steadily more rather than less true. When the first commercial operators appeared on the television scene to test the waters in the early 1980s they were marginal in their influence and status. Since then, the situation has been so transformed that their successors are largely determining the shape of the media future, including broadcasting, with government steadily making regulatory concessions. The limits are set by what audiences and advertisers are willing to pay rather than by government rules.

The European project for a larger and unified audiovisual market, coupled with telecom liberalization and the promotion of competition and increasing scale of the media industry, has provided an environment, as intended, for a more business-like approach to the cultural industries. The television directive of the European Union has been more of a success than was predicted in its early stages both for being fairly effective and enforceable in its limited aims and also serving to allay or defuse some public fears about what commercial television would mean. The project as a whole provides a certain legitimacy and source of political support within countries where commercialization and the decline of the public sector remains an issue.

While nearly all the really *new* media technologies have been much slower to evolve into 'exploitable' forms than was originally predicted, the projected increase in demand for 'old-style' television was not exaggerated and this has on its own been enough to break the old mould of non-commercialism. The most important key has been cable, but experience in Britain and France shows that there are other paths to the same goal of channel multiplication and television abundance. The upcoming technologies involve digitalization by terrestrial or satellite means and are likely to continue existing trends rather than chart new futures.

In any case, a large part of 'television' will come to be dominated by distribution technologies and financial arrangements which are very profitable and commercially exploited. Commercial operation will clearly be the new norm for new services, unlike broadcast TV where public service was the original norm. It remains to be seen what digital television will bring, but it will reinforce current trends and involve further commercial challenges to public broadcasting. All this has the effect of implicitly 'deproblematizing' commercialism.

As national media become exposed to the wider environment of global media developments, there is no longer much real choice, either for investors or media professionals, except adaptation to the predominant norm. In respect of television broadcasting, there will be no significant protected enclave of national cultural media kept from the touch of market forces. Of course such enclaves will remain, but they will be increasingly marginal and not very popular with either media professionals or public. The changes in bordering Eastern Europe are going in much the same direction as sketched for Western Europe, only faster and in more extreme degree. This does not have any necessary immediate consequence, but in the longer-term perspective this is an extension of Europe and of prosperous media markets.

In terms of global media industries, there is clearly a large potential market for European enterprise and production and a growing dynamic, as viable lines of development are found. The new rhetoric concerning the electronic superhighway may be largely hot air and smoke, but it puts fresh wind behind the sails of commercially driven discovery and expansion. It is unrealistic to expect the drive towards this future to be a public (or public service) project in Europe, any more than it is in America.

This analysis may overstate the extent of change but if accepted it makes discussions of 'degrees of commercialization' seem rather myopic and possibly a bit irrelevant in a world where most of the actors seem intent on expanding the scope and degree of 'commercialization' for a variety of self-chosen interests (private, national, European), but all sharing pretty much the same liberal philosophy about the need to promote and satisfy mass demand and also create new markets for all kinds of new products made possible by the applications of new communication technology.

The 'commercialization' of European television: expectations and trends

If the preceding assessment is correct we should be able to demonstrate the adoption of a new norm for European television, according to a number of indicators. While concepts of commercialization differ, there is some consensus on what it means for television *supply*, *content* and, to some extent, *audiences*. Thus the main effects of the process are thought to include some or all of the following:

- A significant increase in the amount of television programming available to audiences, irrespective of the 'platform' or means of delivery.
- The expanded opportunity to view television is likely to be reflected in increasing the average time spent viewing. The general effect should be towards a convergence of average viewing time between countries, as inequalities in supply are reduced and national cultural differences submerged.

- A corresponding increase in the total *amount* of imported television product (mainly from America) will occur. This trend does not necessarily mean an increase in the *percentage* of American foreign programming because of the operation of the European directive rules.
- A change in the ratio of light or 'entertainment' programming (games, drama, fiction, confessional talk shows) compared with 'serious' or informational programming.
- A marginalization of the less popular cultural and informational programming (especially for minorities) as a result of unfavourable scheduling and lower budgets.
- In general, a growing convergence in the 'quality' of public and private provision as public broadcasting adopts the style and ethos of private broadcasting in order to keep its audience share.
- A fragmentation of national audiences as viewing time is redistributed across more of the available channels, and also regrouped according to taste, interests and perhaps socioeconomic level.
- A loss of content diversity, especially 'horizontally' in time, as different general television channels compete for the same household audience at the same favourable peak viewing times.
- A larger share of the income of television comes from advertising (or sponsorship). In general, the more production and transmission is paid for by advertising, compared to either public funds or individual subscription, the less freedom there is to make programmes which are altruistic, or critical of business or just not profit-seeking.

In the period between the mid-1980s and the early 1990s there was already plenty of evidence that all of these trends were under way, although the pace of change was very variable between one country and another and difficult to predict.

Structural trends: 'abundance' and finance

The Euromedia Research Group (1991) made an assessment of the general situation of television in Western Europe in 1990 as well as a number of predictions for change until 1995. The 1990 assessment provides some kind of benchmark for assessing the direction and pace of change towards a more commercial system. In general, the predictions were for rather modest and gradual change.

In 1990, we took account of 'established national channels' in assessing the extent of television systems. These were nearly all terrestrial broadcasters, the main exception being Germany, where significant commercial channels were offered by satellite and cable. Our assessment ignored quite a lot of cable-supplied channels without a significant audience and also pan-European channels, thus without a clear home base. The problem of counting channels is more difficult and risks being more arbitrary today, so a direct comparison with 1990 figures in terms of *number* of channels can be misleading. The European Commission's monitoring of television programmes for the enforcement of the television directive counted 148 separate channels (in 1994), although many of these are very minor operations. The report of the European Communication Council (Zerdick, 1997: 301) puts the number of national channels in the same group of countries in 1995 at over 200, mainly by including numerous private channels with small audiences (for instance, 62 in Britain and 22 in France).

In trying to assess the changes in number of channels, as far as possible with the same criteria as were adopted in 1990, comparison is bound to be approximate. One guideline is to include nationally available channels which have at least 5 per cent of the national (or relevant) audience. We can also leave subscription channels aside and deal with international channels (and cross-border viewing) separately. According to this accounting, the total number of (national) channels has increased since 1990 from 50 to 68 in 15 countries, rather more than predicted, although much of the increase is accounted for by smaller countries (for example, Greece and the Netherlands) and is not widely experienced on this scale.

In fact there has not yet been a major distribution of audiences away from the channels that already existed in 1990, although Spain, Sweden, Greece and the Netherlands have experienced a genuine expansion of national television provision. There has also been a general consolidation and often increase in audience share by commercially financed channels everywhere. For those who have cable or want to get satellite reception, there is also a range of international channels, many based in the United Kingdom. Prominent on the list are Euronews, Eurosport, BBC World, CNN International, MTV, Discovery, TV5, NBC Superchannel, and Arte.

Along with the growing number of channels, there has been an increase in the amount of television transmitted, although the main shifts towards day- and night-time television by the established channels had already occurred by 1990 and the increase is now mainly due to the programming of the additional private channels. Figures for transmission time for the German public service channels, for instance, show an increase of 10–15 per cent over the situation reported in 1991. In Belgium, television broadcasting time of three national channels rose between 1990 and 1992 from 19 to 24 hours (Tanghe and De Bens, 1993–4). French television hours of transmission rose between 1983 and 1993 by 80 per cent (Chaniac, 1995).

It is hardly surprising that no new public channels have appeared since 1990, apart from the Gaelic language channel, in Ireland. On the other hand, none of the existing public channels have been privatized (as happened to TF1 in 1986) or have stopped operating. A minor exception to this point is that one of the broadcasting organizations within the Dutch system (Veronica) took advantage of the opportunity to become an independent commercial broadcaster in 1995. Another rare example of a governmentally initiated extension of broadcasting (although long in the pipeline) was the 1997 launch in the UK of a new terrestrial channel, Channel 5.

As predicted, the gradual extension and consolidation of commercial television in Europe has led to a steady increase in the share of a growing advertising spend which goes to audiovisual media and television in particular. Comparative figures for the amount and source of revenue for television confirm a strong commercializing trend in terms of the total advertising budget and audiovisual media's share compared to other media. However, much of the growth is catching up by countries which previously had little or no TV advertising revenue. In countries with well-established commercial systems before 1990, such as Italy and the UK, a temporary ceiling to TV's share of total advertising spend may already have been reached.

The shift in a commercial direction has been accompanied by a further tendency for the public channels to increase their income from advertising relative to the licence fee, although this trend is far from universal. The TV licence fee has risen considerably in some countries since 1990, especially in Austria, France and Germany. In others, it has typically kept up with inflation (Zerdick, 1997). If anything, the dependence of public broadcasting on the licence fee has risen, especially as the advertising market has become more competitive. The turnover of private television has increased much more than the income of public service channels.

The impact of commercialization on content

The following quotation about the effect of change on German television will express what many have observed about their own national situation, although without being able to prove it. It is based on the findings of the Federal President's report, *The Conditions of Television*, of February 1994:

> Most channels distribute programmes for more than 20 hours per day, with many repeats. Both public service and commercial channels have partly converged on a mixture of 'infotainment' and entertainment; public service television – now with its minority share – still broadcasts substantially more information and educational programmes than its commercial competitors. . . . Major tendencies in the programme structure of German television have been summarized as follows: First of all we can observe a surplus of programmes, both in entertainment and information. The TV programme itself has become more sensational, more negative, focusing more on scandals and rituals in politics. Entertainment has become increasingly focused on sex and violence, on simplistic stereotypes, more rapid editing as part of a slowly developing 'video-clip aesthetic', a new confusion of realities and television realities. (quoted in Ludes, 1996: 128)

It is not easy to demonstrate the effects which commercialization has had on content, partly because categorization is never unambiguous and the broadcasting organizations have an interest in demonstrating (by way of programme statistics) that they are keeping up to certain standards or meeting their obligations. There are other reasons, however, including the very scale of expansion of the television offer, which change the significance of percentages and make it more important to know about audiences reached as well as composition of schedules. In a dynamic situation, with changes coming from several sources, including society and public taste, it is also usually impossible to establish direct cause and effect relations between structural and programming changes. In each national television situation, the forces at work are somewhat different and changes (or their absence) often require interpretation in the light of local circumstances.

There are good reasons for believing that most of the earlier content trends (for instance, those reported in Siune and Truetzschler, 1992) are still under way, especially those concerning the differences between public broadcasters and their commercial rivals. The former still do 'better' in terms of cultural and informational content, although they also appeal to popular taste in order to survive in the audience marketplace. Many of these adaptations are not easy to measure objectively. They are often more a matter of style than substance, although they also often reflect a fundamental shift of management purpose.

It is possible, however, that two trends of the early period of commercialization have been halted or even reversed. These concern the import of foreign programmes and the increasing use of older material. The probable explanation lies both in the relative success of the television directive and in the increasing revenue of the commercial rivals to PSB. They can now better afford to make more of their own programmes or buy from national independent producers.

There is no overall systematic body of data available about content changes, although there are some comparative series over time for earlier periods (for example, Kelly and De Bens, 1992), as well as a number of scattered national case studies (for example, for Finland, the Netherlands, Belgium, Italy, France, Norway and Germany), using different methods and having different objectives. These are discussed below. A new source of information on some points are the reports of the Commission of the European Communities on matters covered by the television directive, especially the degree of domestic (and European) production.

The main hypotheses about the effects of commercialization (and competition) on content have concerned the following:

- The absolute and relative share of television time, especially prime time, given to information, education and culture, usually with reference to increased 'entertainment' content.
- The performance of public service television, especially in respect of traditional obligations and degree of convergence on the commercial sector in programming policy.
- Program diversity.

- Reliance on foreign programmes and on 'second-hand' content.
- Standards of 'quality' with particular reference to sex and violence or creativity and originality.

Hypotheses about these issues can be formulated and tested in many different ways and this is one of the reasons for the lack of a clear picture about current trends. We know a good deal about the absolute differences between different channels and between public and private systems as they were at the start of the 1990s but not very much about the direction and speed of change. Whatever the explanation, it does seem from the scattered evidence that the pace of change as it affects the main national channels in many countries, whether public or private, is still rather slow and gradual. There is a good deal of stability in the structure of television programming over quite long periods of time.

This is true, for instance, of the Netherlands, despite some quite large system changes in the first half of the 1990s. Provisional findings by Vochteloo and Emons (1995), comparing the programme schedules of public broadcasting channels in 1986–7, 1990–1 and 1994–5, showed rather little overall change. However, the proportion of output allocated to the 'informational category' had fallen overall from 54 to 48 per cent over eight years and the category of 'shows' (quizzes, games, talk shows) had risen from 9 per cent of total time to 19 per cent. In the case of Finland, Hellman and Sauri (1994) compared public YLE with commercial MTV for the period from 1970 to 1992 and also reported a high degree of stability over time. Here, there is reference to a stable duopoly situation comparable with that obtaining between the BBC and ITV in Britain and before major shocks from new competitors.

In the Norwegian case, where the monopoly was only broken in 1992, comparisons over time and between public and commercial channels have lead to two main conclusions (Syvertsen, 1997). First, the public broadcaster, NRK, has increased the share of entertainment programming and reduced the proportion of prime time given to education and culture. Secondly, in overall terms NRK has maintained its distance in programming from the commercial channels.

A similar pattern of difference and stability seems to emerge from statistics for Italy comparing RAI with Fininvest (RAI, 1997). RAI consistently transmits more television in the content categories 'news, information and culture'. In 1995, the figure was 37 per cent as against 25 per cent for Fininvest. Generally, Fininvest gives consistently more time to the category 'fiction TV': 33 per cent in 1995 compared to RAI's 12 per cent (RAI, 1997: 191). There is some evidence, however, that over time Fininvest channels have converged on RAI in respect of less reliance on imports and more own production. Between 1987 and 1995, the overall proportion of 'own production' for RAI fell slightly from 72 to 69 per cent, while the corresponding figures for Fininvest show a steady rise from 23 to 48 per cent (RAI, 1995: 100; RAI, 1998: 136).

The figures reported by the European Commission for 1994 (Document 15/7/96) show two of the Fininvest channels below the quota level for European content, but the overall average satisfactory. This is another example of a national system, which has had a more or less mature commercial sector for some time, where a stable duopoly operates and where there is little impact as yet from new competitors. RAI and Fininvest have 90 per cent of the audience share between them.

Evidence of programme structure trends in Germany reported in *Media Perspektiven* (1996) confirms some of the trends which have been noted. The comparisons relate to the two public service channels, ARD and ZDF, and the three leading private channels, RTL, SAT1 and Pro7. The overall picture in 1995 still showed large differences between the programme structure of the two public service channels and three commercial channels. For instance, on a 24-hour basis, ARD and ZDF had respectively 40 per cent and 44 per cent information compared with 14 per cent for RTL, 14 per cent for SAT1 and 10 per cent for Pro7. The comparable figures for 'fiction' were 32, 32, 34, 51 and 54 per cent.

The trends in general structure of content between 1986 and 1995 show a fairly high degree of stability of programming in the public service channels, according to several measures. For instance, the balance between 'information and education' and 'fiction' has remained about even over 10 years for the public channels. They also give almost the same percentage of their time to news in each year from 1987 to 1995, hovering around 17–18 per cent. The trends for private television in Germany are somewhat more mixed. On the one hand, two of the channels have increased the proportion of time given to news and education, although the general gap remains, compared to public channels. Private television seems a little more diverse in its content than in its early days. On the other hand, there has been a steady decline in news on television during prime time on RTL and SAT1 (19.00 to 23.00 hours). The proportion of news on the two channels jointly fell from about 13 per cent in 1986–7 to 4–5 per cent in 1994–5. There has been a very large increase in advertising time, compared to a stable situation for public television. Private television is consolidating its position, but not converging on public television.

A recent analysis of the actual content of news in detail tells a somewhat different story. According to Bruns and Marcinkowski (1996), there has been a fairly consistent trend towards convergence of news content and style between public and two main commercial channels (RTL and SAT1) between 1986 and 1994. The commercial channels have increased the proportion of news given to 'political themes' to approach the original much higher norm of ARD and ZDF. RTL and SAT1 also sharply decreased the 'human interest' subjects in their news to match the unchanged public service norm. On several other internal indicators of news type, a distinct pattern emerges of public and commercial moving (up or down) to approach much the same level. This applies, for instance, to the representation of government actors and prominent persons, and to the average number of themes relating to violence and to actual violent sequences.

In Flanders, a longitudinal comparison of programme structures (Tanghe and De Bens, 1993–4) between VTM and BRT (1988–92) shows some features which are familiar elsewhere. The first result of commercial television in Flanders was to cause a general increase in television transmission time, from 11 to 24 hours a day. Secondly, the supply of 'amusement' and 'fiction' is much increased in absolute terms, although in percentage terms the increase is not so large. De Bens (1997) reported that the share of 'entertainment programmes' on the main public channel (BRTN1) increased quite steadily from 48 per cent in 1988 to over 60 per cent in 1995, although there was also a corresponding proportionate decrease in the second public channel. The main Flemish commercial channel VTM increased its entertainment share from 67 per cent in 1989 to over 81 per cent in 1995. According to De Bens (1997: 8), 'public and commercial channels are growing closer in this respect'. The earlier policy of making the second channel (BRTN2) more serious has been reversed since 1996.

We can observe certain changes in the role of the two public (BRTN) channels in response to competition. In general, the proportion of time given to information on public and commercial channels remained much the same over the first three years of commercial competition. As far as transatlantic influence is concerned, the percentage share of American content remained high but did not increase, while there was a modest increase in the share of home-produced fiction. In general, the respective roles of public and commercial channels remained different and largely unchanged over the early years of commercial competition. There has been little sign of programmatic 'convergence', except perhaps in the decreased reliance of VTM on imports as time goes by.

A last illustration can be taken from France where similar trends have been observed over a decade of commercial competition (see Chaniac, 1995). Essentially these comprise a large increase in volume, and much more fiction both in absolute and relative terms (from 19 per cent of output to 38 per cent). The main loss has been of 'information' content on television, from a 26 per cent to a 10 per cent share of total time. The share of 'news' has decreased, but that of 'magazines and documentaries' has increased in amount and share. These very gross measures of change from 1983 to 1993 reflect changes of format of informational content as well as shifts of audience attention from information to fiction content. Over the period the average amount of time per person spent viewing remained almost unchanged at around 3 hours 50 minutes per day.

The evidence reported by the European Commission on national performance for television channels, in terms of representing European content and giving space to independent productions and 'recent works', is generally fairly reassuring. The report (CEC, 1996) concludes that 'in almost all member States the majority of mainstream terrestrial broadcasters (which account for by far the largest share of the audience) achieved or exceeded by a considerable margin, the majority proportion [of European works]'. Most of the channels surveyed (119 out of 148) also complied with the 10 per cent minimum rule for independent productions. In general all trends were in the direction called for by the directive.

From the scattered evidence we can only reach limited conclusions about the consequences for programme diversity. According to Vochteloo and Emons (1995), apart from relative stability, it is clear that competition in Holland has greatly increased the degree of 'horizontal' diversity (more choice at the same time), but not added much, if anything, to 'vertical diversity' (the overall range of content), confirming that what we have is, essentially, more of the same.

The Finnish evidence suggested something similar. Hellman and Sauri (1994: 57) conclude that 'prime time programme structure is undeniably quite stable but, at the same time, it appears to be "streamlining" little by little towards certain strategic categories which slightly narrows the programme range'. The 'strategic categories' referred to are: news, current affairs, series and serials, and light entertainment. The impression created by other national figures for comparative programme offers supports the view that expansion has not increased diversity.

As long as public service television keeps to its remit, as it has in some countries, the expansion of the system could increase diversity. But the more it reacts to competitive pressure by similar programming the more there is a loss of diversity. There has been some degree of convergence, with effects on both sides of the system. Commercial channels seem to perform 'better' by some criteria as they get more established and successful. However, there may have been no substantive gain in diversity as a result of the new abundance, although there is certainly more *choice* for viewers.

Measures of intrinsic 'quality' are still very imprecise and inadequate (see Ishikawa, 1966) and an impression by informed observers of some decline in quality, of the kind cited above from Ludes (1996), cannot really be proved or disproved. The widespread rise of new, more entertaining, personalized and sensational formats for information programming can sometimes be documented. Vochteloo and Emons (1995), for instance, have some evidence concerning this matter, but it is not easy to make an assessment of the degree and significance of changing quality. Again, we have to keep in mind that media culture is bound to change as well as tastes and standards.

Effects on the audience

The changing technology of distribution and reception has many profound consequences for the audience which are not specific to the question of commercialization, but the latter process has been instrumental in stimulating change. The most relevant potential effects which have been predicted include, as noted above, an increase in average time spent viewing, an increased attention to entertainment and fiction and a 'fragmentation' of the former national audience into numerous niche media markets, with consequences for a reduced sense of national identity.

There is insufficient systematic evidence on these points, although the broad picture is clear enough. First of all, it does not seem that there has been any general and significant increase in television viewing time in Europe. There are still large differences between countries, with daily average viewing times varying between two and four hours. The enormous expansion of content supplied has not had dramatic effects, no doubt because of the many other claims on people's time.

Secondly, it seems very likely from some direct evidence, and from the loss of audience share by public channels, that the relative share of viewing time devoted to fiction and entertainment has increased in most countries. This is an indirect result of commercialization but it also reflects the former deliberate policy of public service channels to privilege information, education and 'culture' in their schedules.

Thirdly, although there has been a proliferation of many smaller audiences and much more diversity in audience choice and behaviour, there has been no true 'break-up' of the 'mass audience'. In virtually every European country, a majority of audience attention is claimed by two or three channels and there are still regularly very large audiences indeed for certain programmes. According to Table 4.4 (see Chapter 4, p. 51), two channels alone receive more than 50 per cent of audience share in 11 out of 15 countries. Of the other countries (Germany, Holland, Italy and Switzerland), the audience tends to be rather evenly divided between four or six channels. We are faced, typically, with a more pluriform pattern of media use rather than a fragmented one, which implies a lack of any stable pattern.

The 'loss' of the unified national audience as a result of commercialization might be understood in terms of the much reduced hold of public broadcasting on the audience. While it is now virtually unknown for a single public channel to have a majority share of the audience, in nearly all the cases where two channels dominate, one of these is a public channel. In addition, public channels are still often dominant in terms of 'reach' – the proportion of a potential audience which tunes in during a given time period. As in respect of programme supply and content, we have to conclude that audience change is a result of many different forces, some of which would be at work even without commercialization of the broadcasting system.

Conclusion

Public broadcasting has now nearly everywhere to operate within an extended, expanding, commercial and highly competitive media environment, with inevitable consequences for the character of the public service.

The old broadcasting order has effectively passed away, although without either trumpets or death throes. As a result, we need a more realistic view of the media system which does not assume that public, non-commercial broadcasting is the norm. An earlier approach (McQuail and Siune, 1986) framed developments in terms of 'degrees of commercialism' of media systems, but this is now inadequate in a predominantly commercial environment and it is unduly one-dimensional in its assumptions. This model treats 'caging the beast' of commerce as the overriding dynamic and goal of media policy (see McQuail et al., 1990).

We do not necessarily have to abandon the values applied in the earlier analysis, but the catch-all criterion of 'commercialism' is no longer useful. Quality can obviously vary independently of the means of finance and we can still assess the quality of the media as we choose. But the concept of 'commercialism' is only useful when there is a fundamental distinction between the performance of public and commercial systems which is also clearly recognized by public opinion and supported by expert judgement. Neither condition seems to hold any more.

Bibliography

Blumler, J.G. (ed.) (1992) *Television and the Public Interest*. London: Sage.

Bruns, T. and Marcinkowski, F. (1996) 'Konvergenz Revisited', *Rundfunk und Fernsehen*, 44 (4): 460–78.

CEC (1996) Communication from the Commission of the European Communities on the application of Arts 4 and 5 of the Directive 'Television without Frontiers'. Brussels: COM(96)302 final.

Chaniac, R. (1995) *La TV de 1983–1993*. INA: Paris.

Collins, R. and Murroni, C. (1996) *New Media New Policies*. Cambridge: Polity Press.

De Bens, E. (1997) 'Longitudinal research programme changes of public and commercial broadcasting', Department of Communication, University of Ghent.

Euromedia Research Group (1991) 'Electronic media policy in Western Europe', in J.C. Arnbak, J.J. van Cuilenburg and E.J. Dommering (eds), *Openbare Elektronische Informatievoorziening*. Amsterdam: Cramwinckel. pp. 255–341.

Euromedia Research Group (1997) *The Media in Western Europe*. London: Sage.

Ferguson, M. (ed.) (1986) *Communication Technologies and the Public Interest*. London: Sage.

Ferguson, M. (ed.) (1991) *Public Communication: The New Imperatives*. London: Sage.

Hellman, H. and Sauri, T. (1994) 'Public service television and the tendency towards convergence: trends in prime-time programme structure in Finland, 1970–92', *Media Culture and Society*, 16: 47–71.

Hellman, H. and Sauri, T. (1995) 'Diversity in the prime-time programme supply 1980–1992', in *Audience Research Review 1995*. Helsinki: YLE Oy.

Ishikawa, S. (ed.) (1966) *Quality Assessment of Television*. Luton, UK: Luton University Press.

Kelly, M. and De Bens, E. (1992) 'Television content: Dallasification of content?', in K. Siune and W. Truetzschler (eds), *Dynamics of Media Policy*. London: Sage. pp. 75–100.

Ludes, P. (1996) 'World trade and the restructuring of German television', in A. van Hemel (ed.), *Trading Culture: GATT, European Cultural Policies and the Transatlantic Market*. Amsterdam: Boekman Foundation. pp. 126–34.

McQuail, D. (1996) 'Transatlantic flow: another look at cultural cost-accounting', in A. van

Hemel (ed.), *Trading Culture: GATT, European Cultural Policies and the Transatlantic Market*. Amsterdam: Boekman Foundation. pp. 111–25.

McQuail, D. and Siune, K. (eds) (1986) *New Media Politics*. London: Sage.

McQuail, D., Tapper, H. and DeMateo, R. (1990) 'Caging the beast', *European Journal of Communication*, 5 (2/3): 313–31.

Media Perspektiven (1996) *Daten zur Mediensituation in Deutschland 1996*. Frankfurt am Main: Media Perspektiven.

RAI (1995) *Annuario RAI 1994*. Rome: RAI radiotelevisione Italiana.

RAI (1997) *Annuario RAI 1995–6*. Rome: RAI radiotelevisione Italiana.

RAI (1998) *Annuario RAI 1997*. Rome: RAI radiotelevisione Italiana.

Siune, K. and Truetzschler, W. (eds) (1992) *The Dynamics of Media Policy*. London: Sage.

Syvertsen, T. (1997) *Den store TV-krigen*. Oslo: Fagbokforlaget.

Tanghe, K. and De Bens, E. (1993–4) 'Televisie in vlaanderen: de invloed van de commercialisering op het programma-aanbod', *Communicatie*, 23 (3): 28–48.

Verstraeten, H. (1996) 'The media and the transformation of the public sphere', *European Journal of Communication*, 11 (3): 347–70.

Vochteloo, M. and Emons, J. (1995) 'Diversiteit in beeld: een model voor onderzoek naar diversiteit van het programma-aanbod op televisie', in K. Renckstorf (ed.), *Communicatiewetenschappelijke bijdragen 1994–1995*. Nijmegen: Instituut voor Toegepaste Sociale Wetenschappen, Katholieke Universiteit.

Zerdick, A. (ed.) (1997) *Exploring the Limits: Europe's Changing Communication Environment* (Report of the European Communication Council). Berlin: Springer.

9

Politicization in Decline?

Kees Brants and Karen Siune

Alongside notions of the programmatic diversity, cultural-pedagogic logic and non-commerciality of television, the issue of its delicate and often symbiotic relation to politics is also close to the heart of the European public service broadcasting ideal. 'Broadcasting structures were a creation of the political and cultural (rather than the economic) system, established by law and sensitive to the prevailing political and social climate' (McQuail et al., 1992: 9) and the introduction of public broadcasting in most, if not all, Western European countries has been accompanied by notions of 'politicization' and of 'citizenship'. Both in the broadcasting laws regulating access and content, and in the political rhetoric of the time, there might have been uneasiness about the effects of television, but there was also an expectation that it would enlarge the conditions for political communication as a means of informing from 'above' and as a way of expressing views from 'below'.

Until the mid-1980s, the official and politically dominant discourse about the political role of broadcasting in most countries of Western Europe saw television as providing the 'windows' through which citizens could follow what went on in the world in general and in the political process in particular. It created a platform for, and critical information about, the workings of the political system and its actors. Broadcasting was seen as part and parcel of parliamentary democracy because, in a complex society such as ours, media (and television in particular) are the dominant source of information for citizens.

In providing fair, impartial and balanced news, analysis, critique and opinion – often substantiated within a regulatory framework – television in Europe assumes some responsibility for the well-being of the political process and for the quality of public discourse generated within it (Blumler, 1992: 12). The civic sphere, where the public participates in the formation of society, the definition of its problems and their solution through the authoritative allocation of values, is expected to benefit from this specific definition of the public service function of broadcasting.

But with public television all over Europe in a state of flux, and commercial television putting the pressure of entertainment on it, what about its assumed role in the public sphere? Is politics losing its self-evident place in broadcasting? Has the notion of politicization become obsolete in a broadcasting system driven more by a market than a cultural logic?

Politicization in the 'old order' of broadcasting

In the 'old order' of public service broadcasting, until the mid-1980s, politicization used to appear in two, often related and not always clearly distinguishable, forms: organizational, or the linkage with political bodies, and programmatic, or the representation of politics in programme content.[1]

Political organization

In a study of the first elections for the European Parliament in 1979, Kelly distinguished three different forms linking television to politics:

1 *Formally autonomous systems*, in which mechanisms for distancing political organs from broadcaster decision-taking have been adopted, as in Britain though also in Ireland and Sweden.
2 *Politics-in-broadcasting systems*, in which the governing bodies of the broadcasting organizations include representatives of the country's main political parties as well as of social groups loosely affiliated to them, as in Germany, Denmark, the Netherlands and Belgium.
3 *Politics-over-broadcasting systems*, in which state organs are authorized to intervene in broadcaster decisions, as in Greece, Italy and France (Kelly, 1983: 73).

The organizational form refers, first, to the organization of accountability. Although there might be differences in the main locus and exact instruments and tightness of control, it was mainly through political institutions (ministries, parliaments or one or more parties) and sometimes social groups like labour unions that European broadcasters were held accountable to society for their policies and programming (Mitchell et al., 1992: 208). As these were mostly countries with public monopolies, accountability was more or less self-evident. Even RTL in Luxembourg, which was not a public broadcasting organization, was (loosely) monitored by the Prime Minister's office. In more dual systems, as in the UK, with channels competing for audiences, some form of accountability to the viewer was more common-place.

There would usually be an uneasy balance between the ideal of editorial independence and the political reality of (sometimes direct) powers over finance and appointments. In some countries, the organization itself was highly politicized: appointments of political affiliates were commonplace (Belgium), channels were carved up along party lines (the legally sanctioned *lottizzazione* in Italy) or interlocking directorships existed between broadcasting organizations and political parties as part of the political communication culture (the 'pillarization' of the Netherlands).

Secondly, politicization refers to the organization of access: of government, political parties, as well as oppositional and (ethnic and other) minority views. In a way, this is at the heart of the role of media in democratic discourse. In order to arrive at rational decision-making, an informed citizenry is necessary which can take stock of all opinions aired in society. But those opinions should have access to the platform of communication. Policy here is probably most clear where it concerns access to television of political parties and candidates at election time (ranging from equal to proportional access), since elections are also the bottom line of public participation in parliamentary democracy.

In Italy the broadcasting law until the early 1980s also mentioned access for trade unions, cultural institutions, ethnic and language minorities. Specific interest groups in Austria (the *Sozialpartner*) could claim 1 per cent of the air time, but this was not laid down in law. Because of the highly politicized nature of public television, with strong representation of political parties and specific interest groups in advisory bodies, parties often considered television their playground and used their position to influence political programming (for examples from different countries, see Kuhn, 1985). As a result, television showed a willing responsiveness to party politics, following the issue agenda of political actors and thus adhering to a general party logic (Mazzoleni, 1987).

Access for citizens to the broadcasting system – the bottom-up part of democracy whereby the public can express grievances, wants and desires in the hope and expectation that they be at least noticed and preferably picked up by decision-makers – is usually less clearly operationalized in policy. So-called 'feedback' programmes have existed in the UK since the mid-1960s, but they were more aimed at audiences reacting to specific programmes than raising civic issues. Rarely do broadcasting organizations themselves allow for access; for instance, by having representatives of the public, civic organizations or grass-roots movements on their Boards or programme Councils. Only in the Dutch broadcasting system does the associational structure allow for member participation in the running of the company. However, this does not necessarily result in actual access to programme policy, let alone that these members can air views and opinions on the programmes themselves.

Political content

The other form in which politicization appears is the representation of politics in programme content. Usually, this refers to the role of news and current affairs programmes, their neutrality and independence, and their contribution to political discourse. We distinguish two forms of programmatic politicization: in the regulation of political content and in the actual output.

The first refers to a situation whereby balance, impartiality and openness to minority views are laid down in law or otherwise form part of journalistic conduct. Although in most Western European countries not always specified in law (Austria, where it is part of the Constitution, being a notable exception), notions of objectivity and impartiality are enshrined in professional journalistic ideology. Balance in the presentation of political views at election time are usually well regulated and strictly monitored, but elsewhere the idea of diversity is much more defined in programmatic genres – information, culture, education and entertainment – than in actual content. Openness to minority views is also considered to be part of the journalistic attitude, although some countries set up special arrangements.

Political content is also regulated in the way journalistic autonomy is guaranteed (or not). Politicization refers here to the balance between, on the one hand, communication freedom and programmatic (journalistic) autonomy of the broadcasting organization and, on the other, political control over what information is handed over or allowed access to and what not, and the way governments protect what is often referred to as the 'national interest'.

It is the delicate balance struck (in some countries by Acts or case law, in others through repressive measures) between the people's 'right to know' and the government's 'privilege to conceal'. Galnoor (1976) concluded from comparative research of 10 liberal democracies in the mid-1970s that, although freedom of the press was upheld everywhere as the cornerstone of freedom of expression, the more any channel of communication is publicly controlled, the less it will be interested in the legal protection of the 'people's right to know'.

Looking at the actual output of political content in television programmes, political information has had a central place in the news while in other informative genres too a lot of air time has been devoted to political events. It is also clear that in the heyday of public broadcasting, news and current affairs formed the heart of its programming, both in the sense that they were scheduled at prime time and in the image the organization liked to portray of itself. Informational programmes were the calling card, so to speak, of the companies and central to the cultural-pedagogic discourse of the time and to the potential 'public interest' capacity of the mass media.

'At the core of this tradition', McQuail (1992: 11) notes, 'is the view that public communication . . . has a significant contribution to make to the general welfare of society and carries a corresponding "social responsibility".' Although they had to compete for resources with other, less journalistic and more popular-culture oriented parts of the organization, managers were well aware of the credibility news programmes had with the viewers.

Within this idea of politics, being both central to the informational output and a legitimate part of a wider social system, political advertising was considered unnecessary and almost seen as an insult. Governments, however, did allow for and also subsidized party political broadcasts which were often shown at prime time and were usually of a traditional ('talking heads') informational style. They formed a platform for representative politics and within the democratic ideal contributed to the political cognition of the electorate.

Political communication in an environment of uncertainty

As public broadcasting in Western Europe was regulated mainly – at least ostensibly – for technical reasons (scarcity of channels), its relation to politics involved other, often more covert, arguments. Among these, political reasons weighed most heavily. The public nature of broadcasting was said to require political scrutiny: as the allocation of social values is entrusted to the state, non-material values communicated in broadcasting need some form of political guardianship. This argument had a political-psychological undertone. For a long time the intrusive nature of the medium had been highlighted. Television in the wrong hands might not only send out the wrong signals, but could also have the wrong influence on people.

There was a related, cultural argument too. In order to guarantee pluralism and diversity and, through this, optimal democracy, organizational and journalistic independence had to be weighed against scrutinizing pluralist and balanced content. Implicit in many regulations was also an ideological argumentation, related to the specificity of European politics. Social and Christian democratic parties alike have always had some distrust of the popular nature of television which, they claimed, would lead to massification, degradation, liberal values and, in the end, manipulation of the public.

Because of changes both in the field of politics and of broadcasting, the relation between the two is no longer what it used to be. Politics is confronted with changes in the political system, often referred to as a 'crisis in politics' (Blumler and Gurevitch, 1995) and characterized by:

- the nation state being no longer the sole reference point for political actions
- the diminishing importance of political ideologies as the 'cement' of society
- a growing fragmentation and individualization of the population
- a decline of voter turnout and, generally, less active participation and involvement in party politics
- less salience for politics as an interest or activity in everyday life and substantial cynicism towards politics, policies and politicians
- an increase in support for anti-system parties notably of the extreme right
- a rise of and growing support for single-issue movements and politics
- scandals becoming part and parcel of the daily routine of political life (notably in Italy, the UK, Belgium, Spain and France, but most other countries seem to be affected too).

At the same time, (public) broadcasting is confronted with:

- a transnational communication system and media structure easily crossing political, cultural and social borders
- a multiplicity of competing channels which, among other things, open up means of communication for political actors
- a fragmented audience, now able and keen to zap away from political content
- increasing competition for limited resources in an only slightly growing advertising market and with licence fees losing their legitimacy
- a growing popularity for entertainment programmes and therefore for channels not bound by content regulations prescribing genres and formats which fit public service ideals.

The reality of television – if not by definition then by production and viewing practice at the turn of the millennium – is that it is first and foremost a 'pleasure machine'.

As a consequence of all these trends and developments, we see in European political communication a shift from the party logic, dominant under the highly politicized conditions of public broadcasting, to a media logic which sets the agenda and even the style and portrayal of politics. Moreover, the stiffening of commercial competition might well result in a changing political content in traditional informative TV programmes and more emphasis on the personal qualities (or faults) of political leaders (Mazzoleni, 1987).

A new order of ambiguity and ambivalence

With these changes and pressures over the past 10–15 years, what is the present state of politicization in public service broadcasting? After more than a decade of rocking the delicate balance between politics and television, the question is whether the threefold division put forward by Kelly (1983) still holds true, or whether the introduction of competition and (at least verbally proclaimed) deregulation has created a new and different organizational linkage between politics and broadcasting in different countries. And has the representation and signification of politics changed under commercial influence?

Political organization

According to Mitchell et al. (1992: 208), 'the dominance of political accountability has receded with the advance of commercial television, though the extent of this shift has also varied in different countries and the boundaries and construction of the new framework have mostly been decided in the political sphere'. From this and our own survey we conclude that public broadcasting organizations are still mainly accountable to political (ministers and/or parliament, and indirectly to the European Commission) or politically appointed (regulatory and supervisory) bodies. But we detect four, sometimes conflicting, developments.

First, particularly in northern Europe, we see a growing responsiveness to viewers (be it more as consumers than as citizens). This is, of course, also part of the shift from goal–means argumentations in broadcasting organizations set within a cultural discourse, to a more market-economic and competition-oriented focus. There is increasing use of audience research and taking account of audience complaints and letters. However, a right of reply, which is mentioned in the EC Directive on Transfrontier Television and indirectly in Article 10 of the European Convention on Human Rights, is more to be found in national legal provisions that deal with slander, privacy and so on than in specific broadcasting regulation.

Secondly, governments try to increase their distance from broadcasting by transferring supervision to more or less independent authorities (Robillard, 1995: 267–72). The appointment of the members of these bodies is still mainly a matter for the executive and the legislative, but a new nongovernmental category of social groups is becoming involved in the nomination and sometimes appointment of the members of these regulatory bodies.

The furthest here are Germany (where the ARD *Rundfunkrat*, the ZDF *Fernsehrat* and the *Landesmedienanstalten* of the commercial sector all have representatives of cultural and other interests in society), Greece (with its Representative Supervisory Assembly of Viewers and Listeners which functions as a watchdog of the public broadcaster), Luxembourg (where a *Conseil National des Programmes* is proposed with a degree of representation for civil society) and Portugal (where besides the Board of Governors of RTP there is an opinion council, with representatives from consumer, family and other associations). All these regulatory bodies have party political representation as well (Robillard, 1995: 267–72).

Thirdly, there is a (re)strengthening of party political power in some countries as well, though not in a strictly regulatory but more in a covert form. Next to the *lottizzazione* of RAI in Italy commercial television is politicized, with Berlusconi entering into politics and even trying to neutralize RAI (or regulate according to his ideology). The division between commercial and public channels in Spain has had its own effect on political loyalties, with the public RTE supporting the government (socialist before and conservative after the 1996 elections) and the commercial Antenna 3 supporting the opposition (RTE in reverse). The socialists also gained more control over Antenna 3 through company stockholders (Diez-Nicolas and Semetko, 1997).

Presidential influence on the French (public and private) broadcasting system is not new (many consider France 2 to be more or less a government agency), but has been exercised with a new vigour by President Chirac. It is based on a less overt form of regulation – compared to the case of the old ORTF – and more through the covert exercise of power or a system of reciprocity. In trying to influence political decision-making, this exchange model (in real terms: 'if you give me a licence, we'll give you access') is certainly though not openly used by commercial competitors in some European countries.

Finally, with the growing number of channels, not only the scarcity argument but also the regulation of access has become obsolete, according to some. Access is one of the characteristics of a public service ideal and as such is supposed to be guaranteed by the state. However, apart from political parties at election time, access is rarely prescribed in broadcasting Acts. In Germany, churches have special rights and the Broadcasting Act in Luxembourg vaguely mentions some form of access for relevant organizations in civic society and the sociopolitical field.

In Italy, access was noted for local administrations, trade unions, cultural institutions, ethnic and language minorities, but implementation never worked and it stopped in the early 1980s. In the Netherlands competition with commercial stations forced the 'pillarized' corporations to cooperate more and more, and with the decreasing importance of membership of a broadcasting organization, the notion of the Dutch system as one of organized minorities will probably cease to exist in a couple of years.

With the extension of cable, the start of digital television and the coming of pay TV bouquets or TV *à la carte* and the introduction of the Internet in many countries, the question of access re-emerges and so does discussion of the need and limitations of universal service. One can expect, however, that the issue of access will be transferred from the cultural to the economic domain and that regulation of access will, thus, become an issue of anti-trust and competition policy.

Regulating political content

Communication freedom in the 1990s is still considered a cornerstone of public broadcasting systems. But reservations remain about the intrusive nature of the medium and its supposed political effects. There is still a need to see that balance, neutrality, diversity and openness are adhered to. Governments seem to bet, however, more on self-regulation in order not to have to interfere.

During the monopoly phase of the 'old order' there was already a contradiction between protection *from* government interference, on the one hand, and protection (state guarantee) *for* the existence of a plurality of opinions, on the other. This conflict was 'solved' by the virtual absence in European countries of legal rules *vis-à-vis* content. Professional ethics guaranteed impartiality and diversity. At the same time there was an almost natural tension between politicians and journalists: the former always complaining that the latter were not impartial. When individual journalists or programmes broke up this co-habitation ostentatiously, the threat of regulatory measures was usually enough both for a professional uproar and a temporary climb down.

With public broadcasting in relative crisis, the claim for access to communication outlets for the political elite is less convincing, however, and seems to prompt different strategies among different power holders. The French president has access by definition (or by raising his voice); less powerful actors use more reciprocal means, as did presidential candidate Balladur who appeared frequently on channel TF1 because its owner Bouygues hoped for certain contracts. The German chancellor extends his authoritative influence to the private channels of the Kirch and Springer *Senderfamilie* (SAT1, Pro7). The other 'family' – Bertelsmann/CLT (RTL, RTL Plus) – has (non-interlocking) links with the social democrats. Other countries use direct (referring to emergency powers, police or military secrecy, as the D-notice system in the UK) or indirect (state advertising) forms of political censorship (Keane, 1991: 95–107). All European governments have increased their professionalization of information and political communication *vis-à-vis* the mass media.

Rules regarding balance in political reporting now only exist in Norway, Sweden, Austria, the UK and Germany. In some other countries they are to be found in internal papers or guidelines. Balanced reporting usually refers to the large parties only – if there is proportional representation and/or a multi-party system – and sometimes, as in Germany with the so-called *Ausgewogenheit*, to the recruitment of journalists. But the latter is not legally binding.

With the exception of Norway and the Netherlands, access for minority views is nowhere laid down in law. Channel 4 in the UK aims specifically at minorities as a target audience, but no reference is made to the presentation of minority views. In Denmark and Sweden, minority views are mentioned with regard to local media, while in Germany and Italy it is to be found in internal papers. On the whole, it looks like a northern European attitude: some reference to neutrality, diversity and openness more often found in that part of Europe than around the Mediterranean.

The openness of a system is also dependent on how access to government information is guaranteed: where and in what form a government's 'privilege to conceal' exists. In several countries developments have taken place since the mid-1980s. Sweden, which already had a relatively open system in 1991, introduced an extra Freedom of Speech Act. In Italy (in 1990), Belgium (in 1994) and the Netherlands (in 1992), three countries in which freedom of information was already a constitutional right, specific Acts on public access to government information were introduced, while in Ireland a Freedom of Information Act is in the making. Ireland also has an Official Secrets Act, according to which all government information is secret, unless a minister decides otherwise. The Austrian Secrecy Law names specific interests such as public order and security which, if violated, prohibit disclosure of requested government information.

Two countries have seen a development towards a more closed political communication system. In Luxembourg, a written instruction from the Prime Minister has existed since 1992 explicitly prohibiting civil servants from dealing and speaking directly with journalists. In the UK, the Official Secrets Act was revised in the late 1980s; in addition, in 1988 a broadcasting ban was introduced on interviews with Sinn Fein members, which was only lifted in 1996. The Labour Party promised a Freedom of Information Bill in their manifesto, but it was one of the first plans shelved when they were elected to government. In Germany and France, where all official information is legally confidential, nothing much seems to have changed.

Output of political content

Although comparative content analysis of European TV news is very limited (Heinderyckx, 1993, is a notable exception, although his comparison of eight countries focuses mainly on public channels), separate country studies give a generally ambiguous and sometimes contradictory picture of programmatic convergence between public and commercial channels. First, contrary to what one might expect, news and current affairs programmes on the public channels have not moved outside prime time in order to compete with popular drama on commercial television. Instead, most commercial channels have followed the public schedule and seem to compete with public broadcasters on their 'home ground'. Legitimizing the channel as a serious television station and thus attracting the same (for certain advertisers particularly interesting) audiences seems to have been the driving force.

Secondly, as expected, in most countries commercial television at the outset did marginalize political news, but now that commercial channels have become established this is no longer generally the case. Pfetsch (1996) found conflicting proof for the hypothesis that German public channels would follow commercial stations in their entertainment focus. Instead, both public and commercial channels have increased their political information since the mid-1980s, the latter even doubling political references in their news, thereby putting it almost on a par with public news. In Denmark, Powers et al. (1994) also found little distinction between the public DR TV and the commercial TV2, but their research was not longitudinal.

On the other hand, Van Poecke and Van der Biesen (1991) found a marked difference in political news between the Flemish public BRT and the commercial VTM (23 per cent and 16 per cent respectively). In Sweden, Hvitfelt (1994) also noticed that airtime devoted to politics had declined sharply between 1990 and 1993. For the Netherlands, van Engelen (1997) did not find such a development with the public NOS news or RTL news, but De Vries and van Praag (1995), in looking at campaign news at three consecutive elections, found a marked decrease in politically informative news on the public channel and, alternatively, an increase in coverage of campaign ritual and treatment of the campaign as a 'horse race' between 1986 and 1994.

Thirdly, several examples of the adaptation of public news to the style and mode of presentation of the commercial channels can be identified.

Pfetsch (1996) notes this for Germany. Brants and Neijens (1998) found entertainment style and format elements in both commercial and public TV news in the Dutch 1994 election coverage. In comparing Dutch and Belgian public and commercial stations, Canninga (1994) concluded that the latter usually show shorter items, a tendency noticed elsewhere too (by Hvitfelt, 1994, for Sweden). But in the Netherlands and in Germany the tendency is the opposite: the items have become longer and of a more narrative nature.

Next to the more 'serious' news, we see, fourthly, the growing importance of conflict and scandal, partly following the example of the tabloid press, as in the case of the UK. In Belgium (Canninga, 1994), Sweden (Hvitfelt, 1994) and in Denmark (Powers et al., 1994) there is evidence of more sensationalism in news reporting (in the choice of items, for example, more crime news, and/or in news angle and visuals), as well as more 'soft' news and dramaturgically crafted techniques of story-telling. This trend is clearer with respect to commercial rather than public channels, however.

There are signs that the form sensationalism takes will be more that of reality TV type news reporting (local TV stations, in particular, in some countries seem to copy the American example) and/or an emphasis on investigative reporting combined with personal scandal. So far there is hardly any tabloid TV, but the German tabloid newspaper *Bildzeitung* and TV producer Endemol in the Netherlands clearly saw this as a niche when they combined forces in 1997.

Fifthly, in most countries (perhaps with the exception of the UK, France and Ireland) there has been a steady decline in audience ratings of the traditional current affairs programmes. At the same time there has been an 'upgrading' of more 'infotainment' type programmes such as talk shows and variety (breakfast, coffee) shows and magazines. Pfetsch (1996) claims that in Germany 'serious' politics on television is reduced to the traditional news format, while new genres have appeared that blur the boundaries between political information and entertainment.

With the fragmentation of audiences, politicians feel more or less obliged to use all channels of political communication available. And as President Clinton showed in the USA, most politicians feel that talk show hosts are far less critical than the traditional political 'watchdogs'. However, as Brants and Neijens (1998) found for the Netherlands – and several other countries confirm this – at election time, and when politicians are address-ing the nation with 'serious' problems, they use a 'serious' format. Then, TV news is still favoured most.

A final change in the content of political information can be seen in party political broadcasts. Traditionally, most countries in Western Europe have had a form of party broadcasts which fitted the public broadcasting system: they were usually longer than advertisements, the 'talking head' was commonplace and the emphasis was on cognition rather than affect. Political communication was done via persuasion through information; the electorate had to be convinced with arguments. With the coming of commercial television, several countries have seen parties 'go over to the other side' with shorter, more image-focused political TV spots which bear more resemblance to American political spots than traditional European party political broadcasts. Party spots on commercial TV are, though, still an exception (Kaid and Holtz-Bacha, 1995).

New ways of looking at politics

Politicization in public broadcasting is manifold: it refers to the relative control of political actors over the communication process, to the informative and educational role of TV in addressing citizens as active participants in a parliamenary democracy and to the organization of a responsible and balanced representation of different views. As such, the notion of politicization is enshrined in the ideal of democracy and the ideas of democratic theory: collective decision-making through deliberative communication, namely, through discussion and debate among members of the citizenry under conditions of openness, fairness, mutual respect and concern for the common welfare (Price, 1992: 2).

A prerequisite for a well-functioning democracy acording to this theory is an actively participating citizenry that knows something about the actual issues on the political agenda and thus has access to relevant information. For decades mass media have been the prime source of information, making people aware of issues and influencing the agenda of the most important political themes of the day. Broadcasters were expected to address their audiences as citizens, informing and thus equipping them for rational participation in the public sphere, that discursive, opinion-forming domain. Democracy thus has high hopes and expectations of the mass media.

Among the more significant functions and services the media should perform for the political system in democratic theory (Blumler and Gurevitch, 1995: 97) are:

- surveillance of the sociopolitical environment and holding officials to account for how they have exercised power
- reporting developments likely to impinge on the welfare of citizens
- forming a platform for debate and dialogue across a wide range of views
- giving citizens incentives to get involved rather than to follow the political process
- a sense of respect for the audience member, as potentially concerned and able to make sense of his or her political environment.

On the whole, these functions refer to an idea of public interest which sometimes 'connotes one particular form or media arrangement, that of

"public service broadcasting", and is invoked in defence of that system'
(McQuail, 1992: 3). In his colourful account of the demise of the public
sphere, Habermas (1962) has sketched a gloomy picture of publicity in
democracy under industrial capitalism, which has been elaborated by
Keane (1991) and Golding (1994).

With an interventionist state and interest groups and large organizations
taking over the role of the public, mass media have become more a basis for
consumption than for discussion where information is being presented to a
critical public. Publicity has been turned into public relations, journalism
has lost its critical role and the audience is only expected to identify and to
acclaim instead of forming an informed opinion on social issues.

Whether turning a blind eye to or being unaware of this critical evaluation, the idea of politicization in public service broadcasting and the
salience of democratic theory are still prominent among political actors and
broadcasters alike. Where, on the one hand, political commentators are
quick in asserting such labels as 'Americanization' to elements of the
modern publicity process in Europe (see Swanson and Mancini, 1996), they
still very much adhere to broadcasting's informational and educational role
in liberal democracy. Although the foregoing analysis of the changes in
politicization have given a rather ambiguous and hybrid picture, there are
some lines to be distinguished and lessons to be learned.

Rethinking citizens in the public sphere

First, there is a slow and hesitant change in the way governments keep their
distance *vis-à-vis* broadcasting organizations. Kelly's (1983) threefold
typology of television's links with politics therefore needs some revision.

With the increase of (semi-)independent organizations, the first form,
formally autonomous systems, has gained in importance. The second form,
politics-in-broadcasting, seems to have lost its significance, with governments in Denmark, the Netherlands and Belgium keeping their distance and
party affiliations losing their importance too. Only Germany still 'occupies'
this type and Chancellor Kohl has even tried to extend it to private
channels. It is these private channels, of course, that have upset the idea of
linkage more dramatically. Despite Berlusconi and Murdoch, in most of
Europe the idea of organizational politicization is anathema to the
commercial discourse.

The third form, *politics-over-broadcasting systems*, is both gaining in
importance and changing in character. With the introduction of independent authorities and keeping their distance, presidents and governments
realize that they have lost their self-evident access to the platform of
political communication. With more covert forms of pressure and the
emergence or enlarging of the 'public relations state', power-holders try to
make up for lost ground.

Secondly, the viewers have changed; that is, the idea of who he/she is and how they should be treated. The growing number of channels and the competition between them have scattered audiences over a range of stations, which they zap and graze in search of pleasure more than political information and education. This has forced both politicians and broadcasters to show a greater responsiveness to the viewer. Where traditionally they knew what the public needed, they now take more seriously what they want. This does not necessarily mean a loss of citizenship in favour of consumer sovereignty, more a rethinking of the traditional idea of the citizen.

This idea is based on the assumption that all people are political animals, thus treating citizenship not as an empirical but as a moral category, making it a universal norm shared by 'all democrats' (Frissen, 1997). This is building disappointment into your definition or morally dichotomizing between the consumer and the citizen, which Murdock (1993: 527) so nicely caricatured:

> On the one side stood the crowd, emotional, seduced by dramatic images, acting in concert, bargaining by riot and demonstration. On the other side stood the citizen, rational, open to sequential argument, making considered personal choices and registering preferences soberly, in the solitude of the voting booth.

Times have changed. For one, there are 'new' citizens such as migrants who miss the basic element of citizenship – the right to vote – and might occupy a different discursive sphere, or cyber citizens who live and discuss in virtual communities, and thus fulfil the prerequisites of a *burger*, but who might well be excluded by their own choice from the traditional platforms of rational debate. Classic notions of citizenship may have become less adequate to analyse contemporary relations within the public.

> We would do well to shy away from a singular conception of citizenship and allow for the play of multiple versions, at least as far as it has to do with a form of identity. The postmodern notion of plural and contingent subjects provides a useful link to understanding citizenship as a specific form of identity, while at the same time opening the door, theoretically, to the idea of a common, minimalist res publica. (Dahlgren, 1995: 146)

The romanticizing of the citizen comes partly from the idealization of the bourgeois public sphere of the eighteenth and nineteenth centuries, so vividly described by Habermas (1962). The public sphere is in theory a space between the formal, decision-making authority and the private sector or, more down to earth, the coffee bars and tea houses where in a continuing public debate and exchange of views public opinion was formed. In this idea, there is a distinction between the public sphere – with the media now as core institutions – and the private sphere, where affect, emotions, popular wisdom and pleasure are to be found. The distinction between the public and the private is gradually imploding, however, not least because television – with talk shows, infotainment and forms of reality TV – is making the private visible and public. And people seem to like it, for one because audiovisual spaces like talk shows give 'experience experts' like themselves a platform.

It would be too easy just to dismiss this as a shift from a party to a media logic. With sociopolitical and media changes in society, traditional dichotomies like citizen–consumer, public–private, rationality–emotion, information–entertainment are becoming more and more problematic. This is bound to have an effect on the traditional notion of politicization in public broadcasting in Europe.

Note

1 Unless otherwise indicated, the following overview and analysis is based on a survey among all members of the Euromedia Research Group.

Bibliography

Blumler, J.G. (ed.) (1992) *Television and the Public Interest*. London: Sage.
Blumler, J.G. and Gurevitch, M. (1995) *The Crisis of Public Communication*. London: Routledge.
Brants, K. and Neijens, P. (1998) 'The infotainment of politics', *Political Communication*, 15 (2): 149–65.
Canninga, L. (1994) 'Een vergelijkende analyse van de nieuwscultuur in de buitenlandse berichtgeving op BRTN, VTM, NOS en RTL', *Media & Maatschappij*, 4 (1).
Dahlgren, P. (1995) *Television and the Public Sphere: Citizenship, Democracy and the Media*. London: Sage.
De Vries, H. and van Praag, P. (1995) 'De inhoud van het campagnenieuws', in K. Brants and P. van Praag (eds), *Verkoop van de Politiek*. Amsterdam: Het Spinhuis. pp. 151–69.
Diez-Nicolas, J. and Semetko, H. (1997) 'For whom the bell tolls: competition for audiences in Spain's election campaigns', paper for the American Political Science Association, Washington.
Frissen, V. (1997) 'Somewhere between forum and supermarket: relocating citizenship in the information society', Department of Communication, University of Amsterdam.
Galnoor, I. (1976) *Government Secrecy in Democracies*. New York: Harper and Row.
Golding, P. (1994) 'Telling stories: sociology, journalism, and the informed citizen', *European Journal of Communication*, 9 (4): 461–84.
Habermas, J. (1962) *Strukturwandel der Oeffentlichkeit*. Neuwied and Berlin: Hermann Luchterhand.
Heinderyckx, F. (1993) 'Television news programmes in Western Europe: a comparative study', *European Journal of Communication*, 8 (3): 425–50.
Hvitfelt, H. (1994) 'The commercialization of the evening news: changes in narrative techniques in Swedish TV news', *The Nordicom Review*, 2: 33–41.
Kaid, L.L. and Holtz-Bacha, C. (eds) (1995) *Political Advertising in Western Democracies*. Thousand Oaks, CA: Sage.
Keane, John (1991) *The Media and Democracy*. Cambridge: Polity Press.
Kelly, M. (1983) 'Influences on broadcasting policies for election coverage', in J.G. Blumler (ed.), *Communicating to Voters*. London: Sage. pp. 65–82.
Kuhn, R. (ed.) (1985) *Broadcasting and Politics in Western Europe*. London: Frank Cass.

McQuail, Denis (1992) *Media Performance: Mass Communication and the Public Interest.* London: Sage.

McQuail, Denis, de Mateo, Rosario and Tapper, Helena (1992) 'A framework for the analysis of media change in Europe in the 1990s', in Karen Siune and Wolfgang Truetzschler (eds), *Dynamics of Media Politics.* London: Sage. pp. 8–26.

Mazzoleni, G. (1987) 'Media logic and party logic in campaign coverage: the Italian general election of 1983', *European Journal of Communication,* 2 (1): 81–103.

Mitchell, Jeremy, Bundschuh, Anja, Mounier, Philippe and Woldt, Runar (1992) 'Comparing the countries', in Jeremy Mitchell and Jay G. Blumler (eds), *Television and the Viewer Interest.* London: John Libbey. pp. 207–27.

Murdock, G. (1993) 'Communications and the constitution of modernity', *Media, Culture & Society,* 15: 521–39.

Pfetsch, B. (1996) 'Convergence through privatization? Changing media environments and televised politics in Germany', *European Journal of Communication,* 11 (4): 427–51.

Powers, A., Kristjansdottir, H. and Sutton, H. (1994) 'Competition in Danish television news', *The Journal of Media Economics,* 7 (4): 21–30.

Price, V. (1992) *Public Opinion.* Newbury Park, CA: Sage.

Robillard, S. (1995), *Television in Europe: Regulatory Bodies. Status, Functions and Powers in 35 European Countries.* London: John Libbey.

Swanson, D. and Mancini, P. (eds) (1996) *Politics, Media and Modern Democracy.* New York: Praeger.

van Engelen, Marcel (1997) 'Televisienieuws onder Druk', MA thesis, University of Amsterdam.

Van Poecke, L. and van der Biesen, W. (1991) 'Programme and news supply in BRT and VTM', in *Strategies of Public versus Commercial Broadcasters.* Paper of the thirteenth Flemish Conference for Communication Science, Ghent. pp. 24–48.

10

Media Use in the European Household

Mary J. Kelly

The household as a major site for leisure was confirmed throughout the 1980s and into the 1990s as European consumers bought more television sets and VCRs, radios and CD players, home computers and video games, and hooked up to cable and satellite television services. It is also the proposed site for the purchase and use of many new communications, multimedia and digitalized technologies. This chapter looks at the patterns of purchasing and usage of existing media technologies in the home and asks what these patterns might lead us to expect regarding the take-up of new technologies and services.

For corporations developing and hoping to exploit these technologies commercially this is vital but highly uncertain terrain, for it is these domestic consumers who, it is hoped, will fund the huge cost of developing and distributing new media services. However, it is also highly complex terrain, differentiated by class, gender and generational factors and by how these factors interact both within the domestic context of the home where new media are used, and the market economy where they are bought. Furthermore, all these elements are open to change as individuals explore various lifestyles, as households and families negotiate lifecycle and other changes, and as producers and markets find that their enthusiasm for new technologies is not necessarily reflected in the marketplace.

This chapter asks who decides within the household what media to buy and how to use these new purchases? What are the patterns of interaction and negotiation involved in these decisions? How are they related to patterns of power within the household, especially as structured by gender and age? How are they influenced by the broader contextual factors of class and ethnicity? Furthermore, how do household consumption and use patterns articulate with, on the one hand, the market economy in which new technologies are produced and marketed, and on the other, the democratic public sphere.

Household practices and decisions regarding the purchase and use of new communication technologies are located within the broader institutional spheres of the market economy and the state. The concept of lifestyle is particularly helpful in examining linkages between households, their purchase and use of new communications technologies and these contexts. In its simplest form, lifestyle can be defined as that set or repertoire of norms, symbolic forms and everyday practices which form 'taste cultures'. Taste cultures can differ widely between groups. Rosengren (1994: 9) has proposed three sources for these differences. They may be due to macro sociocultural differences between groups, such as national, ethnic or religious differences. They may be due to a group's position within society, for example differences due to gender, class or generational position. Or they may be due to individual choice. He argues that actual patterns of individual actions reflect all of these.

While lifestyle is a helpful concept in linking domestic practices and the marketplace, linkages between usage of new media technologies and the democratic public sphere may be usefully examined by raising questions concerning culture and politics. What cultural and subcultural values do different audiences bring to the purchase and use of new media? How do usage patterns articulate with the national, regional and ethnic identities of audiences? In particular, to what extent do the forms of knowledge and symbolic cultures offered by new media technologies contribute to or lessen political pluralism and tolerance between social groups?

The argument of this chapter is that new media technologies are actively domesticated and responded to by media consumers and users. It is important to understand the context in which this domestication occurs: the immediate context of family negotiations as well as the broader social, economic and political contexts. It is also the argument of this chapter that the examination of domestication of new media technologies to date may enable us to make more informed predictions regarding the future adoption of the newer media technologies. In particular, it allows us to question some of the more technologically driven assumptions concerning the future adoption of the 'superhighway' within the home. It will be argued that the increasingly unequal and fragmented society of the 1990s will not provide the same kind of mass market as that of the 1950s, which so rapidly and happily incorporated television into the home, and which some hoped would similarly facilitate widespread and rapid take-up of new communication technologies.

This chapter looks at how new media technologies enter the home and come to be used routinely within it. The first section examines the structure of European households. We then move on to look at how producers and marketing experts envisage the potential buyers of media technologies and to compare this with how the dynamics of lifestyles and negotiation patterns within the home actually influence purchasing decisions. Following this, patterns of media usage in the home are examined, and how they differ across class, gender and generations. The consequences of these patterns, as well as the influence of one's own culture or subculture, for the way in which media-mediated cultures are used as a means of actively negotiating social and cultural identities are then addressed. A case study method is used here, looking in particular at how migrant ethnic groups use a wide range of media technologies and draw upon local, national and international media to negotiate identity. Given patterns of usage and interpretation, and given that these are mediated through the domestic familial context, the chapter concludes by asking to what extent new media technologies are contributing, or may contribute in the future, to the vitality of the democratic public sphere.

European households and lifestyles

The lifestyles and related patterns of purchase and usage of media technologies might be expected to differ quite radically across different household types. Meyer and Schulze (1995a) have identified nine household types, each with its own media needs. These may be grouped into three main sets. I have added details of the size of each of these sets within the European market as a whole and give these below, as well as giving some indication of the differences between European countries.

Household types

1   Single-person households, including (a) households with younger singles, and (b) households with senior citizens. This is a growing set of households across Europe, as in the USA. An examination of Eurostat (1995) indicates that single-person households constitute over a quarter (27 per cent) of all European homes, with 10 per cent of the population living in these homes. There are quite large variations across Europe in household composition. In particular, northern European countries can be contrasted with those in southern Europe and in Ireland. To take two of the more extreme examples, household composition in Sweden and Ireland: in Sweden 40 per cent of all households are single-person households (with 19 per cent of the population living therein), while the comparable percentages for Ireland are 20 per cent and 6 per cent respectively.
2   Couple households, including (c) young couples without children, (d) older couples without children, and (e) couples whose children have moved out. These constitute a quarter (23 per cent) of all European households, with 18 per cent of the population living therein. Again there are differences across Europe, exemplified by the fact that in Sweden couple households constitute 30 per cent of all households (with 31 per cent of all persons living therein), compared with 14 per cent and 9 per cent respectively in Ireland.
3   Family households, including (e) households with children under 10, (f) households with children over 10, (g) single-parent households, and (h) households with more than two generations. In Europe as a whole this is the largest set of households, constituting almost a half (45 per cent) of all homes, while two-thirds (65 per cent) of all Europeans live in these homes. In Sweden the figures are 26 per cent and 46 per cent respectively, in Ireland 59 per cent and 79 per cent. There has been an

increase in single-parent households in all countries. They now constitute 7 per cent of all homes with 10 per cent of the population living therein.

To summarize, the European market is characterized by household type as follows: a quarter are single-person homes, a further quarter couple households and a half family homes. If we look at how the population is distributed in these homes, we find that one in every 10 lives in a single-person home, two in every 10 lives in a couple home, while almost seven in every 10 lives in a family home. Thus while recognizing the increased incidence of single occupancy households, and especially their frequency in northern European countries, none the less the great majority of individuals in all European countries live with others, with all the consequences this entails for the negotiation of lifestyle patterns and the purchasing and usage decisions for household items.

Age, gender and class also, of course, differentiate the market in Europe, and the various lifestyle preferences of these categories have major implications for the purchase and use of media in the home. One market clearly characterized by lifestyle differences is the youth market. Expressed in terms of consumption, these lifestyles include a desire for novelty, for fashion, for entertainment products marketed globally and for hi-tech equipment, although, as we shall see, this is strongly differentiated by gender. This market is clearly targeted by global firms in teen-magazines, on MTV, by radio and television, and, in particular for boys, by video games and in home computer stores and hobby journals. It is, however, a numerically declining market segment in Europe, and declining especially rapidly in northern European countries (see Hassan et al., 1994: 67–9).

The equating of hi-tech with masculinity and modernity make men an easier marketing target for new media technologies than women. Women are thought to vary in their general purchasing behaviour and in lifestyle orientation according to whether they are employed outside the home, their age and education (Bartos, 1994). These gender differences will be discussed in considerable detail below.

A numerically rapidly growing segment of the market is those over 65. They constitute 15 per cent of the total population. In terms of attitudes to the use of technologies in the home and to the adoption of new media technologies this segment tends to be highly conservative (Johnsson-Smaragdi, 1989; Meyer and Schulze, 1995b). However, it might also be noted that early retirement is increasing. In West Germany, France, the UK and the Netherlands, one out of every three men between 55 and 59 is no longer in the labour market (Guillemard and Rein, 1993: 474). A similar trend towards early exit from the labour force exists for women. It is perhaps appropriate to note that not only are the retired heavy television users but that increasing proportions of this group on retirement will bring from work computer literacy and skills. It is perhaps not surprising therefore that in the USA in 1996–7, research by the Nielson Media Research

Group showed that those over 50 are among the fastest growing groups of Internet users – from an admittedly very low base. The other fast-growing group are women, particularly those over 55 who are using e-mail to keep in touch with children (Swartz, 1997). It is thus appropriate to begin to ask if we are entering into a second phase in the marketing and usage of new media technologies, one oriented to both women and older age groups, especially if well off and well educated.

The third major differentiating factor influencing consumption and lifestyle patterns is social class. Occupation and income are two of the more important indicators of class. In Europe as a whole there are wide variations in income levels and consumption both within and between countries. Household consumption per individual is lowest in Portugal, Greece, Ireland and Spain (Eurostat, 1997: 48). Inequality in income distribution is also higher within these latter countries (Atkinson et al., 1995: 80; Eurostat, 1995). The available income left for spending on new communications technologies is thus considerably less, especially among the poorest groups in these countries. Thus in 1992, while on average 60 per cent of households in the six wealthiest countries had VCR equipment, the percentage for the five poorest countries was 40 per cent (Euromonitor, 1995).

Income level, however, needs to be related to occupation and education before it can begin to be a useful indicator of lifestyle. Both sociologists and marketing experts have pointed to the differing lifestyles and related purchasing practices of two high-income groups. One consists of those whose income and occupation depends on cultural and educational capital and whose public claims to status superiority tends to be based on attendance at and knowledge of high culture and the arts. Here the increasing role of university level education in contributing to income and status inequalities should be noted (Atkinson et al., 1995: 84). The other group consists of those whose income depends on economic capital who make public claim to status superiority through high spending on material objects (see Bourdieu, 1984). A middle income, *petit bourgeois* lifestyle tends to be more traditionalist.

At the bottom of the class hierarchy is what some would see as an underclass with little economic or cultural capital and prone to unemployment. This class is particularly frequent in southern European countries, Ireland and to some degree the UK. Strongly over-represented in this group are women. Not only are there many older women, lone mothers and unemployed women in this category, but also women in poor rural areas, women employed in low-income segmented labour markets and in low-paid part-time work (see Lewis, 1993; Hutton, 1994). Furthermore, inequalities in income appear to be increasing in many countries (Atkinson et al., 1995: 59).

A fourth factor influencing lifestyle preferences is ethnicity, especially perhaps among immigrant groups. Patterns of new media usage among these groups will be examined below in terms of the extent to which immigrant groups see some forms of media use as contributing to maintaining ethnic identity and links with their country of origin. Other forms of use are seen as contributing to negotiating variable patterns of integration into the host country.

The production and marketing of new media technologies

Many communication technologies now in daily use in the home were not originally designed for domestic usage but for industrial, commercial or military reasons. This leads to what Wajcman (1992) has called the 'double life' of technologies: on the one hand, what their designers intended and, on the other, their rather different adoption and usage in the home. The telephone is an interesting example of this process. Initially, in the latter half of the nineteenth century, it was primarily used to link banks, professionals, businesses and other commercial interests. When it began to move into private upper-class homes, it was business interests again that predominated as businessmen used it to link home and office. Women began also to use it to order household goods. By the turn of the century the use of the phone, especially by home-based women to maintain interpersonal contact, began to surface, especially in the USA, and became, by the 1930s, the main reason women wanted a telephone (see Flichy, 1995). This pattern of broader domestic diffusion and use was not to occur in Europe until the 1950s and 1960s, due to a range of factors including state policies and those of nationalized telephone companies, different rates of social change and urbanization, as well as class and social attitudes. The present gendered use of the telephone and the feminine culture surrounding its domestic usage by women to maintain familial and friendship networks over widely dispersed space (see Moyal, 1995) was certainly not originally conceived of by either its designers or marketers. Similar patterns have been observed regarding the design and subsequent use of the gramophone and radio (Flichy, 1995).

However, the lack of recognition of women's role in the take-up of new media technologies may vary considerably. Spigel (1992) has analysed the very rapid domestication of television in the USA between 1948 and 1955 by which time nearly two-thirds of US homes had purchased a set and by 1960, 90 per cent. She examines a wide range of sources through which television was popularized including magazines, advertisements, newspapers, television programmes and films, all mainly aimed at the white middle class. In particular, she argues (1992: 39), home magazines 'helped to construct television as a household object, one that belonged in the family space. More surprisingly, however, in the span of roughly four years, television itself became *the* central figure in images of the American home; it had become the cultural symbol par excellence of family life.' Furthermore, the attraction of television for women working in the home was confirmed by providing programming (often soaps) for 'Mrs Daytime Consumer'.

However, recent researchers into this process of production and marketing of new media technologies, in particular VCR, cable and satellite, computers and video games have noted how women and the domestic context became the 'absent actors' (Gatzke, 1995: 2; see also Berg, 1994) not only at the design and production stages but also the marketing stage. The gendering of new technologies in the marketplace, and in particular the association of hi-tech with masculinity, has been noted by many researchers (see Cockburn and Ormod, 1993; Meyer and Schulze, 1995b). Advertising, specialist magazines as well as shops identified youth and masculinity with a techo-modernist lifestyle. And indeed they have responded accordingly. Graber (1996) in her research on World Wide Web and Internet usage in the USA and Canada, examined age, gender, socioeconomic and educational differences among users and non-users. As has already been noted in Chapter 6, young, white, educated and affluent males predominate. However, the question may be raised as to whether this gender and generationally biased production and marketing represented an early adoption phase in the 1980s and early 1990s. We now appear to be moving into a second phase where these biases may be considerably lessening.

Gender differences are reduced considerably within some educational and age groups. Young women, especially if well educated, are much less hesitant in adopting hi-tech products than elderly women (Meyer and Schulze, 1995a, 1995b; Hellman, 1996), and indeed elderly men. Although, again, we need to differentiate here between an expanding group of 'young' early retired and older groups. The former, especially if affluent, may be increasingly interested in extending their consumption of new media in the home. Even with the latter older group, however, familiarity with, for example, computers will increase through their use in public libraries and in home-based telephone alarm systems.

Buying new media technologies

Within this context of markets and lifestyles differentiated by age, gender and class, how do households negotiate purchasing decisions? Control over purchasing, especially over non-routine and relatively major items, may be seen as a strategic power resource within the household. Recent British research on the political economy of households has shown that power over financial decision-making is highly correlated with who manages the household's finances overall – whether husband or wife or by the more equal pooling of resources (Vogler, 1994). The degree of equality or of male dominance over the management of resources was found to be related to two factors. One was the extent to which the husband held traditional or non-traditional attitudes regarding who was ultimately responsible for family income generation (i.e. the breadwinner role) and for domestic housework, and secondly the extent to which he held sexist attitudes to women's employment outside the home (Vogler, 1994).

Not only are the southern European countries characterized by more multi-occupancy households and more frequently have children living in them but they are also more likely to have a traditional division of labour in the home. Eurobarometer (1992: 86) research indicated that only a minority of women saw themselves as the main household breadwinner in Spain (18 per cent), Italy and Greece (both 23 per cent), Ireland and Luxembourg (both 24 per cent) or Portugal (26 per cent). In contrast, for example, in Denmark almost half (47 per cent) of women saw themselves as the main breadwinner. Likewise men in southern European countries and Ireland were less likely (on average 15 per cent) to see themselves as the main person responsible for housework. In contrast, a third of Danish men saw themselves as so responsible.

These attitudinal patterns would lead us to expect that, especially in southern European countries and Ireland, ultimate authority over major purchasing decisions such as the buying of new communications technologies is likely to be unequally gendered in favour of the male. This, along with male-oriented marketing of new media technologies, undoubtedly contributed to the widespread pattern of males rather than females being predominant among the early purchasers of these new technologies. However, this pattern of male dominance varies across Europe and is decreasing as more women enter the workforce. Recent research by Bergman (1996) in the Netherlands found that here the pattern of decision-making is more equal. She found that the buying of new communication technologies is a process in which both partners and older children, if present, tend to participate. However, it is men who tend to do the product research and the investigative shopping.

Class, income and education, along with household type and whether there are children living in the home, all play a role. Take the example of buying a home computer. MacKay (1995: 329–35) found that the ideal-typical British household which purchases a home computer is a higher-income 'family household', with the couple aged between 35 and 44 and with children. Meyer and Schulze (1995a: 7) describe how, in Germany,

> In order to meet the demands of this specific situation, households of families in middle age develop an openness to innovation; somewhat older children encourage an innovative spirit and are often the driving force behind new acquisitions in the communications- and entertainment-sector. Whereas women mostly regard such suggestions critically and favour the acquisition of work-saving technologies, fathers often endorse the suggestions of their children and adolescents. This coalition of interests explains the purchase of expensive equipment in the entertainment sector even in families whose financial means are not particularly 'rosy'.

There were undoubted gender differences in both purchase and use of computers in the first phase of their entry into the home (see Murdock et al., 1992; Wheelock, 1992). Parents more frequently bought computers for sons than for daughters, and even when bought for both, they were more frequently used by sons and over a longer period of time. Also, boys rather than girls tended to use computers to generate and interact with networks of friends and to join computer clubs. Within the family as a whole, wives and mothers were the least frequent users. This was also the pattern with regard to computer and video games. Researchers have argued that heavier use by males of these technologies reflect their heavily male-oriented content and their consistently aggressive and destructive themes (see Kubey and Csikszentmihalyi, 1990: 97). Cultural orientations both within schools and generally with regard to computers and technology again tended to be masculine based. Hellman (1996: 7) concludes:

> the social relations of technology are gendered. In the social division of labour and power, technology has become an essential part of male identity, whereas women's identity is not enhanced by their use of technology. The male sex dominates the discourse of technology, thus determining what is technology and what is not. It is men who control the whole chain of technology from design and production to marketing and ways of using it.

These linkages between male-oriented content, a favoured techno-modernist lifestyle and masculinity also contributed to the promotion of cable and satellite services. The heavy emphasis on sports programmes – as well as news and films – is a major selling point here.

As argued above, however, this may be changing – if slowly. For example, the development of video games for girls is being actively explored, following the success of the *Barbie Fashion Designer* CD-ROM launched in late 1996. Ideas include following through on television shows popular with 12–16-year-old girls, and games which emphasize relationships rather than competition and winning. In the main, small companies are developing these. However, they complain that the major manufacturers and retailers who have never seen young girls buy software are more difficult to convince than the young girls themselves (De Witt, 1997). Women are not necessarily techno-phobes as the purchase of domestic 'white technologies' for the kitchen as well as the use of computers at work shows. The question is the development of services that they see as useful and pleasurable in the home.

Major factors influencing computer-purchasing decisions both at the present time and most likely into the future are income and class. At a macro level this can be seen across Europe with an average of twice as many households in the richest six EU countries owning computers than the four poorest (Euromonitor, 1995: 392; see also Gatzke, 1995: 11). Furthermore, richer households are more likely to own more expensive and versatile machines with the capacity for a wider range of self-generated uses including programming, word processing, printing, and not simply games. There also tends to be more private space available in upper- and middle-class homes allowing more convenient usage, while networks of friends and contacts with similar computer equipment with whom to share and swap, and as sources of support when in difficulty, are more frequently available in upper- and middle-class areas and schools (Murdock et al., 1992).

Computer usage in such households tends to be more frequent and to continue over a longer period of time, while cheaper, less versatile and more typically games machines are tired of sooner.

The interaction of class and gender might be noted here. Within high-income households, women working outside the home contribute a higher proportion to family income than do those in low-income families (Atkinson et al., 1995). These are likely to be well-educated women in professional and managerial positions, and also likely to use computers at work. If they perceive new technologies as enhancing their lives at home, they will buy them. Contrasted with this group are low-income households which tend to be headed by women with fewer financial and educational resources, and, if not elderly, to have more children in them. This group will continue to be the most discriminated against by the development and spread of new communication technologies into the home.

Using new media technologies in the home

As we have described above, purchasing new communications technologies is influenced by difference in lifestyles that are themselves structured by gender, age and social class. A central contributor to the promotion and maintenance of these lifestyle differences is the operation of the consumer market. Lifestyles are important not only in terms of the meaning and value thereby invested in material objects and social practices and the sense of identity thus engendered (Csikszentmihalyi and Rochberg-Halton, 1981), but also because lifestyles are a statement to others – a statement about difference and about claims to recognition and status.

Consumer markets in advanced industrialized societies operate through the promotion of lifestyles. It is thus that they invade or colonize the household not only through lifestyle purchasing decisions but also by influencing how these purchases are used in the home. In the home, however, new purchases meet with existing domestic and familial norms and practices, and it is within this dual context of marketplace definitions and existing household routines that the product is domesticated.

One of the major factors influencing the domestication of new media technologies as they enter the household is how the home is seen and defined by different members, and in particular the different ways in which men and women see their home and use their time within it. Women frequently see their home as a place within which they work, while men see it as a site for leisure. This is, of course, due to women's traditional housekeeping role, a role that has continued despite the increasing partici-pation of women in the paid workforce outside the home. Gershuny et al., (1994) have found that in the eight countries they studied, including France, Finland, Norway, the Netherlands and the UK, women working outside the home still do considerably more housework, shopping and childcare than men. While the proportion of housework done by men has increased over the past three decades, this still does not equal that of women (Gershuny et al., 1994: 183–6). Indeed, women's proportion of the *total* of paid work outside the home *plus* unpaid work in the home has increased over the past three decades and thus their leisure time has decreased. For most women, whether employed or not, housework constitutes a large segment of each day. Employed women in Britain spend, on average, four hours per day in routine housework, shopping, domestic travel and child-care. Men spend two and a half hours (Gershuny et al., 1994: 178). The figures for urban France are very similar (Coré, 1994). Women working solely in the home spend almost seven hours per day in domestic work compared with four hours by unemployed men.

This amount of time spent in domestic work inevitably has implications for how women see the home, their somewhat sceptical attitude to the home as a place of leisure and how they use both old and new media technologies. Furthermore, the definition of women's role as primarily familial and an expectation that women are concerned with and highly competent in interpersonal relationships, while men's primary role is defined in terms of their job outside the home, also has major consequences for media use in the home.

Despite an increasing number of television sets in the home, watching television continues to be primarily a familial and communal activity (Gatzke, 1995: 8). Thus patterns of family interaction influence which programmes are viewed, attitudes towards them and the terms in which they are discussed. Bryce (1987: 133) concludes that rather than seeing television as dominating family life, families 'use television as one medium through which to establish social meetings and carry on the acculturation process'. Some of the most significant family interaction patterns in the context of television viewing include differential gender uses and preferences, differential negotiation patterns between parents and children regarding viewing within various family types, and differential patterns among children depending on age. As these patterns may well continue to influence the domestication of new media technologies, I will briefly review them here.

Women's relationship to television viewing has been found by Morley (1992), among others, to be quite different from that of men. Men more frequently carve out a leisure time and space for themselves and their television viewing. They more frequently than women plan their pro-gramme choices, more frequently enforce their programme preferences despite that of others and view attentively. Indeed, the extent to which husbands dominate programme choice and the remote control has led some researchers to argue that television viewing in the family living room is a masculine domain. Women view differently. They tend to integrate their viewing into household routines except for a few highly favoured pro-grammes. Thus, for example, they knit or iron while viewing, talk and get children ready for bed and tend to accommodate husband and children's programme preferences. They may feel guilty if they carve out a leisure space and time devoted to the pleasure of viewing, especially if they see this as excluding what they see as their primary familial responsibilities.

The ease with which men carve out a space for themselves while viewing will undoubtedly enable them to adopt the more active style of interactive television if they so desire. This appears to be the market on which inter-active service providers are focusing at present, building interactive ele-ments into those male-preferred programmes of sports and news (Blake, 1997). However, it is again important to note that when women find an application for a new communication technology which tallies with their interests and for which they can create a space, they use it. An interesting example here, although not home based, is their use of the usually office-based Internet to establish a news group entitled RATS (Recreational Arts Television Soaps) which is devoted to the recreational discussion of daytime soaps and is one of the 15 highest newsgroups in the USA (Baym, 1995a, b).

The context within which children view television is part of the pleasure of viewing. Buckingham (1993) has reported how seven to 12-year-olds recount with enthusiasm watching particular programmes within a familial setting, while also enjoying viewing alone after school or on a weekend morning when they are free from adult constraint. While many of the children he interviewed had second televisions in their homes, the prefer-ence in this age group was for viewing on the best-quality colour set in the living room with other family members. Buckingham (1993) also notes that while some research has indicated that women and children consent to adult male domination over programme preferences, he found that children were not entirely passive in this regard, nor were they passive regarding mothers' attempts to regulate viewing. Children resisted both parents through developing finely tuned interpersonal skills, used for example to pester or to align with one parent against the other. They also avoided parental dominance or control through viewing on other television sets, with friends or by taping to view later.

As children reach adolescence they frequently use the media to create a private space within the home, distancing themselves from family participation and norms. While listening to popular music is a very typical way to do this, new communications technologies, including VCRs, second or more television sets, and the greater availability of more terrestrial, cable and satellite service programming of their interests, may bring about increased viewing by this group. The Media Panel Study in Sweden, which followed children through to young adulthood from the 1970s to the 1990s, has given a particularly detailed account of the response of adolescents to these new media as the communication environment has changed (Roe, 1987, 1989; Rosengren, 1994). Researchers report how each successive wave of new media – VCR, cable, then satellite television – was rapidly adapted by them for their own purposes. For example, as VCRs became available in their homes, teenagers began using these to view hired videos with peer group friends. VCRs were thus used to reinforce peer group friendship and autonomy, and as a way of circumventing both parental and cinema censorship and hence distancing themselves from adult authority. Viewing hired videos with friends was found to be particularly frequent among young working-class males who were low school achievers and alienated from school. Horror movies were a particular favourite. As the availability of cable and satellite television increased, these new media were taken up rapidly by adolescents and the viewing of television increased, beginning to equal time spent listening to music. Again, heavy viewing was a particular characteristic of working-class boys. Rosengren (1994: 71) concludes that 'changes in media structure, then, seem to have added to already existing differences between young people from different walks of life'. It might be expected that the mid and later 1990s would include adoption of video games and computers, the World Wide Web and the Internet following the same pattern of active adoption, but within the contexts and constraints of existing peer group lifestyles and the structural differences of gender and class.

Examining the incorporation of the VCR into the household offers an excellent opportunity to examine how this is shaped by a matrix of gender-based norms, family interaction and consumer ideologies. Gray (1992: 243) has explored how 'a combination of the masculine address of VCR advertising, the relative freedom of male leisure in the home, and male economic power' have contributed both to male prerogatives in purchasing VCR equipment, their tendency to become competent in its operation sooner than women and hence to control its use. Women, on the contrary, Gray argued, resented its intrusion into the household, did not want the extra responsibilities regarding its use, resented men's ability to switch off from domestic chores and responsibilities through television and video viewing and would rather have spent more leisure time going out.

While Gray's research showed strong gender differences in attitudes to and use of VCR equipment, Meyer and Schulze's (1995b: 3–4) longitudinal data show that changes in gender norms and patterns over the past 10 years have shifted gendered attitudes to domestic technologies. Although women as a whole are still not as favourably disposed to media technologies in the home as men, younger women, especially if in professional employment, are much more familiar with new media technologies, do not rely on men to instruct them in how to use them but work it out for themselves with the instruction manual, and are not hostile to their use. Likewise women with higher education – if their partner also has higher education – tend to be more similar to them in their programme and video preferences (see also Hellman, 1996). Thus attitudes among women are strongly differentiated depending on age and education, with older and less-educated women still quite traditional, fearful and resentful of new media technologies intruding into the home, but younger and well-educated women much less so.

As has been noted a number of times above, it is not only gender and generation which influence media consumption but also social class. Its influence can be seen at a number of levels. First at the level of afford-ability, which is based at least to some degree on income levels. Secondly that of status, in which ownership and use of new media is used as a claim to superiority or membership of a particular status group. Marketing lifestyles particularly focus on this level. And, thirdly, at the level of class structuration and reproduction. Here the role of education is well recog-nized. The way in which the educational system classifies and differentiates the educationally successful from the educational failures is a process that has major class consequences. But perhaps what is less clearly recognized is the role of the educational system in structuring the media audience. This is clearly seen among young people, where the educationally successful and the educational failures tend to have different media preferences. Thus it is not only the consumer market and its ideologies which may impinge on the family, but the educational system – a compulsory system as defined by the state – which classifies children as successes or failures and hence structures both their longer term futures and the adolescent media audience.

What has been reviewed above is the extent to which the adoption and domestication of the new media are influenced by existing domestic practices, particularly by gender and generational norms and interaction. They are influenced by stages in the family lifecycle and by the pleasures associated with familial and communal viewing as a group, as well as the need of some family members to create space from the family by viewing or discussing media consumption with peers. Changing societal values and cultures, for example changing gender cultures, also influences them, and hence the marketing of new media technologies by identifying them with masculinity may be less successful in the future. It has been the argument of this chapter that it is existing domestic practices and socially structured class, gender and generation patterns which influence both consumption and use of media technologies. New media technologies are used further to confirm and articulate these social patterns rather than changing them in any radical way.

New media technologies and the public sphere

This chapter has attempted to identify those factors, mediated through the domestic context, which influence the consumption, use and cultural con-sequences of new media technologies. I have already identified a range of factors: broader structural factors including class, income and education; age and gender; the structure of the domestic sphere including family composition, stage in lifecycle and familial interaction and pleasures; as well as economic factors including production and marketing of media products. A further factor to which I now turn is that of cultural identity, again as mediated through domestic family dynamics. Of particular interest here is how the cultural identity of users may articulate with local, regional, national and global modes of address, as they become available through new media technologies. The approach taken to this analysis is, as above, within an active audience frame: new media technologies are seen as a cultural resource which audiences may actively use in constructing and negotiating a sense of cultural and political identity. Access to these resources is structured by the social, familial and economic factors already discussed, as well as being mediated through the family.

One possible prism through which to begin to examine this articulation of cultural identity and usage of new media technologies is to look at the use of new media by minority ethnic groups, especially immigrants. In particular it is of interest to examine how they may use new media to negotiate complex forms of ethnic *and* cosmopolitan identity, using these media to maintain social and cultural linkages with their country of origin and with the wider ethnically based diaspora, as well as using them to negotiate forms of integration with the dominant society. This prism can begin to establish a range of appropriate questions to raise regarding cultural and political identity, new media and the public sphere.

Immigrant-based cable and satellite services have grown rapidly in those countries with the largest immigrant inflows – France, Germany and the UK – as has their take-up. In France, immigrants 'after providing plenty of business for video hire clubs . . . have been flocking to buy satellite dishes which enable them to pick up channels from North Africa, Turkey and Pakistan' via Entelsat (Abdallah, 1995: 54). The French government in a counter-move has established a cable pay channel, Franco-Arabe Câble, with an emphasis on encouraging integration with French society. In Germany, VCRs were also rapidly taken up by Turkish guest workers, with very high levels of Turkish video viewing (Gillespie, 1995: 79). The majority of Turkish homes can now receive, through cable, the Turkish state channel (TRT-INT) beamed at Turks living abroad. They can also receive private Turkish channels, with viewing of the latter believed to exceed that of TRT-INT (Frachon and Vargaftig, 1995: 176–7). Also receiving a high level of viewing are the Offener Kanale (local access channels) for example in Berlin. The majority (75 per cent) of the programmes offered here are in Turkish, SerboCroat, Pakistani, Sri Lankan and Polish (Frachon and Vargaftig, 1995: 176). In the UK, the cable and satellite channel Asia TV, among others, provides mainly bought-in films and series from India, Pakistan, Bangladesh and Sri Lanka, broadcasting in Indian languages.

Marie Gillespie, in her research on adolescents in Asian families living in London in the 1980s and early 1990s, examined in detail their use of local, national, international and ethnically based media. Asian families in London bought VCRs as early as 1978, well before most households in Britain. Gillespie (1995: 78) describes how video equipment was 'appropriated by Asian parents and grandparents . . . as a means of recreating cultural traditions in Britain'. The majority of Asian adolescents watched Indian films at least once a week, although this varied between three-quarters of adolescent girls and just under half the boys. Viewing was done within the communal family setting, often across three generations and with considerable discussion. This discussion tended to be articulated around such opposed categories as tradition and modernity, morality and vice. But while many adolescents enjoyed familial viewing and discussion, they also feared that the viewing of Indian videos might isolate them from mainstream British life. This fear of ghettoization was also expressed with regard to listening to the ubiquitous local Asian radio station, Sunrise. It addressed its audience as 'British Asian' and aimed to foster Asian identity by keeping its listeners informed of news from the Indian subcontinent as well as news concerning 'Asians' in Britain.

The media were used not only to explore a sense of Asian identity but also to explore what it meant to be British and to be a part of Western global teenage culture. The frequent viewing of TV news bulletins with the family opened up questions of what it meant to be Asian and a British citizen, to be Muslim and black, especially in terms of these groups being represented as a 'problem' both nationally and internationally. The viewing of Australian soaps, particularly *Neighbours*, which two-thirds did often with mothers present, opened up discussions comparing on-screen morals and those of Asian families. The enjoyment and exploration with friends of global teenage popular culture offered a further site for the discussion and negotiation of potential contradictions and conflicts between family-based identities and being an adolescent within the Western capitalist marketplace. Gillespie argued that the London Asians she studied developed a self-conscious ambivalence and reflexivity regarding the received categories of British and Asian, and noted the complexities of these young people's sense of hybrid national and cultural identity. Furthermore she found – not for the first time – that the global teenage media culture was being used as a cultural wedge to attempt to open up closed social barriers and ghettoization.

Gillespie's research, examining as it did the use of media as a resource, indicated how consumers drew on the particularities of local, national, ethnic and global media in constructing and negotiating identities. These negotiation processes were mediated through family dynamics, socially structured roles and cultural values. This construction of identities may have political consequences. Gillespie (1995: 17) argued that the ethnic situation of London Asians, as well as the use they made of a range of media, 'necessitate a reflexive attitude, producing a very acute awareness of cultural differences – what Gilroy . . . refers to as a "double consciousness", [and] the sense of "dual identity"'. She further argued (1995: 21) that it led to 'cosmopolitanism' or openness to other cultures among these young people, and thus contributed to the development of self-consciously pluralistic identities.

While it may be attractive to align oneself with such an optimistic per-spective, an active and politically engaged cosmopolitanism may be difficult to sustain. The fragmentation of cultures and identities on which it is based may quite easily slide back into the security of group identity politics, bounded, shut and committed to maintaining one's own 'difference' even if domination of others is required to do this. Also the 'cosmopolitanism' of minority groups requires at least equal levels of 'cosmopolitanism' among dominant groups if a more democratic public sphere is to be established. Furthermore, the cultural fragmentation of postmodern consciousness may become so excessive as to be disabling and disempowering.

While it is the role of the media in democratic states to contribute to encouraging pluralistic and politically active perspectives, the media is by no means all powerful in this respect. Much more influential is the nation state (among other institutions) which has a central role in constructing, maintaining and reinforcing particular identities, through, for example, its immigration, welfare, educational, law and order, as well as media policies. It is also central, along with other political forces, in structuring access to political power and hence influences forms of political mobilization and empowerment. It is again central in elaborating the political and national ideologies that legitimate these policies and power structures. The national media tend to reproduce these ideologies.

National identity has traditionally been one of the main ideologies articulated by the state and national media to legitimate policies and mobilize consent (see Scannell, 1989; Schlesenger, 1991). With the weakening of the dominant position of national media, especially public service broadcasting, by new media technologies and media privatization over the past two decades, as well as the focus of new media on entertainment rather than information programming (De Bens et al., 1992), concern has been expressed regarding the loss of the traditional role of the national media as a major articulator of national identity. Rather than looking to the past, however, it may be more relevant to examine the definition of national and other identities which was and is being offered by state and media and to ask whose interest is being served by these definitions. In particular, is the concept of national identity that informs state and media cultural policies open to the self-definitions of a range of different groups? Are its policies and practices informed by the principles of access, diversity and accuracy (see McQuail, 1992), and does it offer a forum for the exploration and discussion of differences? Hence, to what degree is it operating as a democratic public sphere?

Conclusion

The market for new media technologies and services is highly fragmented. It is not only fragmented by class and ethnic lifestyles, by gender and by generation, but by household type. I have concentrated in this chapter on family and couple households rather than single-person households, and on the patterns of negotiation and decision-making regarding purchase and use of new media in these homes. The household as the site for new media leisure is one that has changed rapidly over the past 30 years. These changes have included rapidly increasing numbers of women in the labour force, an increasing level of family break-up and reformation, declining fertility and increasing single parenthood. Nevertheless, the great majority of the population still lives with others in family and couple households, and it is within these homes that complex patterns of negotiation are played out in deciding how money and leisure time are spent.

The post-war introduction of television into the home was greatly facilitated by its pervasive marketing as a symbol of family togetherness, while also confirming the role of the mother as an integrative force. On the contrary, the new media technologies and services are marketed predominantly in a highly individualized and gendered style to the affluent and white male consumer. There is at present no similar clarity regarding a potential family or female market for new media. This perhaps reflects the rapidity of the changes that have occurred within the family and in relation to women's roles. Some of these changes undoubtedly have implications for new media markets including:

1   Increasing time pressures on women in the home, especially if they have children and are in full-time paid employment. Women frequently carry a disproportionate 'second shift' of domestic work and childcare, leaving little time for leisure and indeed much less time than in the recent past. This may be mitigated somewhat by part-time employment which is particularly frequent in northern European countries.
2   An increasing divergence between well-educated and relatively high-income women and those at the bottom of the class hierarchy who have been caught in the trap of the feminization of poverty, especially those who are rearing children alone. While the former may well be able to afford new media, this is certainly not the case for the latter group and the considerable number of children whom they parent.
3   An increasing number of older women who may be divided into two groups. One is that of relatively young retirees from 55 upwards. Some of these will increasingly bring from work considerable computer literacy. The second is an older group who may, if sufficiently affluent, constitute a market for more passive forms of computer link-ups, through, for example, telephone alarm systems.

The majority in each of these categories, except perhaps the last, lives with partners and/or children. Purchasing and using new media in the home is frequently motivated at least in part by a desire to confirm or improve these and other existing social relationships and social patterns. Thus telephones and e-mail are used to maintain close social relationships; video games to play with peers and siblings; television viewing to cement family relationships; purchasing each new media as it comes on the market – at present access to the World Wide Web and the Internet – as a statement of status superiority.

These patterns of differentiated domestic contexts and interests contribute to highly fragmented media markets – a pattern that is likely to continue. The market is further fragmented by the macrosociological variables of class and ethnicity, again mediated by the family. The desire among migrants to stay in contact with their ethnically based home culture, and to rear their children according to its values, offers a strong motivation to buy those new media technologies and services that facilitate this. It is not known if this will contribute to a continuing strong level of commitment to immigrant ethnic cultures which in the past tended to lessen in the second and subsequent generations. Gillespie (1995) argues that among the second generation adolescents she studied there was considerable interest, especially among girls, in their parental culture, but also an interest in British mainstream and global teenage cultures. It can be argued that the self-conscious moving between a number of cultures contributes to growing reflexivity and cosmopolitanism, creativity and dynamism. Alternatively, if boundaries between cultures become closed, intolerance and cultural impoverishment may be the consequence. National media policies, and those of international media corporations, need to address and support those media forms that celebrate cultural differences, cultural hybridization and cultural and political tolerance.

Mediating and influencing how household composition and ethnicity articulate with the take-up of new media is income level and its increasingly unequal distribution. At the top of the class hierarchy, high- and dual-income families will undoubtedly explore the possibilities offered by new media services. They will in particular hope to give their children an educational head-start in doing so by buying PCs and related information services. Those at the bottom, and the increasing number of children located there, will have few such home-based opportunities. This is likely to constitute between a quarter and a third of the population. In the public interest, we need to ask whether this is the direction we want to take, and what economic, social, educational and media policies we need to counteract it.

Bibliography

Abdallah, Mogniss, H. (1995) 'Networking for migrant perspectives on television in France and Europe: the IM média agency's experience', in Claire Frachon et al. (eds), *European Television: Immigrants and Ethnic Minorities*. London: John Libbey. pp. 45–59.

Atkinson, Anthony B., Rainwater, Lee and Smeeding, Timothy (1995) *Income Distribution in OECD Countries, Evidence from the Luxembourg Income Study*. Paris: OECD.

Bartos, Rena (1994) 'Marketing to women around the world', in Salah Hassan et al. (eds), *Global Marketing, Perspectives and Cases*. Fort Worth, TX: Dryden Press. pp. 119–45.

Baym, Nancy K. (1995a) 'The emergence of community in computer-mediated communication', in Steven G. Jones (ed.), *CyberSociety: Computer-mediated Communication and Community*. Thousand Oaks, CA: Sage. pp. 138–63.

Baym, Nancy K. (1995b) 'From practice to culture on usenet', in Susan Leigh Star (ed.), *The Cultures of Computing*. Oxford: Blackwell. pp. 29–52.

Berg, Anne-Jorunn (1994) 'A gendered socio-technical construction: the smart house', in

Cynthia Cockburn and Ruza Furst-Dilic (eds), *Bringing Technology Home: Gender and Technology in a Changing Europe*. Buckingham: Open University Press. pp. 165–80.

Bergman, Simone (1996) 'Communication technologies in the household: the gendering of artifacts and practices', paper presented at the Granite Workshop, Amsterdam, February.

Blake, Pat (1997) 'Whose going interactive', *Telephony*, 13 January. pp. 18–22.

Bourdieu, Pierre (1984) *Distinction: A Social Critique of the Judgement of Taste*. London: Routledge & Kegan Paul.

Bryce, Jennifer W. (1987) 'Family time and television use', in Thomas R.L. Lindlof (ed.), *Natural Audiences*. Norwood, NJ: Ablex. pp. 121–38.

Buckingham, David (1993) *Children Talking Television*. London: Falmer Press.

Cockburn, Cynthia and Ormod, Susan (1993) *Gender and Technology in the Making*. London: Sage.

Coré, Françoise (1994) 'Women and the restructuring of employment', *OECD Observer* 186 (February/March): 5–12.

Csikszentmihalyi, Mihaly and Rochberg-Halton, Eugene (1981) *The Meaning of Things: Domestic Symbols and the Self*. Cambridge: Cambridge University Press.

De Bens, Els, Kelly, Mary and Bakke, Marit (1992) 'Television content: Dallasification of culture', in Karen Suine and Wolfgang Truetzschler (eds), *Dynamics of Media Politics*. London: Sage. pp. 75–100.

De Witt, Karen (1997) 'Girl games on computers', *The New York Times*, 23 June.

Eurobarometer (1992) *Public Opinion in the European Community*, no. 38. Brussels: European Community.

Euromonitor (1995) *European Marketing Data and Statistics*. London: Euromonitor.

Eurostat (1995) *Statistics in Focus: Population and Social Conditions*. Luxembourg: Office for Official Publications of the European Union.

Eurostat (1997) *Basic Statistics of the European Union*, 33rd edn. Luxembourg: Office of Official Publications of the European Union.

Flichy, Patrice (1995) *Dynamics of Modern Communication: The Shaping and Impact of New Communication Technologies*. London: Sage.

Frachon, Claire and Vargaftig, Marion (eds) (1995) *European Television: Immigrants and Ethnic Minorities*. London: John Libbey.

Gatzke, Monica (1995) '"Electronic markets": where are the private households', paper presented at the PICT Conference, Westminister, London.

Gershuny Jonathan, Godwin, Michael and Jones, Sally (1994) 'The domestic labour revolution: a process of lagged adaptation?', in Michael Anderson, Frank Bechhofer and Jonathan Gershuny (eds), *The Social and Political Economy of the Household*. Oxford: Oxford University Press. pp. 151–97.

Gillespie, Marie (1995) *Television, Ethnicity and Cultural Change*. London: Routledge.

Graber, Doris A. (1996) 'Disparity in information resources: the widening gap between rich and poor', paper presented to the American Political Science Association, San Francisco.

Gray, Anne (1992) *Video Playtime: The Gendering of Leisure Technology*. London: Routledge.

Guillemard, Anne-Marie and Rein, Martin (1993) 'Comparative patterns of retirement: recent trends in developed societies', *Annual Review of Sociology*, 19: 469–503.

Gunter, Barrie et al. (1993) *Television and the Public's View, 1993*. London: John Libbey.

Hassan, Salah S. et al. (1994) *Global Marketing: Perspectives and Cases*. Fort Worth, TX: Dryden Press.

Hellman, Heikki (1996) 'A toy for the boys only? Reconsidering the gender effects of video technology', *European Journal of Communication*, 11 (1): 5–33.

Hutton, Sandra (1994) 'Men's and women's incomes: evidence from survey', *Journal of Social Policy*, 23 (1): 21–40.

Johnsson-Smaragdi, Ulla (1989) 'Sweden: opening doors – cautiously', in Lee B. Becker and Klaus Schoenbach (eds), *Audience Responses to Media Diversification*. Hillsdale, NJ: Lawrence Erlbaum. pp. 109–32.

Johnsson-Smaragdi, Ulla (1994) 'Models of change and stability in adolescents' media use', in

Karl Erik Rosengren (ed.), *Media Effects and Beyond: Culture, Socialization and Lifestyles*. London: Routledge. pp. 97–130.

Kubey, Robert and Csikszentmihalyi, Mihaly (1990) *Television and the Quality of Life*. Hillsdale, NJ: Lawrence Erlbaum.

Lewis, Jane (1993) 'Introduction: women, work, family and social policies in Europe', in Jane Lewis (ed.), *Women and Social Policies in Europe*. Aldershot: Edward Elgar.

MacKay, Hughie (1995) 'Patterns of ownership of IT devices in the home', in Nick Heap et al. (eds), *Information Technology and Society*. London: Sage. pp. 311–40.

McQuail, Denis (1992) *Media Performance*. London: Sage.

Meyer, Sibylle and Schulze, Eva (1995a) 'Smart home in the 1990s: acceptance and future usage of private households in Europe', paper presented to the EMTEL Workshop, Amsterdam.

Meyer, Sibylle and Schulze, Eva (1995b) 'The smart home in the 1990s: a new lesson in gender and technology', in *Granite Newsletter*, 8: 2–4.

Morley, David (1992) *Television, Audiences and Cultural Studies*. London: Routledge.

Moyal, Ann (1995) 'The feminine culture of the telephone: people, patterns and policy', in Nick Heap et al. (eds), *Information and Technology in Society*. London: Sage. pp. 284–310.

Murdock, Graham, Hartmann, Paul and Gray, Peggy (1992) 'Contextualizing home computing resources and practices', in Roger Silverstone and Eric Hirsch (eds), *Consuming Technologies: Media Information in Domestic Spaces*. London: Routledge. pp. 146–60.

Roe, Keith (1987) 'Adolescent media use', *American Behavioural Scientist*, 30 (5): 522–32.

Roe, Keith (1989) 'School achievement, self-esteem and adolescents' video use', in Mark R. Levy (ed.), *The VCR Age: Home Video and Mass Communication*. London: Sage. pp. 168–89.

Rosengren, Karl Eric (ed.) (1994) *Media Effects and Beyond: Culture, Socialization and Lifestyles*. London: Routledge.

Scannell, Paddy (1989) 'Public service broadcasting and modern public life', *Media, Culture and Society*, 11 (1): 135–66.

Schlesenger, Philip (1991) *Media, State and Society*. London: Sage.

Spigel, Lynn (1992) *Making Room for Television: Television and the Family Ideal in Postwar America*. Chicago, IL: University of Chicago Press.

Swartz, Jon (1997) 'E-Mail bringing families together', *San Francisco Chronicle*, 8 July.

Vogler, Carolyn (1994) 'Money in the household', in Michael Anderson, Frank Bechhofer and Jonathan Gershuny (eds), *The Social and Political Economy of the Household*. Oxford: Oxford University Press. pp. 225–6.

Wajcman, Judy (1992) 'Domestic technology: labour-slaving or enslaving', in Gill Kirkup and Laurie Smith Kelly (eds), *Inventing Women: Science, Technology and Gender*. Cambridge: Polity Press. pp. 238–54.

Wheelock, Jane (1992) 'Personal computers, gender and an institutional model of the household', in Roger Silverstone and Eric Hirsch (eds), *Consuming Technologies: Media Information in Domestic Spheres*. London: Routledge. pp. 97–112.

11

The Media in the Age of Digital Communication

Els De Bens and Gianpietro Mazzoleni

The electronic superhighway and digital communication technology have led to a real media hype: the digital communication age will ultimately lead to the definitive end of the analog Gutenberg era. In this chapter we want to consider a number of critical questions concerning this so-called 'digital revolution'. It is certainly not the task of a communication researcher to describe, analyse and evaluate in detail the actual digital communication technologies. We assume that the know-how for digital, multimedia, inter-active communication technologies is available today. Therefore, the digital communication age is not primarily a technological matter, but mainly a social one. Technological change without social change is impossible. The user must be prepared to accept the new media applications and the adop-tion process is the result of negotiation (Silverstone and Haddon, 1993).

In recent years more attention has been paid to the residential user because he or she plays a crucial role in this adoption process. The micro-cosm of the household is an extremely interesting research environment because in the household a multitude of variables come into play during the adoption process. However, it remains difficult to predict the behaviour of consumers and their needs because it is not easy to question users about media products with which they are not yet familiar. The so-called 'technology assessment' approach has worked out a number of methods to evaluate the adoption of new communication technologies as well as possible (Van Doorn and Van Vuyst, 1978; Slack, 1984).

According to Hamelink (1988), it remains risky to recommend certain choices with respect to new communication technologies. In his book with the very significant title *The Technology Gamble*, he stresses the fact that our knowledge is often too limited to make solid predictions. It is hard to prepare oneself for the unexpected, the inconceivable. He especially fears the obstinacy of the 'obsessional gambler', the technologist or politician who wants to control the situation, who wants to be the first and who is very obstinate, even if after some time it becomes obvious that the road taken is a dead end. An example is the way in which the European Commission stubbornly kept recommending and imposing the analog colour standard MAC as a preparatory step towards HDTV, even after it had become clear

that neither the hardware nor software industry or the suppliers and consumers were in favour of this system. In the meantime, MAC and the related
analogue HDTV story has cost the community billions.

Even so, we would like to make a careful attempt to draw the outlines of
the digital communication age. We rely on an extensive literature search, a
research survey on the needs and expectations of the residential user with
respect to new communication technologies, especially video-on-demand, as
well as on in-depth interviews with experts (De Bens and Van Landuyt,
1996).

Towards a uniform digital platform

For a number of years the digitilization of the telecommunication networks
has been under way, more particularly with respect to telephone and
satellite networks and soon also cable networks. The transmitted data are
coded in a binary way so that speed, amount and accuracy have increased
enormously. The ATM (asychronous transfer mode) standard for digital
transmission can transmit different types of information (voice, data,
images, video) through different transmission carriers (copper wires, coax
cables, glass fibre networks or wireless transmission). In addition, the
transmission capacity of the networks is greatly increased by compression
techniques. For the compression of images a world standard (MPEG,
Motion Picture Experts Group) was developed. This international standard
will undoubtedly have a stimulating effect. Digital compression increases
capacity, speed and quality.

The most important effect of all this is that there will be a convergence
between the different transmission channels, such as telephone and cable
networks, and the software designers so that the media sectors are
becoming exchangeable (see Chapter 7). In the past, in the analog world,
the content of the media was produced, distributed and received in different
ways. The media developed into separate business sectors with their own
production methods and their own distribution networks. In the future,
traditional networks such as telephone and cable and traditional media
sectors will operate in each other's fields of activity. Telephone companies
prepare to offer video-on-demand; cable companies want to offer telephone
facilities. This convergence will thoroughly change the present telecom and
media landscape. The convergence between cable and telephone companies
even now manifests itself in the superhighway hype.

Rhetoric about the electronic information highway

In recent years we have been swamped with rhetoric about the electronic
superhighway, particularly from the United States. The information

highway, according to the Clinton administration, will lead to a real revolution in the way Americans work, relax and live. People will be better and more efficiently educated, and democracy will benefit; cultural and geographical boundaries will fade so that people from all over the world will be brought closer to each other (Gore, 1994: 5). New communication technologies seem to feed optimism.

The euphoria concerning the superhighway reminds Europeans of similar rhetoric that could be heard at the beginning of the 1980s in France with respect to 'Le Grand Plan Cable', which was to provide France with a complete broadband glass-fibre net: France would become the first information society in Europe. The costs that had to be invested were so high, however, that neither the government nor the private sector wanted to take the risk. In the 1980s its rhetoric was still heard in the European Commission through the RACE project which would provide Europe with a complete broadband glass-fibre net.

Today, because of the progress of technology, a somewhat more modest plan seems feasible. In fact, a lot of telephone and cable companies are interested in getting involved in the electronic highway. It is no longer necessary to bring the fibre to the home, only the main lines and the main branches will be glass fibre. The large network operators especially – the telephone and cable networks – suggest themselves as possible partners. Partly because of the liberalization policy of the European Commission, traditional monopolies are threatened. New regulations have to be worked out in order to make the free telecom market possible, but also regulations that guarantee the public interest role of the media.

The realization of the highway, which will carry a large number of services, still has a long way to go. The problems usually begin with extra expensive excavation works, which are often very time-consuming and costly. In particular, the software that has to make the highway function must be able to offer a multitude of functions. The platform of the highway must be able to support different servers and information equipment. The so-called 'upgrading' of the cable and telephone networks into a fast, connected, two-way road that carries telephone speech, text data, sound and images is much more complex than is sometimes believed. It requires investments in billions. Calculations have been made that show that in order to connect the 100 million households in the USA to the highway, approximately 120 billion dollars are needed. It is obvious that the superhighway will be no freeway and that economic profitability will be of the utmost importance (Dizard, 1994: 182).

Finally, we must not forget that electronic highways are not the only solution for fast data transport. The largest bandwidth known is still a lorry full of CD-ROMs being transported on a highway. You cannot transport bits any faster at the moment, or in other words, free-standing digital information carriers such as the CD-ROM can also offer the residential user a lot of information without the use of a network (De Jonghe, 1996).

Convergence: more concentration

To be competitive in national and international markets, convergence of the telecom networks will stimulate concentration. Large mega-mergers are to be expected and especially the network operators, cable and telephone networks will enter the production and suppliers' market. New partners such as electricity and water companies will also want to participate in these new media concerns (Mansell, 1993). As the mega-mergers will enter into vertical as well as horizontal alliances, this convergence will also be combined with an increase of internationalization. In the United States a number of mega-mergers between the telecom and the audiovisual-production industries have recently been concluded. The biggest media concern, Time Warner, which had already entered into a horizontal and vertical concentration (Warner Bros film studio, Warner Music, Home Box Office cable and movie pay channel, Warner Cable, Time Inc. books) drew up an alliance with the electronic hardware company US West (separated from AT&T). US West bought 25 per cent of the shares of Time Warner, and paid 2.5 billion dollars, and 50 per cent of Warner Cable's shares.

In May 1995, MCI (the second biggest American telephone company) bought a share of two billion dollars in Murdoch's News International (Print, 20th Century Fox, Fox TV stations and so on). This participation should lead to a worldwide distribution of entertainment and education. From this point of view, it is interesting to mention that MCI signed a joint venture with British Telecom, although this was subsequently annulled. Disney drew up an alliance with a number of so-called regional telephone companies, the 'Baby bells' (Ameritech, GBC, Bell South and GTE). Together they want to invest (500 billion dollars) in new television and video services offered by the telephone companies and the new cable networks. Their competitor is Hollywood Creative Artists Agency with Bell Atlantic, Pactel and Nynex, also regional telephone companies. The recent alliances among the big television networks illustrate the vertical integration strategies (ABS and Disney Co., Turner and Time Warner, NBC and Microsoft, and CBS and Westinghouse Electric).

Finally, there are many actual or potential alliances between American and European network operators (such as MCI and British Telecom, Sprint and France Telecom and Deutsches Telecom, AT&T and Unisource). This list is not complete and certainly not definitive. Most of the mergers within the hardware industry and software industry want to control the complete communication process. At the same time it is a clever way to avoid several national limiting regulations as well as intellectual property rights. Transparency has never been so remote and mega-mergers can escape from the prevailing regulations because these usually apply only to specific, traditional media sectors, of which the fields of application are fading today.

What changes will the traditional printed and audiovisual media undergo as a result of new digital technologies? According to a number of authors, it is the traditional newspaper that appears to be most threatened in the digital era.

Will the traditional newspaper disappear?

In his book *Being Digital* (1995), Negroponte, Professor of Information Technology at MIT, gives a long funeral oration for newspapers. They are replaced by digital information, to be obtained via networks: the information becomes bit-based, the bit is the DNA of information. According to Negroponte's bit-based theory, readers will in fact no longer want to consult the whole newspaper, but only specific parts that interest them and for which they are prepared to pay. The consumer will be in control. He or she will not choose one newspaper, but will navigate between *The Times*, the *Guardian* and the *Daily Mail* and pick whatever interests him or her. As a result of this development, the newspaper market will become very segmented. The reader will no longer subscribe to a newspaper as a whole, but buy separate numbers and articles. Journalists will become 'information brokers'. In the summer of 1993, a number of large American newspaper concerns invested 100,000 dollars each to make a personified newspaper the 'Daily Me'. The initiative was taken by Knight Ridder who firmly believed in such a newspaper. The publishers agreed to offer separate packages from their newspapers. The 'newspaper' was subdivided into special interest categories, such as economics, art, sports, leisure, fashion, gastronomy, travel and so on. It soon turned out that the 'Daily Me' became a kind of mix in which the reader was no longer able to find his or her 'own' newspaper, his or her 'own' companion. As a result, the 'Daily Me' experiment certainly cannot be called a success (Willis, 1994: 111–12).

Most authors are convinced that the traditional newspaper will continue to exist. The newspaper reader wants to touch his or her newspaper, leaf through it and read it in all kinds of locations. Especially with respect to skimming – the zapping through a newspaper – the reader has no need for a digitally programmed menu. The newspaper is a companion to be put aside and picked up again. Another Knight Ridder experiment, in which the newspaper is downloaded from a PC onto a portable PC, also encountered user resistance. In fact, newspaper publishers have spent a lot of effort and will continue to do so to make the lay-out of a newspaper even more attractive, including the use of colour.

In the coming decades, the readers of the paper newspaper will remain the most important target group to be invested in. Research on advertisers has shown that the traditional newspaper has not been written off as a medium for display advertising (brand name). The newspaper publisher does realize, however, that with respect to classified advertisements, the on-line services can become serious competitors. This type of advertising lends itself extremely well to bit-based communication.

The newspaper publishers will concentrate mainly on complementary, digital services. One of the most important of these consists of offering certain information packages electronically. Already in 1988, Knight Ridder began a specialized financial economic service that competed with Reuters' and Dow Jones' financial electronic information services. In addition, newspapers often dispose of extra source material and input about certain topics, which can be offered to interested readers as an extra. Certain information lends itself well to being offered via an interactive search menu, for example, a TV guide, sports results, classified ads and so on.

The videotex experience in France shows that newspapers can tap new market segments via digital applications. The newspapers were among the first enthusiastic information suppliers of videotex in France. Above all, they have developed new complementary services. For them, videotex was a complementary activity; in other words, they extended certain information packages or developed completely new services (games, quizzes). The *messagerie rose*, the most consulted videotex service in France, was actually an initiative of the newspapers. The experience of newspaper publishers with videotex in France could prove to be particularly instructive for those newspaper publishers who want to start up digital activities (Charon, 1992).

In addition to on-line services via networks, newspapers also use CD-ROMs. They use them as an archiving medium: the newspaper is digitally stored and the reader can consult certain columns by means of an interactive system. This filing system is also important from a bibliographical point of view because it has been shown that it is difficult to store cheap newsprint, especially the recycled kind.

Are the new digital TV programmes different?

The transmission channels, the air waves, cable and satellite remain the same: telephone networks are added. In fact, digital transmission and compression do not make much difference: only the number of channels increases incredibly and technology makes it possible to offer more on demand; in other words, the public is expected to select more individually, more *à la carte*.

Will the boom of a multifold of new channels trigger drastic changes? Today the cable networks and DBS satellites have already greatly increased the number of channels. Audience research in several countries has revealed that, in spite of the increased supply of TV channels, viewers remain loyal to a limited number of TV stations, especially to their own national stations. In Flanders, where cable penetration is 92 per cent (the highest percentage in the world) and where for many years 25 channels have been on offer, the viewing patterns show very strong channel loyalty: 80 per cent of viewers watch the three Flemish channels during prime time (De Bens and Van Landuyt, 1996). For the production process, too, there is little that changes. The time and costs needed to create good programmes remain the same, the creativity needed to make a good product is the same whether it is produced digitally or not. Consequently, many authors believe that to fill the thousands of hours of the 500 TV channels one will have to resort to many re-runs, repeats of old programmes (Jankowski and Fuchs, 1995: 157).

In Europe, the experience of an increase in channels via cable or satellite has shown that this situation has indeed led to ever more re-runs and especially to an increase in American programmes. The American TV market disposes of the largest number of affordable and, for the viewer, attractive titles (Silj, 1988; Sepstrup, 1990; Biltereyst, 1991; De Bens et al., 1992).

Will the interactive character of digital TV bring about a big shock? In the near future, will the viewer indeed choose from a 'menu' instead of from the familiar programme schedules? Today, for many viewers, the programme schedules to a large extent determine their choice; they serve as a guideline, a support. For the broadcasting networks, the system also offers considerable advantages. It allows them to develop a certain strategy: for example, new programmes are deliberately placed between two popular programmes so that the viewer becomes familiar with them. Via the programme schedules the broadcasting company can work on viewer loyalty. In the menu system, however, it becomes more difficult to influence viewer loyalty. Here it is the viewer who is almighty because he or she is 'freed' from the programme schedules of the broadcasting companies and selects his or her programmes autonomously. According to Negroponte (1995), the broadcasting companies will disappear anyhow. Instead of 'broadcasting' there will be 'narrowcasting' and especially 'bit-casting'. The viewer will select bits, that is, certain programmes. In his book *Life after Television*, George Gilder (1992) too asserts that viewers will put together their own programmes. Gilder believes in the very active viewer, who will put together a do-it-yourself package from the programmes. As early as 1994, the *Frankfurter Allgemeine Zeitung* (15 April) ran the headline 'Every TV viewer becomes a programme director in his own right' (*Der Fernsehzuschauer wird sein eigener Programmdirektor*).

Probably only a small active minority, mainly light viewers with little time to watch television, will use the interactive system to put together their own programmes. Most authors are convinced, though, that the large majority of viewers are too passive, too little motivated to compose their own TV evening. The fact that the interactive search menus will be offered in digital text will discourage potential users. It will be difficult to inform the user about the hundreds of programmes on offer. An electronic menu is not always as user-friendly and as conveniently arranged as one thinks. Most authors tend to conclude that the majority of viewers will continue to prefer the programme schedules of the broadcasting companies. For a number of thematic products, such as films, sports, the news and children's programmes, the situation is different. These specific interest categories are not new and the thematic channels that have played to those needs control part of the market today. Probably, these thematic programmes, which even today aim at specific target groups, will easily be replaced by on-demand services. These on-demand services will actually function as a kind of substitute for the present thematic use of the media.

Advertisers also have doubts about narrow bit-casting. Target groups that are too small are not worth reaching by expensive TV spots: 'A 500 channel world is one in which 490 services will fight each other over even smaller audience fragments' (Jankowski and Fuchs, 1995: 161). In the future, the advertising cake will definitely be cut up thinly by the new on-demand and on-line services. The eroding of the advertising market in the digital communication era will jeopardize the chances of survival of many traditional and new media. Advertising experts have doubts about the so-called great opportunities of the future for all sorts of marketing activities aimed at the finely woven target groups of the digital society (De Bens and Van Landuyt, 1996). Bill Gates sounds naive when he highlights the advertising opportunities for teddy bears in a teddy bear magazine (Gates, 1995). According to media and advertising experts, the consumption market will never become that fragmented.

Will the viewer watch his or her programmes on a television set or on a computer? Opinions differ on this. Still, there is a majority which is convinced that the television and computer cultures will remain separate in the living room. Television culture is more connected with entertainment, computers with data and all sorts of on-line services. Obviously, people will spend more time being entertained, and consequently with watching television, than with consulting data and all kinds of computer network services. For the programme industry there is more money to be made in television entertainment culture than on-line services (Gomery, 1994: 17). A person who has a television set and a computer will in the end look for different kinds of gratification and will possibly do so in different rooms. One should not forget that there is still a difference between what technology 'can' offer and what the user ultimately wants.

However, other scenarios are possible in which, in a somewhat remoter future, both the television set and the PC will be replaced by a *multimedia terminal* which will simultaneously fulfil the function of television set and computer. For Negroponte (1995), the television set definitely belongs to the past. In *Life after Television*, Gilder (1992) also dismisses the television set definitively. Consumer surveys have shown that viewers are not interested in such a multimedia terminal and that users wish to keep the television and computer cultures separate.

It is evident that new technologies that are related to traditional media, such as VCR and video-on-demand, will be more easily adopted. New media applications that have less in common with existing media, such as videotex and the Internet, will meet more resistance. New media must have an added value: for example, the CD offered better sound quality, a user-friendly interface and a longer playing time than the traditional vinyl record. The added value, however, also has a symbolic dimension: the purchase of a PC, for example, often has symbolic value because it means that the family enters the information age. The adoption process also refers to lifestyles and values.

Video-on-demand: a killer application?

Many authors consider video-on-demand (VoD) as the ultimate 'killer application' for ICT (information and communication technology). VoD is an interactive system for on-demand services that are distributed by the telephone networks. Most commercial trials offer feature films, so that VoD is considered as an important competitor for video rental or video sale, as well as for film pay channels. VoD, however, can offer all kinds of services: TV programmes, video games and so on. The VoD programme is selected by means of a menu and the waiting time is very short, only a few seconds. The requested programme is switched to a so-called set-top box. This set-top box decompresses the digital video signal and reconverts the signal to PAL, so that the output can be generated on the TV screen. The set-top box offers the same functions as a VCR: stop, rewind and forward, so that the interactivity increases. Meanwhile, the telephone line can still be used for voice telephone. For all this – the programmes, the set-top box and the use of the network – the user has to pay.

VoD seems to be an attractive medium because it meets the demand for individual, segmented media use. The user also considers VoD as a substitute for video rental, video sale and film pay channels. VoD is perceived as a new technology, but the content – feature films, TV programmes – is not new. For the user, VoD offers an added value. VoD's *à la carte* system and very short waiting times are attractive. In the case of a feature film, the advantages are manifest: the film is available, no visit to the video shop is required, there are no fines for returning the video late, and there is no dependency on broadcast programme schedules. VoD fits in very well with the need for time management within the available leisure time. The success of the VCR can mainly be explained because it has liberated the user from the compulsive programme schedules of broadcasters. VoD offers the same opportunities for time management. VoD also responds to the increasing need for leisure time within the microcosm of the family. After the age of 25, more and more leisure time is spent at home.

Nevertheless, VoD has to cope with several obstacles. First of all, there is the obstacle of price. The user has to pay for VoD. A Belgian research survey, commissioned by Belgacom, revealed that the consumer is not prepared to pay more for VoD than for hiring a video at the video shop (De Bens and Van Landuyt, 1996). The price of the set-top box, estimated at approximately $500, can also cause problems. Expenses for leisure time in the household budget are not very flexible. In Europe, the TV viewer is not yet used to pay-per-view systems, and is only acquainted with the concepts of the licence fee and the fixed price for subscription (pay channels).

The VoD user will not only have to pay for the on-demand services, but at the same time he or she will be forced to pay a subscription in order to get access to the VoD services. Telephone companies seem to stick to the subscription formula. Experts, however, consider the subscription system to be too rigid, especially for potential VoD viewers who want to make use of VoD in a flexible way. The Belgian research survey has shown that the consumer considers a monthly subscription rate of around 14 dollars as the maximum he or she is willing to pay (De Bens and Van Landuyt, 1996).

Video shops and film pay channels, especially pay-per-view systems, the direct competitors of VoD, are of course preparing a counter-attack. Video shops will lower the price of video for rent. The industry of video for sale will also fight back. The price of video cassettes and, in the near future, digital video and CD-ROM will decrease. The purchase of video makes the user fully independent of all kinds of programme schedules and on-demand services. Negroponte (1995: 169) is one of the few authors who still believe firmly that VoD will in time replace video for rent and video for sale completely.

The intentions of Hollywood towards VoD are not yet clear. Video rental and sale are important spin-offs for the Hollywood film industry. Holly-wood has the largest share in the 21 billion dollar video sale and rental market. It has so far hesitated to engage in VoD services or participate in existing VoD supply services (Sherman, 1995: 139). There is also a great deal of uncertainty with regard to film and distribution rights for VoD services.

Pay channels also are developing an anti-VoD strategy by means of pay-per-view (PPV) systems. In recent years, PPV has been expanding in the USA.The recent collaboration between BSkyB, Bertelsmann, CLT, CanalPlus and Havas, with the aim of offering digital pay TV, PPV as well as near-VoD together, shows that pay channels are preparing them-selves to compete with VoD.

Cable networks are one step ahead of telephone companies. The modi-fication from pay-per-view to near-VoD is small (Dizard, 1994: 113). Cable companies do not have a switched network (point-to-point) necessary for full interactive VoD, as the telephone companies, but, as a result of their large bandwidth and digital compression techniques, cable companies can distribute feature films at regular times, every 10 or 15 minutes. The waiting time is somewhat longer than for VoD, but the system is cheaper. Experts have mixed feelings and argue that both cable networks and telephone companies are capable of offering VoD (De Bens and Van Landuyt, 1996).

Another important obstacle for VoD is the passive use of TV by the average TV consumer. More than 40 years of passive TV culture has made the viewer dependent on the programme schedules of the broadcasting institutions. Many authors doubt whether viewers will be willing to make use of the menus that offer a teletext-like long list of programme titles.

VoD arrives in a period of saturated television culture. The average European watches three hours of TV a day, and only disposes of three to four hours of leisure time. In many European countries, watching television is stagnating. Even in the USA, TV consumption seems to have reached saturation point. 'As much in love with television as America seems to be, there may well be a point of saturation' (Willis, 1994: 87). The competition among TV channels and all kinds of audiovisual media (VoD, CD-I, CD-ROM) will be very fierce. Future VoD consumers will have to be lured away from other audiovisual media. The Belgacom survey revealed that, among the early adopters, we can distinguish two target groups (De Bens and Van Landuyt, 1996). The first group consists of young adults with a rather low educational level but a good income. They are the heavy viewers. In the past they were the early adopters of VCR and they often have a subscription to a film pay channel. These heavy viewers are characterized by passive TV behaviour and they will probably not be in favour of the menu-system of VoD. The second group of early adopters consists of a very small market segment: light viewers with a high educational level, who have little time for watching TV and who will occasionally be interested in VoD because of specific interest categories. This small group obviously offers poor VoD market prospects.

Recently, VoD seems no longer to be considered the ultimate 'killer application'. The video industry, both sale and rental, as well as the film pay channels will fight back. There is too much uncertainty about the price, the better service, the number of available programme titles and so on. The average TV viewer is not ready to make use of the 'do-it-yourself' formula of VoD. Worldwide, the VoD hype is cooling down. Several trials have been postponed or scaled down. Time Warner has reduced its project in Orlando from 4,000 connected households to 60. Meanwhile, the American regional telephone companies have cancelled their VoD plans. Pacific Bell has decided not to start its trial. The only regional telephone company that has actually launched VoD, Rochester Telegraph, has decided not to expand the 52 connected households (*Cable & Satellite*, April 1995). British Telecom, which is involved in an important trial, has recently announced that entertainment and feature films seem not to be the killer applications for VoD. They now believe that non-entertainment VoD services will offer better market opportunities. Conclusions from other VoD trials indicate that educational and professional applications could be more promising. The VoD technology is available but the consumer does not seem ready to use it.

Internet: the real breakthrough?

The activities of networks through the electronic superhighways will cause social changes. Today, the most successful network is the Internet.

Launched in the early 1970s by the Pentagon, and later on elaborated by enthusiastic academic researchers into an open network, the Internet has become a worldwide web today. Thanks to governmental subsidies, academic staff could use the World Wide Web (WWW) freely (telecom infrastructure), and sites are still offered freely. Citizens who want to make use of the Internet have to subscribe to an access provider and must pay for the use of the telecom infrastructure, but only a local call is charged, so that the worldwide use is cheap.

In France, too, where the government subsidized videotex (people could get hold of a Minitel without paying for it), videotex boomed. An efficient marketing and information campaign attracted many suppliers of services. Videotex in France proved not only to be an information service, but users invented all kinds of social activities through videotex: the use of videotex was indeed also triggered by typical entertainment and erotic services, such as the *messagerie rose*. The sudden boom of the Internet can be compared with the French Minitel case. The Internet is an open network that stimulates the creation of new types of communication.

The most recent significant change in the Internet is the rise of commercial sites. Enterprises began using the Internet for marketing objectives. Through the Internet, new types of communication have arisen. Some authors (Katz, 1992: 9) consider cyberspace to herald the end of traditional journalism. It is no longer the journalist who selects the topics, but on-line users themselves. The interactivity of networks like the Internet can indeed create new, active, horizontal communication groups, exchanging ideas and views about a certain topic. Journalists are no longer needed. They do not participate any longer. On the other hand, journalists will become more important than ever because they will have to select the 'newsworthy' events out of an endless, chaotic information flow, and they will have to comment on and interpret it. Bardoel (1996: 299) argues that

> the profession is one of the last strongholds of generalism in an increasingly specialized and fragmented society. Greater individual freedom for citizens produces, more than ever, the need for common orientation. This might be the most important mission for journalists in the future – a mission that calls for responsibilities and skills beyond the present journalistic practice.

Many authors and politicians firmly believe, however, that cyberspace will stimulate more democratic participation and emancipation. Gore, the US vice president, recently declared: 'Clinton and I are committed to making the benefits of the communication revolution available to all Americans across all sectors of society' (Gomery, 1994: 18). This, of course, sounds like empty rhetoric. In the USA alone there are already 10 million illiterates and millions of people do not even have a telephone connection (Dizard, 1994). Access to the Internet is not a necessary or natural state of affairs. It has to be organized or created (Street, 1997). Technologists sometimes sound quite naive. Bill Gates, for example, is convinced that the gap between the poor and the rich countries will narrow. According to Bill

Gates, the underdeveloped countries will catch up, and join the electronic information society (Gates, 1995: 281). Participation in cyberspace, however, requires electricity, telephone infrastructure, computer and software know-how, literacy and a certain standard of living (Van Bolhuis and Colom, 1996). The problems of access and imbalance will be reproduced in the new electronic age. The most important reason why people will use or not use the Internet will be income. An NOP survey in 1995 in the UK revealed that a third of the respondents who use the Internet earn more than £25,000 annually (Golding, 1996). Golding underlines that 'as communications are driven into the marketplace, the widening inequalities of economic fortune are translated into cultural and political disadvantage' (1996: 78). The Internet's 'net' is not so worldwide. The Internet Society estimated that in 1994 there were 0.002 Internet users per 1,000 inhabitants in India (compared with 48.9 in Sweden) and most African nations have no Internet access.

Many authors still consider access and interactivity with the media as one of the great challenges of the information society. As early as 1969, Jean d'Arcy wrote that the citizens had to claim 'a right to communicate'. This right to communicate should stimulate communication among citizens and government in the digital area (Kleinwachter, 1995: 110). The commercialization of the Internet could be a threat to these 'cyber-rights'. Governments have a social responsibility to make the Internet infrastructure available to all citizens. At the same time the new technology has to be regulated. The Internet offers the possibility of uncontrolled access, but the emergence of pornography, 'undemocratic' political babble and the infringement of intellectual property rights, threaten cyber-democracy.

Finally, the whole Internet hype has to be analysed in a critical way. Today, the Internet is still in the launch phase and only reaches the happy few. The Internet is used worldwide by 26 million people and this is a very small, white-collar elite. Kroker warns us that an analysis of technotopia and cyberspace has to remain critical: 'How can we turn the virtual horizon in the direction of substantive human values: aesthetic creativity, social solidarity, democratic discourse and economic justice?' (Kroker, 1996: 169). Many authors doubt whether the Internet will stimulate participation in the political process and will finally enrich democracy.

The digital communication age will not turn out to be a real breakthrough. We are now experiencing the very first phase and are approaching very slowly the substitution stage, during which domestic users will exchange traditional media for new digital media applications. McLuhan (1964) drew our attention to the fact that we enter the future backwards: 'The content of a new medium is an old one'. For the next decades, the traditional media will continue to reach the majority of citizens.

Technologists will persist in their search for the ultimate 'killer applications', but the innovation process is complex and multidimensional. The final adoption of a new technology is the result of a dynamic process with several variables, such as a user-friendly interface, the price to pay, the flexibility of the family budget, the availability of a world standard, the expected added value, the place in leisure-time activities, lifestyle and values. Technology is not something that exists on its own and our ways of life are not determined by technology. Technology isn't 'the message', but technology operates in a cultural, societal environment.

The recent hype about the Internet and the electronic superhighway is inspired by technological, one-sided optimism. The use of the Internet will remain the privilege of highly educated people with a good standard of living. The thesis that the Internet will stimulate and revitalize the democratic process is undermined by market mechanisms, limited access and cyber-individualism. Real democratic policy-making should implement the G7 declared objective of 'the highest possible levels of participation of citizens', avoiding the emergence of two classes of citizens. In a word, the 'public interest' should be on top of all other legitimate interests of all involved actors in the huge business of the information and communication technologies.

Bibliography

Arnbak, J.C. (1995) *Athena en Arache: Bestuurlijke patronen in de toepassing van netwerktechnologie*. Amsterdam: Cramwinckel.

Bardoel, J. (1993) *Zonder pen of papier: Journalistiek op de drempel van een nieuwe eeuw*. Amsterdam: Cramwinckel.

Bardoel, J. (1996) 'Beyond journalism: a profession between information society and civil society', *European Journal of Communication*, 11 (3): 283–302.

Biltereyst, D. (1991) 'Resisting the American hegemony: a comparative analysis of the reception of domestic and US fiction', *European Journal of Communication*, 6 (4): 469–97.

Blumler, J.G. (1992) 'New roles for public service television in Western Europe: challenge and prospects', *Journal of Communication*, 42 (1): 20–35.

Charon, J.M. (1992) 'Les Français et leurs media: le doute toujours', *Mediapouvoirs*, 25: 24–35.

Cronberg, T. (1994) 'The social construction of home technology: the case of the home information network in Denmark', in K. Bjerg and K. Borreby (eds), *Home-oriented Informatics, Telematics and Automatisation*, Proceedings of a Cross-disciplinary International Working Conference, University of Copenhagen, 27 June–1 July 1994.

Curran, J. (1991) 'Rethinking the media as a public sphere', in P. Dahlgren and C. Sparks (eds), *Communication and Citizenship. Journalism and Public Sphere, the New Media Age*. London: Routledge.

Davies, D.E.N. et al. (1993) *Communications after AD 2000*. London.

De Bens, E. and Van Landuyt, D. (1996) *Video-on-Demand: A User Oriented Study*, 4 vols. Brussels: Belgacom.

De Bens, E., Kelly, M. and Bakke, M. (1992) 'Television content: Dallasfication of culture', in K. Siune and W. Truetzschler (eds), *Dynamics of Media Politics*. London: Sage. pp. 75–100.

De Boer, C. and Brennecke, S.I. (1995) *Media & Publiek*. Amsterdam: Boom.

De Jonghe, E. (1996) 'Barco Electronics Demo'. Unpublished lecture, University of Ghent, Ghent.

Dizard , W. (1994) *Old Media – New Media*. New York: Longman.

Feldman, T. (1994) *Multimedia*. London: Chapman & Hall.

Gates, B. (1995) *De weg die voor ons ligt*. Meulenhof: Kritak.

Gilder, G. (1992) *Life after Television*. New York: Norton.

Golding, P. (1996) 'World wide wedge: division and contradiction in the global information infrastructure', *Monthly Review*, 48 (3): 70–85.

Gomery, D. (1994) 'Potholes and passing lanes: the information superhighway', *Current*, 368: 16–21.

Gore, A. (1994) 'Forging an Athenian age of democracy', *Intermedia*, 22: 2.

Habermas, J. (1993) *Faktizität und Geltung: Beiträge zur Diskurstherapie des Rechts und des demokratischen Rechtsstaat.* Frankfurt-on-Main: Suhrkamp.

Hamelink, C. (1988) *The Technology Gamble.* Norwood, NJ: Ablex.

Jankowski, G.F. and Fuchs, D. (1995) *Television Today and Tomorrow.* New York: Oxford University Press.

Katz, E. (1992) 'The end of journalism: notes on watching the war', *Journal of Communication*, 42 (4): 5–14.

Keane, J. (1991) *The Media and Democracy.* Cambridge: Polity Press.

Kleinwachter, W. (1995) 'Is there a need for right to communicate in cyberspace?', *The Public Javnost*, 2: 107–15.

Kroker, K. (1996) 'Virtual capitalism', in B. Martinsons and M. Menser (eds), *Technoscience and Cyberculture.* New York: Routledge.

McLuhan, M. (1964) *Understanding Media: The Extension of Man.* New York: McGraw-Hill.

Mansell, A. (1993) *The New Telecommunications: A Political Economy of Network Evolution.* London: Sage.

Negroponte, N. (1995) *Being Digital.* London: Hodder & Stoughton.

Sepstrup, P. (1990) *Transnationalisation of Television in Western Europe.* London: Libbey.

Sherman, L.B. (1995) *Telecommunications Management: Broadcasting, Cable and the New Technologies.* New York: McGraw-Hill.

Silj, A. (1988) *East of Dallas: The European Challenge to American TV.* London: BFI Publishing.

Silverstone, R. and Haddon, L. (1993) 'The individual and social dynamics of information and communication technologies: present and future', Project Vissex, SPRV Report for CEC, RACE Project 2086.

Slack, J.D. (1984) *Communication Technologies and Society: Conceptions of Causality and the Politics of Technological Intervention.* Norwood, NJ: Ablex.

de Sola Pool, I. (1990) *Technologies without Boundaries.* Cambridge, MA: Harvard University Press.

Street, J. (1997) 'Remote control? Politics, technology and electronic democracy', *European Journal of Communication*, 12 (1): 27–42.

Van Bolhuis, H.E. and Colom, V. (1996) *Cyberspace Reflections.* Brussels: VUB Press.

Van Cuilenberg, J.J. (1994) 'Een toekomst vol informatie en communicatie', in A.C. Zijderveld (ed.), *Kleine geschiedenis van de toekomst: 100 thesen over de Westerse samenleving op weg naar de 21e eeuw.* Kampen: Kok Agora. pp. 146–54.

Van Doorn, J. and Van Vuyst, Fr. (1978) *Forecasting: Methoden en technieken voor toekomstonderzoek.* Amsterdam: Van Gorcum Assen.

Willis, J. (1994) *The Age of Multimedia and Turbonews.* Westport, CT: Praeger.

PART IV   POLICY RESPONSES

12

Debating National Policy

Claude Sorbets

The changes in the electronic and broadcasting media sector, initially brought about by the recomposition of national media systems, in turn linked to the development of new media and general contextual changes, have resulted in a re-mapping of the media landscape of Europe. *De facto*, in every country a coherent overall trend can be observed, evidenced in such commonplace terms as 'public tendering' and 'deregulation'. However, even if there is no debate as to the general direction of this movement, what does give food for thought is the existence of differences in the *how* and *when* of these reforms in national media systems. We also need to pay attention to the fine detail of these inter-country differences.

The factors that account for national shifts of media sites are well known, especially the new technological and economic trends that are transforming cultures and influencing policy. This line of analysis is generally convincing. Techonological advances in media support systems, such as digitalization, and the secondary social effects described by such terms as the 'computerization' of society and 'digital man' are well identified and leave little room for doubt that they are part of a process of changing civilization.

The floating economic situation of the past 25 years has been a source of constant uncertainty. On the one hand, some European countries have been faced with mass unemployment and plunged into a quagmire of social crisis from which one could hope to find a way out, at the top, by way of a sharp recovery of growth or, at the bottom, by sharing out the jobs available. On the other hand, the future economy will find itself increasingly having to do without a human workforce because of the increasing use of computer-driven robots. In addition to this, computerization tends to eliminate time and space considerations, thus engendering new problems related to the de-location of production activities.

In these circumstances, any debate must surely turn on the one crucial issue, namely that there must be a political dimension at all levels, every-where and at all stages. The first question is to ascertain what powers the political actor would need to get things done. Would national governments drift along ineffectively, at the mercy of changes by which they have been overtaken, or could they play an active role? If so, what would this active role be? Secondly, there will have to be some evaluation of the procedures by which public sector policies are elaborated and implemented. In a political context, which experiences in a continental frame have already been elaborated (for example, the EU), what is left to be dealt with at a national level may seem rather secondary, compared to working from a principle of subsidiarity, one which presupposes that one should hand up to higher authorities only those matters which could not be dealt with at a lower level.

In this chapter we shall consider the local adaptations to national media systems which will enable us to take into account certain dimensions which are, paradoxically, becoming partially or wholly obsolete. These include certain differentiations of positions or options between parties of the left and those of the right. Everything seems to be happening in a generalized climate of fatality, such that the principal actors are giving up and doing no more than making proposals to adapt to the inevitable. From one political market to another, these proposals could provoke debate but still lead to the same conclusion, namely that no more can be done but simply try to manage the situation.

One might wonder if the general changes occurring do not, on the one hand, contribute to the singularity of each of the national sites (change is simply a function of where one is, the particular situation and particular state) or, on the other hand, help to account for the conditions shared by the various national authorities. In the latter case, this would lead to a re-assessment of the status of this sector and thus of the way the public sector should handle it: is a sector necessarily driven by market forces and if so what should the role of the authorities be?

Media landscapes and political history

An overview of the comparative literature on national media systems (Ostergaard, 1997) affords a retrospective evaluation of the path taken by various European countries over the past 15 years. A very marked tendency can be discerned in all countries, namely the reshaping of the national landscape in a commercialized and privatized direction. At the same time it should be emphasized that there is much opening up and diversification. The opening up results from joining in the flux of transnational system developments. The diversification occurs as new media support systems appear that both render each other superfluous and also engage each other in a more or less fierce competition (Sorbets, 1985). Besides this commonly observed phenomenon, the 'medialogical' product is transformed (Debray, 1991). The pace of change varies from one country to the next, and information-oriented media products vacate or replace each other in an ever-expanding communication space. This can weaken the concept of a 'culture and education providing public service', whose goal is to stimulate and enhance from above rather than allow the drift towards entertainment. The latter depends heavily on a lowering of cultural sights (socializing from below) which is based on the shared values typical of social intercourse within closely knit communities or communities which are very similar and closely identify with each other.

No doubt the way audience markets are divided up into specific segments arises from the tendency of our societies to gather together behind entirely different demarcation lines than before. Surely what distinguishes present-day developed Western societies is that everyone feels that they belong to a wide variety of groups, implying that former historical social divisions, based on class and other once significant factors, have to be discarded. Considerations such as these raise the question of 'lifestyles', which in our modern societies are perceived as complex and multiple. They exist at many levels and they are liable to a multiplication of modes of action that may be brought into play more or less at random.

Political scientists are very familiar with the recurrent problem posed by the political crisis that seems to be symptomatic of the current state of political affairs. There is a crisis of representation which corresponds to a reduction in political debate and hence a loss of articulation in the political system with the expectations, beliefs and values of the population being faced with new problems. Then there is the stigmatization of those marginalized sections of the population who find themselves tempted to play the 'exit card' (see Hirschman, 1970, on the exit solution). Public authorities desperately seek more effective and efficient bases from which to make new endeavours work and to find new configurations of actors. In a political science interpretation of this situation one has to take into account constitutive reform efforts (see Lowi, 1972) to remould politico-administrative structures; for example, decentralization and/or regionaliza-tion. There are other reforms, proposed at the same time as those that concern the media system and which are seemingly directly related. We have only to think of reforms designed to tackle urban problems. Consider the new concept of urban engineering (Martinand, 1986; Sorbets, 1988) which now extends the role and responsibility of engineers from that of being technicians to being global urban experts, a broadening of their role brought about entirely because of the general computerization of our societies.

Ambivalence is well known to be one of the best heuristic keys to help us understand the contradictions of our present-day societies. Thus the increase in the professionalization of politics – the rise of a political pro-fession – could go hand in hand with an increased power of experts, and no doubt could also lead to the population feeling that they want to be more actively involved in public initiative procedures. In such a situation, we should never fail to insist on the problematic consequence: that a politi-cian's authority is formally founded on legitimizing electoral rites much more than on whether he or she can grasp the facts and knows what to do in given decision-making processes.

In the media field, where public officials in some countries have found themselves having to take fast and far-reaching decisions, under the influence of experts or the pressure of interest groups or sometimes both, there is inevitably much conjecture and speculation about the predicted outcomes. The anticipation of new technological development, the ability to obtain future returns on investment for a particular enterprise and the need to keep up with neighbouring authorities are no doubt among the list of explanations for actions which could have been dictated by the context or which, in other situations, would have been postponed (Elias, 1991). These situations include those in which 'keeping the initiative' could take the form of holding off in a state of extended expectation. Whatever the case, political leaders may find themselves subordinated both in terms of their electoral milieu and by their own staff.

The singularity of the new electronic media is no doubt that these media, as support systems and as particular technologies, are already themselves the instigators of what should be decided *for* them. Either the services attached to support systems are already defined or the support systems are developed along with the economic and social measures for their implementation. In the same vein we cannot help but recall the Palo Alto School's use of Gregory Bateson's analysis according to which there is a multiplication of critical political situations in which public officers, either individually or in groups, find themselves in a double bind (Bateson and Ruesch, 1988). They are caught between the tendency to do or not to do that which they are called upon to say or get done. Here we find ourselves with a situation which is frequently encountered by politicians, namely having to let through numerous political decisions – which would have to be rationalized later – to cut back both on public sector monopolies as well as public sector institutions or audiovisual projects inspired by a public service philosophy. The dilemma arises when these same politicians actually belong to 'political families' among whose political beliefs deregulation, privatization or commercial programming were anathema.

In this respect, the well-known position which holds that policy-making is the whole or essence of political governance (Bergeron, 1977) (going beyond a possible reductionism pertaining to some schools of thought about which we will speak later) indicates a general line of interpretation of public action. This is, on the one hand, beyond reproach since it presents government teams as decision-makers and regulators of society who use adaptive strategies. But, on the other hand, this line is rather questionable, since it fails to take full stock of the conditioning of the political actor by his or her milieu and vice versa. This conditioning can only be measured by an in-phase analysis; that is, by taking into account the action involved and the moment it occurred. All in all, it is manifestly useful, not to say necessary, to observe the main trait of 'new governance' (Rhodes, 1996), namely the polarization and clear sectorialization of public action and the relocation of the public authority into other institutions created within the territorial jurisdiction. These basic dimensions of the new conditions for public action could be expressed by the analytical model whose acronym IMPACT (institutionalization of the mode of production of public action through the local authorities) could be the signifier (see Sorbets, 1994).

The reductionism referred to above concerns distortions which could be brought about by neo-institutionalist generalizations as well as by simplifications of the strategic approaches coloured by a 'rational choice' paradigm, reframing both the 'politics' and the 'polity' dimensions to the format preferred for conceptualization in policy-making. In this way, an interpretation of public action along the lines of the Jones (1970) sequential analytic model might be preferred. This considers the moment at which various governmental political agenda were elaborated and does not take account of data concerning the political society in question or the origin and field of the considered action. An alternative, this time a 'substantial' approach to public policy, suggests that we first and foremost consider global-sectoral frames of reference and the action of 'mediators' on the determination of public actions (Muller, 1991).

A national interpretation of public policies for the media, in one or other of these perspectives, effectively runs the risk of actualizing (as opposed to potentializing or modalizing) these analytical difficulties. In this respect, the presentation, both in its original and second corrected version, of the '*plan cable*' policy by Brenac et al. (1985) shows up the difficulties of an in-phase analysis and of conceptual tools of this type. In order to provide a more complete analysis we would no doubt have to consider a multitude of parameters. We can list the set of questions or a complete description of this field of analysis.

Levels of analysis

In the first place it will be necessary to ascertain which targets would be chosen by the decision-makers. In other words, who or what does the government intend to target first? The order of hierarchy reflects a prioritizing of targets in time and space. For example, a decentralizing reform could be first targeted at the local authorities or the administration, at elected representatives or community leaders. As far as media matters are concerned, this question will no doubt generate different responses from one country to the next, from one moment to the next and from one government team to another.

Anyway, this question will vary as a function of the public action involved. A constituent of the 'giving up of public monopoly' type would certainly not have the same parameters as would apply in a regulative type, to adopt Lowi's (1972) categorizations, an example of which would relate to the allocation of radio frequencies. A distributive type of action, for instance policy governing advertising and licence fees, would differ from a 'redistributive' type of action such as transferring regulatory responsibility for the audiovisual sector from one authority to another. Such a transfer might be from a ministerial to an independent authority, or to one at another territorial level (regional, local or even supranational). An example here is the European level organization of controls on progamming laid down in the 'Television without Frontiers' directive.

Secondly, any reflection on the conditions and size of national initiatives which become public policies should, it would seem, take on board the significant fact that a public action *generally* follows in the wake of previous actions which it is intended to correct or replace. The use of the adverb 'generally' leaves the field open for new public policies. Indeed, it is new public policies that interest us here, or at least differential public policies, either because they indicate a particular desire for action which would be innovative or which would require an unusual orientation in a given politico-territorial site.

In this respect, policy-making theorizations generally seem to fall into the follow-on category, even if the question is not put in these terms: public actions of some importance are shown to be sector adjustment actions. This may appear from the references which are made to the setting up of a 'governmental agenda' – from the moment that the scope of the problem is defined to the moment of its evaluation at the end of the process. Or it may be apparent from the adoption of a perspective of making a sector coherent in respect of the whole society. For our analytical reasoning, it is advisable to go beyond noting a serial and diachronic logic and consider another, that is a contextual and synchronic, logic. This could be expressed as enabling us to enter a 'get into phase/get out of phase'. In other words, it helps us to take into account the discursive and symbolic dimension that is concealed behind and within any public action.

In this respect, the difficulties involved in objectivizing the room to manoeuvre that public officials actually have *in situ* are perhaps less important at the end of the day than are the decisions *not* to take into account – other than for the record, one could say – political effects which either had been or could have been anticipated by the politicians concerned; for example, 'the impact of announcing' a particular political action or a presentation of an action with a particular political slant (emblematic in a strategically/tactically relevant way). In the kind of sector that concerns us here, the part played by values and symbols is in fact intrinsically – perhaps 'naturally' – very important, be it only because of the collective identity impacts which are produced or effected. This should be understood in the light of proclamations for the defence or the promotion of culture, with regard to national languages and traditions, that have been formulated by government teams in various countries of Europe.

A third level of investigation to be considered here is how public officials construct the list of needs that they will undertake to satisfy. This refers to the choice of needs that they take to be legitimate and which should be tackled first. Indeed, we know that public decision-makers may also be seen as 'non-decision-makers' (cf. Bachrach and Baratz, 1969). Only part of the spectrum of demands – and the needs which they express – ever gets into the field where they could be written into the political agenda or included in the frame adaptation procedure. With regard to the needs–demands that will be taken into consideration and/or be dealt with by government bodies, it is obvious that all the parameters mentioned – including the geographical location, the dimensions of the economy and/or the existence of a state industry in the sector, the effects induced by belonging to various groups and so on – will condition the choice made by authorities in the name of the defence of national interests.

In this respect one could say that the rationalization process that Weber so imaginatively described as an 'iron cage' runs the risk of inducing an over-reductive vision of how effective a public action can be (Bouretz, 1996). It is enough to mention interpretations which use as a key the 'end of ideology' or today 'the decline and fall of missionary endeavours' in our so-called postmodern societies. These are societies which relinquish messianic expectations and promises within a population which has become not so much disillusioned as rather pragmatic with respect to governmental actions. Such interpretations, in some instances at least (for instance, by harping on emotional factors: Braud, 1997), eclipse the material interests of groups to which they happen to be related. These interests are, to a certain extent, masked by political rhetoric which is an integral part of the policy-making process.

The fourth level of our investigation should lead us to a reconsideration of the first question but this time posed in its globality. This concerns the *posture* in which the decision-makers operate with regard to the entirety of their field of action. By this we mean that every public policy decision is taken after a presentation of what the problem is, a diagnosis and proposals made by the various *ad hoc* commissions set up for this purpose from which the government takes advice before every major reform. In the media sector, the newness of systems and layouts, which is no doubt greater than in other sectors, has led to a generalization of the resulting Green papers. Those advocates of a 'substantial' interpretation of policy make use of these commissions as the privileged sites in which the 'global/sectoral frames of reference' are rationalized and requests transmitted by the 'mediators' are put in working order.

Back to national differences

Prior to these organizational efforts to reach agreement which are intended to reduce uncertainty or to reconcile preferences, and which certain analysts would describe as the conditioning of public officials towards the wishes of interest groups, we find other phases. These are times when relations between politicians and the society are structured and when general schemes of the representations of the public interest and of private interests interact. One could say that the practices of consensus-making, which are becoming hegemonic these days, fall essentially into one of two distinct analytical models. They could certainly be linked to the 'incrementalist' model for the formation of public policies. Let us recall that this model is generally considered to be characteristic of the Anglo-Saxon tradition of government, as distinct from the Jacobin tradition influenced by the French 'habitus'. The latter is exemplified in the so-called rational French practice (see Green, 1984) in which there is state control and a centralized definition of goals and means. The authoritarian nature of this kind of procedure is modified by the set of arrangements that allow for exceptions to the rules, which are formulated in general and universal terms. This French practice may be preferred to one in which interested parties come together to define their own means and goals.

In this respect politicians, just like ordinary citizens, work within a frame of reference from their own experience (see Goffman, 1991) in each different country, within which the variations and usual behaviour patterns differ endlessly according to geographical location, social category and, of course, the political currents of the moment.

At this point we should perhaps recall the work of specialists in social political interactions who have exposed the dynamics and also the very particular topography of the tension created by the two types of social-ization, one from the top the other from the bottom. We may add a reminder of the way in which audiovisual programmes are perceived to have perverse or dangerous effects – to use Hirschman categories – because they either homogenize culture or are culturally integrating and hence can produce dire consequences. Consider the theme of violence and/or sex in television programming and the branding of programmes as variously 'authorized' viewing, providing good models to follow and setting them apart from content which could traumatize the young, fragile or sensitive viewer.

Beyond these personal cultural differences, political actors, public officials and citizens alike are in fact both the mirrors and the interpreters of public opinion – by virtue of their knowledge of the state of public opinion – for the formation of public arenas. In this respect, the media as a field of intervention of public action is particularly sensitive to the democratic reality, whether by way of information (access, diversity) or by the under-lying effects of control because the media are the source and vector of communication in society.

Everything concerning political competition, the political regime and political institutions necessarily involves the media sector and can suffer the consequences thereof. For this reason the sensitivity with which politicians are liable to intervene in the decision-making process concerning this sector is very understandable. For the protection of various interests, regulatory bodies are often set up by law. Various demands for protection can be made in order to guarantee the g eneral division of powers; for example, between European and national levels, but also within nation states between central and local levels or from federal to federated state. Generally, the extension and globalization of effects, which are either the cause of or are caused by decisions concerning the media sector (Descombes, 1995), lead to tensions and crises which then appear on the list of 'causes to be defended', ranging from the defence of ideas and particular opinions to special positions of established interests or instituted prerogatives. In this respect, the 'national' solutions which appear to constitute the new media national regulatory systems, both in the provisions of which they are the substance and in the institutional bodies set up to monitor them, are the indicators of the way things are done in systems of public action.

The tempo of public policies, with regard to national society – the champions in the various sectors – and the opinion found there, with regard to what is done elsewhere, can, in its turn, lead to excessive rationalization of the processes of recomposition carried out by politicians. In this respect, one should no doubt recall the generally heuristic character of the 'garbage-can' model proposed by Cohen et al. (1972). Numerous public decisions could be described as 'opportunistic' since they take advantage of the frameworks that happen to be at hand for their elaboration and in their implementation.

In this way, media systems are becoming normalized or, conversely, more voluntarist. One could oppose the normalized (what happens naturally) or voluntarist situations to others which 'are forced upon us by circumstances' or 'defined by external constraints'. In such a case there are no politicians who would ever admit that something was thrust upon them since they consider their principal preoccupation to be to discover – or to preserve – the degree of initiative for themselves or for those of their constituents. At the national policy level, the leaders have lost their grip on the control levers because of the multiplication of actors, support systems, programmes and external driving forces.

Conclusion

The national answers as to what should be done and how it should be done in respect of the new media ought at least to be related in a complementary way to more or less global logics, in particular economic ones which condition the public and private actors in the media sector. Specific variations, which can be noticed here and there, compared to what could be considered as the European norm, undoubtedly depend on several parameters. These include being a small or large country, located in the north or in the south of the continent, belonging to one or other subcontinental grouping of states, or owning some transnational company. These variables, and probably others (for instance, different levels of prosperity between countries), influence the conditions of the restructuring of national communication systems.

A strategic view of media sectoral change would underline the unequal resources and constraints that states can use to implement more or less autonomous policies, albeit that the autonomy of each may be limited to the ability to negotiate the conditions of submission to the common regulation. Significant echoes of these modulated interpretations are to be found in the various tones of national debates and rhetorical arguments that refer to the 'market' and the economic process of relating the local to the global. Uncertainties about the ins and outs of such a new general economic process can lead to the belief that most public authorities present themselves as pretending to rule over what is actually escaping them and as partly manipulating external 'challenges', whose potency and strength of destiny they exaggerate.

Bibliography

Bachrach, P. and Baratz, R. (1969) *Decision and Non-decision: An Analytical Framework of Political Power*. Roderick Bell.

Bateson, G. and Ruesch, J. (1988) *Communication et société*. Paris: Editions du Seuil.

Bergeron, G. (1977) *La gouverne politique*. Paris: Mouton.

Bouretz, P. (1996) *Les promesses du monde: la philosophie du Max Weber*. Paris: Gallimard.

Braud, P. (1997) *L'Emotion en politique*. Paris: Presses de la FNSP.

Brenac, E., Jobert, B. et al. (1985) '"L'Enterprise publique comme acteur politique": la DGT et la genese du Plan cable', *Sociologie du Travail*, 3: 291–304.

Cohen, M.D., March, J.G. and Olsen, J.P. (1972) 'Garbage can world of organizational choice', *Administrative Science Quarterly*, 17 (1): 1–25.

Dahl, R. (1971) *Qui gouverne?* Paris: Armand Colin.

Debray, R. (1991) *Cours de mediologie generale*. Paris: Gallimard.

Descombes, V. (1995) *La Denrée mentale*. Paris: Editions de Minuit.

Douglas, M. (1987) *How Institutions Think*. London: Routledge.

Duran, P. and Thoenig, J. (1996) 'L'Etat et la gestion territoriale', *Revue Française de Science Politique*, 46 (4): 580–622.

Elias, N. (1991) *Qu'est ce que la sociologie?* La Tour d'Aigues: Agora.

Goffman, I. (1991) *Les Cadres de l'expérience*. Paris: Editions de Minuit.

Green, D. (1984) 'Industrial policy and policy-making', in V. Wright (ed.), *Continuity and Change in France*. London: Allen & Unwin.

Hirschman, A.O. (1970) *Voice and Loyalty*. Cambridge, MA: Harvard University Press.

Jones, C.O. (1970) *An Introduction to the Study of Public Policy*. Bellmot: Duxbour Press.

Lowi, T. (1972) 'Four systems of policy, politics and choice', *Public Administration Review*, July–August: 298–310.

Martinand, C. (1986) *Le genie urbaine*. Paris: La Documentation Française.

Muller, P. (1991) *Les politiques publiques*. Paris: PUF, Qui sais-je?

Ostergaard, B. (ed.) (1997) *The Media in Western Europe*. London: Sage.

Rhodes, R.A.W. (1996) 'The new governance: governing without government', *Political Studies*, 44 (4): 652–67.

Sorbets, C. (1985) *Thomson et la politique de nouveaux médias: rapport préliminaire*. Bordeaux: CNRS-DGRST.

Sorbets, C. (1988) *Traitements – Rapport de synthese: programme urbanisme et technologie de l'habitat*. Paris: Plan Urbain.

Sorbets, C. (1994) *Valeurs des termes: rapport pouvoirs et territoires*. Recherche collective: IEP de Bordeaux.

Taylor, C. (1987) *Grandeur et misere de la modernité*. Quebec: Bellarmin.

13

Media Concentration: Options for Policy

Josef Trappel and Werner A. Meier

Media concentration and its irritations

The history of European media policy can to a certain degree be regarded as a continued debate about the effects, results and consequences of media concentration. Besides having affected the print media in regular cycles, concentration has also affected broadcasting because private television competes with public service broadcasting and the latest development touches upon the convergence between broadcasting, telecommunications and computer-related information within a 'global information order'. American and Japanese consortia have provided the world press with spectacular headlines following giant mergers between the hardware manufacturers, telecommunication operators and content providers such as film production companies. Sony/Columbia Tristar, CBS/Westinghouse, ABC/Disney just top the list of giant mergers.

In Europe, the market introduction of digital television has stimulated the desire of large companies to combine. In Spain, a public debate questioned the move of Spanish Telecommunication to join a digital television consortium in 1997. Germany went through this debate in 1994 and 1998 when Deutsche Telekom, Bertelsmann and Leo Kirch arranged to cooperate over digital television. The European Commission, however, twice declared the cooperation incompatible with the internal market (1994 MSG decision; 1998 DF1/Premiere decision). The deal would not only have included the second largest media company worldwide but it would have tied in the production with the physical distribution of television programmes by cable and satellite. This was regarded as an unique concentration of the power to edit and distribute television programmes under one roof. In a similar case (Nordic Satellite Distribution) the Commission reaffirmed in 1995 its strict view on these vertical concentration processes. However, these top-level cooperations are joined by small- and medium-scale mergers, affecting in varying degrees all media at the local, regional, national and international level.

Media concentration and media power will inevitably proceed under the prevailing structural conditions. Whether media enterprises themselves, media professionals, professional organizations, trade unions, national governments or the European Commission can construct a case for action seems to be more than questionable. Is indifference, helplessness or resignation prevailing, considering the complexity and dynamics of the two phenomena, media concentration and media power? Or are some dominant actors encouraging this development on purpose?

When one analyses media concentration against the background of national and international restrictions and promotions, a range of *contradictions, difficulties* and *particularities* is actually encountered, as follows:

- *Extension from controllers and observers to political actors*   Political influence and importance accompanies the growth of media conglomerates which incorporate several different media. Media conglomerates tend themselves to become more distinct political actors; their power expands from observing and controlling the political elites to active participation in politics.
- *A reluctance to engage in transnational regulation*   In many European states dominant national media enterprises are restricted from further growth by national legislation. Consequently, transnational activities of media enterprises (mergers, joint ventures, cooperation agreements) constantly increase, while transnational media regulation is no more than in a project stage.
- *A lack of legislative flexibility and adjustment*   National media merger regulations – if they exist at all – are based on the media's performance in the 1980s. Meanwhile, the media have changed their economic structure and continue with accelerated speed (for example, digitalization of the media). Transnational and national regulation attempts are not keeping pace with the media industry.
- *A reluctance to put media concentration on the political agenda*   Media concentration is at the same time a positive and a negative development for the political power elites. It is *positive* because political messages and public relations activities can be focused and targeted to only a few multiplying agents and it is easier to keep control of and have influence on a few than on a large variety of media. It is *negative* because the political influence of each media company increases when their overall number decreases. Making politics the object of surveillance of highly concentrated media puts the political actors at the mercy of these media. Because of these interrelations, the political system is not eager to put media concentration on the political agenda at all.
- *A reluctance to execute media concentration regulations*   Media politics in general and media concentration policy in particular are politically highly sensitive issues. The political system therefore acts cautiously in implementing policy initiatives, even when they are institutionalized in

media law. It is most difficult to pass legislation in the media sector, but it is even more difficult to execute its provisions.

Media concentration and its regulation at the national level

Such odds and evens with regard to political action on media concentration have dominated the debate for decades. '[T]here is certainly no agreement as to what steps, if any, should be taken by the government to deal with the situation. While many persons believe that strong government action is necessary, many others fear that this would do more harm than good' (Eaman, 1987: 98). Since Eaman's statement no major progress has been made at the national and European level. There is still an important controversy going on at the political level, and the various political initiatives within the European states have not succeeded in stopping media concentration. However, some states categorically reject the idea of limiting media companies in their growth, while other states implement strict competition rules, different from the general competition legislation applicable for other sectors of the economy. Different lines of action and restriction have therefore been enacted in various states.

Against this background of conflicting interests and few generally agreed principles, *states* have developed certain instruments for intervention in order to enhance competition, diversity and pluralism. Government actions against media concentration processes are implemented at different levels as follows: (a) limits to horizontal concentration; (b) limits to vertical concentration; (c) favouring effective competition; (d) restricting media ownership; (e) favouring internal pluralism; (f) favouring content-related diversity; and (g) enabling transparency in respect of media concentration.

Limits to horizontal concentration

In order to prevent an enterprise within the same media area – in particular with regard to the press, radio and television – controlling several channels, the majority of European countries have limited licensing, ownership or financial participation. In Germany, one television broadcaster may control any number of television channels up to a combined maximum of 30 per cent of the audience market share. In Spain, the participation is limited to one single channel per person or enterprise. Restrictions within the print media, however, are rare. In France, a take-over of a daily paper is not permitted if thereby the publishing house or group would gain control over more than 30 per cent of the circulation of all newspapers in France. In the United Kingdom, the transfer of ownership of a newspaper to a person already controlling newspapers with a circulation of more than 500,000 requires the prior consent of the Secretary of State for Trade and Industry

(Humphreys, 1996: 94). Italy adopted in 1981 anti-trust legislation specific to the press restricting any company from controlling more than 20 per cent of the national market (Sánchez-Tabernero, 1993: 216).

Limits to vertical concentration and cross-ownership

Regulations designed to prevent monopolies in more than one media area are widespread all over Europe. These 'cross-ownerships' are of importance particularly under aspects of competition because cross-marketing provides a substantial competitive advantage. Some European states released limits to this type of integration. The owner of a print medium in one of the German *Länder* having a dominant position in its market, may not, according to *Länder* legislation, exercise dominant power over a broadcasting programme in the same area. The relevant *Länder* regulations differ to some extent. In Hamburg and Bremen publishers have access to radio and television only within the framework of joint ventures, holding less than 25 per cent of the shares. In Baden-Württemberg there are no access limits, but internal pluralism is requested for those companies which are controlled by dominant print media.

In the Netherlands, publishers are refused broadcast licences if the enterprise already controls 25 per cent of the daily press market. The Austrian Regional Radio Act of 1993 and the Cable and Satellite Act of 1997 limit the participation of press owners to a maximum of 26 per cent of the shares in a radio station and a cable/satellite broadcaster. Persons or companies holding more than 25 per cent of shares in the newspaper in question are taken into consideration (Kogler and Traimer 1997: 105). Likewise, in the United Kingdom, newspapers with more than 20 per cent of national circulation are prevented from having more than a 20 per cent interest in national and regional television services (Broadcasting Act 1996). The same rule applies to local newspapers with regard to Channel 3 (ITV) services. Any newspaper applying for radio and television licences are furthermore subject to a *public interest test*, which is applied by the ITC (Independent Television Commission) and the Radio Authority. If the bodies conclude that the suggested control of newspapers in radio or television services is against the public interest the required licences are not granted. Among the criteria of the test are the promotion of plurality of ownership and the promotion of diversity in the sources of information.

In Belgium, legal regulations tend rather to support than to limit the concentration process and to institutionalize monopolistic structures. In the Flanders region, a consortium of newspaper publishers was originally granted the exclusive licence for private television, providing them with a monopoly for almost the entire advertising market. Radio advertising is limited to one station for the whole of the Flanders region. Similarly, Denmark has favoured cross-ownership: regional and national daily papers are exempted from the general provision that excludes 'relevant influencing control' of profit-oriented organizations from local radio or television. In turn, these service providers are obliged to offer 'open discussion fora' and to waive programme networking.

Favouring effective competition

Horizontal, vertical and diagonal concentration processes are usually followed by the allocation of existing resources within the control of only a few enterprises, potentially advancing to dominant positions in the different media markets to the detriment of open competition. Restrictive trade practice legislation, together with merger control regulations, are designed to prevent concentration processes limiting competition. Germany introduced its merger control law in 1976, considering such a control as necessary: 'In the press sector, which depends in particular on the variety within the regional and local area and which is composed predominantly by medium-sized and small enterprises, a merger control legislation affecting only large enterprises is not sufficient' (justification of the government on 11 December 1974 in the *Bundestag*). The law had been adopted to prevent further concentration between publishers and the development of dominant positions by a single enterprise. Despite specific provisions for the press, the same objectives as in the general merger control law apply: 'The purpose of the merger control is to prevent any concentration of enterprise from influencing the conditions of competition to such an extent that the chance for recovering from a low level competition becomes even worse' (Thiel, 1992: 128).

Whether pluralism or the diversity of opinions is affected is not the subject of discussion at all. The debate is centred around two questions: first, what do the relevant markets look like and is the result from the planned fusion a dominant position on the market? And, secondly, is an existing dominant position on the market further strengthened? The identification of the relevant advertising and readership markets proves to be the key problem. This field lacks generally accepted definitions; each individual case requires its own operational definitions.

In 1993 Austria introduced specific provisions on media mergers. In general, mergers can be prohibited if they lead to the emergence or reinforcement of a dominant position on the market. Media mergers can also be prohibited when it is expected that, as a result of the merger, media diversity would be impaired (Wessely, 1994: 88). Media mergers are compulsorily notifiable when the combined turnover exceeds some 1 million ecu. In assessing the merger's effects, only generally relevant factors of competition such as market share, financial power, market access barriers, but not media or sociocultural considerations, are taken into account. The main weakness of the media merger regulation lies in the fact that at the time of entering into force the most important mergers had already been implemented and no *ex post* measures are foreseen (Wessely, 1997: 36).

Restricting media ownership

There are different models of media ownership restriction. First, limits are set as to the capital controlled by one person or enterprise. In several countries, the maximum financial participation of a single shareholder within a broadcaster is determined by law. Thus the influence of the majority shareholder is reduced and a variety of shareholders is demanded, hoping that thereby diversity and pluralism can be promoted within the programme. In France any legal person cannot own directly or indirectly more than 49 per cent of the capital or voting rights of a company holding a national television service. More restrictive is the Norwegian rule on the ownership of the private channel TV2. The participation is limited to one-third of the capital per shareholder. In Spain, Law 10/1988 provides that no natural or legal person can own more than 25 per cent of the capital of a national radio or television programme. A similar 25 per cent rule for television services was implemented in 1990 in Portugal.

Secondly, specific restrictions apply to individuals or groups. In Denmark, companies from outside the media sector, with the exception of publishers, may not exert 'dominant influence' on local radio and television stations. Additionally, the majority of the board members of a broadcaster must be resident in the area of distribution. In Austria, political parties, state agents like universities and the public service broadcaster are excluded from applying for local radio licences and from cable and satellite television services.

Thirdly, restrictions apply to the involvement of foreign capital. In order not to lose control of their own media system, several countries restrict investment by foreign capital, originated from non-EU member states. In Switzerland, applicants for radio and television licences must either be of Swiss nationality or, in the case of a company, must have a registered office in Switzerland. In France, there is a 20 per cent shares and capital restriction on foreign companies owning publications in French language or radio and television services. Any applicants for broadcasting licences in the United Kingdom have to be resident nationals of a European Economic Area member state.

Favouring internal pluralism

This form of national intervention may have the longest tradition in the history of mass media. Most European states have introduced radio and television as a public service (with the exception of Luxembourg). The statute of public service broadcasting normally includes provisions enabling different points of views to be presented and reported. The Austrian broadcasting law (Article 2) stipulates that the ORF has to inform the public about all relevant political, economic, cultural and sporting events in an objective manner. Furthermore, the broadcasting law ensures the principles of objectivity and diversity and guarantees the independence of all persons working for the ORF. The legal provisions are backed up by the strong position of employees in the ORF and their representation.

In the United Kingdom, the government published its White Paper on the future of the British Broadcasting Corporation (BBC) in 1994. It proposed that the BBC should broadcast a wide range of programmes for people with different tastes and interests and ages. All programmes should aim to be of a high general standard and much emphasis is placed on the need to reflect the interests and cultural traditions of the UK. In particular, the BBC's output should reflect the needs and interests of all of the population, including those of ethnic and other minorities.

At the Fourth European Ministerial Conference of the Council of Europe dedicated to 'the Media in a Democratic Society' (Prague 1994), the participating states stressed the importance of internal pluralism for public service broadcasting by stipulating that 'the independence of public service broadcasters must be guaranteed by appropriate structures such as pluralistic internal boards or other independent bodies' (Council of Europe, 1995: 36). Furthermore, the ministers called upon governments to develop procedures providing for regularly published information on the activities of public service broadcasters and allowing viewers and listeners to comment on them.

These classic 'public service principles' are in some European states also applied to the private sector, if private media have to perform public tasks or if horizontal media concentration has left only monopolistic media. The German State Broadcasting Treaty of 1996 (*Dritter Rundfunkstaatsvertrag*) can be read in this tradition. The broadcasting market was already highly concentrated when the Treaty came into force on 1 January 1997. It therefore stipulates that any television broadcaster with a national audience market share of more than 10 per cent has to allocate a minimum of 260 minutes of weekly airtime to an independent third party. This measure is intended to 'safeguard pluralism in television' (the heading of the chapter in the Treaty).

Favouring content-related diversity

In order to counterbalance the absence of competition in countries where television is still in a monopolistic position, programme diversity is traditionally legally required. The exclusive objective for private regional or local television programmes in the Flanders region is the distribution of programmes with a sociocultural and educational character. Their legal obligations comprise the promotion of information, culture, education and the maintenance of close links with the local population within their area of distribution, as well as the contribution to the overall social and cultural development of the region.

In Denmark, the national broadcaster TV2, which includes eight regional companies, is obliged to commission the major part of its programme –

with the exception of news, current affairs programmes and sports – with independent production firms. Beside the restrictions on ownership for example in the German *Länder* Hamburg, Bremen and North-Rhine-Westphalia, internal pluralism at the programme level is also required, in particular balanced and broad coverage of different points of views. In Switzerland, the authority granting broadcasting licences can require a representative composition of the board and the implementation of an advisory programme commission.

Enabling transparency of media concentration

In the majority of European countries, information from media enterprises on business activities are used as a basis for state intervention and measures. In Denmark, according to a competition law from 1989, all agreements and decisions are to be announced 'potentially or effectively constituting dominant influences on a certain market'.

In Switzerland, applicants for radio and television licences must prove their sound financial background and their conviction not to endanger the variety of choice and opinion before approval by the authority. In addition, applicants have to commit themselves to communicate prior to its effectuation any changes in ownership structure (starting from 5 per cent of the share capital) or any transfer of the licence to third parties. The applicant is finally requested to inform the authorities on their request about the balance of programming, sponsoring, profits and so on. Refusal of the duty to supply information or making false statements is subject to fines.

Transnational regulation of media concentration

Any quick look at media development in the late 1980s and the first half of the 1990s confirms the fact that product innovation and entrepreneurial initiative were overwhelmingly carried out across national borders. Not only was satellite broadcasting in Europe from its beginning a transfrontier business, but also innovation in programme scheduling and print media formats have been frequently imitated or even copied by media in other countries. Even content has shown a tendency towards increasing uniformity, in print media by similar agenda-setting and in electronic media by economic constraints following the deregulation of broadcasting and as a result of the multiplication of available channels and their demand for programmes.

Despite the rather long period of constantly increasing internationalization at the media company level, this trend has not found its counterpart in the regulatory framework. Evidently the major actors in the field have so far successfully hampered any restricting regulation at the transnational level. The assumption that market forces alone determine transnational media concentration, without interference by public policy, is supported by examining the way in which the European Commission regulates the transnational flow of media. There can be no doubt about the awareness of the Commission of the potential effects of pan-European media concentration. The Commission has on several occasions not only received critical observations, but has at some point even integrated into the secondary Community legislation low-profile elements of concern as regards media concentration.

The most significant attempt was launched in December 1992 when the Commission adopted a Communication to the Council and the European Parliament on 'Pluralism and media concentration in the internal market – an assessment of the need for Community action'. This Green Paper makes reference to the need to complete the internal market also in the area of mass media and consequently a possible need for action in order to fulfil the requirements laid down by the Single European Act, in particular in Article 7a of the Treaty establishing the European Community. This Article contains the obligation to establish progressively the internal market over a period expiring on 31 December 1992 by defining the internal market as 'an area without internal frontiers in which the free movement of goods, persons, services and capital is ensured in accordance with the provisions of this treaty'. The Commission's obligation to establish the internal market also in the media sector by the end of 1992 was not met by the Green Paper on pluralism and it has not been met for the subsequent years. In the Green Paper on pluralism the Commission proposed three options and asked all interested parties to comment on them. These options were:

1   taking no action;
2   proposing a recommendation to enhance transparency;
3   proposing the harmonization of national restrictions on media ownership by (a) a Council directive, (b) a Council regulation, or (c) a directive or a regulation together with an independent committee. (Commission of the European Community, 1992: 9, 112ff.)

Consequently and unsurprisingly, the consultation process yielded controversial and voluminous results and a second Communication from the Commission was adopted by October 1994, summing up the reactions in professional circles (Commission of the European Community, 1994b). This document adds another perspective to the problem of media concentration. Not only do the traditional media have to be examined against the background of potentially harmful effects on pluralism, but also the development of the European section of the global information highway has to be incorporated into the considerations. This aspect might be one of the single most important elements for the slow and hesitating approach of the Commission.

In fact, this link is discussed in length in the 1994 Green Paper. Between the publication of the 1992 and 1994 Green Papers, the European Council decided in Brussels, in December 1993, on the implementation of an action plan with respect to information infrastructures and new applications, which was adopted by the Commission in July 1994 on the basis of the so-called 'Bangemann Report' on the information society, entitled 'Europe and the global information society – Recommendations to the European Council, Brussels, 26 May 1994' (Commission of the European Community, 1994a). These two documents have evidently directly affected the conclusions drawn from comments on the first Green Paper received by the Commission.

In discussing the different options, the following statement highlights the importance attached to the concept of the information society:

> In this respect it is clear that the current situation as regards media ownership could have a negative effect on the launching of projects relating to the information society. . . . The greater the prospects for the profitable operation of bundles of varied services with a high added value (education, culture, distance selling, health, games, entertainment, practical guides, etc.), the easier it will be to recoup investment in infrastructure. Sound and audiovisual media and multimedia services will have an essential role to play in the short term. (Commission of the European Community, 1994a: 33)

Following this argument, it is not very likely that any kind of stricter rules on media ownership and media concentration would result in *positive effects* for the information society. Indeed, media concentration would even have to be promoted in order to achieve the necessary scope and scale for successful operations.

However, the Commission has pointed out already in the 1992 Green Paper that media pluralism *per se* is no objective of the Community and measures for its safeguard do not fall within the competence of the Community according to the Treaty establishing the European Union. 'The sole objective of safeguarding the pluralism of the media, as such, is neither a Community objective nor a matter coming within Community jurisdiction as laid down in the Treaty of Rome or the Treaty on European Union' (Commission of the European Community, 1992: 59). In the Green Paper much more attention is devoted to the question of whether certain national regulations aimed at the maintenance of diversity and pluralism might potentially harm the single market objective of free circulation of services and the right of establishment. This limited conceptual view of the rather complex problem of effects of media concentration in a democratic society has been criticized in professional circles. In its comments addressed to the Commission on the Green Paper, the European Broadcasting Union (EBU) puts it as follows:

> The concept of pluralism laid down in the Green Paper seems to lead to the following question: which measures to safeguard pluralism can be justified despite the fact that they limit the commercial freedom of media owners? Instead, the real question should be: which measures to safeguard pluralism must be taken to achieve freedom of expression and to protect the democratic process of opinion forming? (European Broadcasting Union, 1993)

This comment by the EBU clearly points to the fact that there are important dimensions linked to media concentration other than just the internal market, reflected upon in the Green Paper.

Up to mid-1998 business alliances had succeeded in their resistance to Community action against media concentration. A new proposal elaborated by the responsible Directorate-General XV had already been rejected and postponed at the level of the Commission in March 1997 and did not even enter into the long and cumbersome process of decision-making. This delay (no proposal under formal consultation for more than six years) has led observers to harsh criticism.

> The Community has so far not acted positively despite long-standing and multiple calls. An approach fraught with inconsistencies, featuring an endless stop-go-stop modus operandi was displayed by the Commission. . . . So far, the Commission has (1) caused a deterioration of pluralism as defined by public interest representatives, (2) disadvantaged small and medium-sized enterprises and cultural/linguistic areas, (3) allowed concentration and anti-competitive trends by granting strategically precious time to already dominant players, resulting in irreversible market distortions. . . . (Kaitatzi-Whitlock, 1996: 477)

But the problem of media concentration and its potentially harmful effects on the media system in the member states has also been addressed in several other policy areas of the Community. First, the Council regulation no. 4064/89 on the control of concentrations between undertakings of 21 December 1989 dedicates a specific importance to media mergers. In Article 21 of this regulation the plurality of the media figures among those legitimate interests which justify appropriate measures at the level of the member states, thus going against the general principle that the Commission has the sole competence of taking decisions in the area provided for by the regulation.

Secondly, competition policy in relation to the merger control regulation 1989 is of increasing importance to Community media policy. According to this regulation, all intended mergers above a quantitative threshold of combined turnover and with a Community dimension have to be notified to the Commission, as far as the merger would create a dominant market position. The responsible Commissioner Karel Van Miert expressed his concern that more and larger cases were submitted to the Commission in the early 1990s and that the likelihood of the Commission taking a more restrictive view is increasing (Reuters, 13 September 1995). According to Van Miert, this is particularly the case for the media sector. Of the four mergers the Commission has blocked between 1990 and March 1996, three have been media joint ventures (Van Miert at the EBU Conference on the Information Society for All, Brussels, 7 March 1996).

Thirdly, the Council directive on transfrontier television also makes reference to the protection of pluralism of the media. Article 19 of the directive 89/552/EEC allowed for the adoption of stricter (advertising) rules for broadcasters under the jurisdiction of a specific member state in accordance with the public interest, *taking account in particular of the protection of pluralism of information and of the media.* This view is generally maintained in the revised directive 97/36/EC of 19 June 1997 but the new directive refers to pluralism only in the recitals (nos 16 and 44). The suggested wording of a new Article 3, explicitly mentioning the *need to safeguard pluralism in the information industry and the media* had not been maintained in the final text (Commission of the European Community, 1995b).

Fourthly, vertical concentration is a major concern for the European support programmes in the audiovisual sector. By the end of 1995 the MEDIA programme expired and was replaced by a restructured programme, aiming at the encouragement of a European programme industry, capable of satisfying the information society's cultural and economic requirements. In its Communication the European Commission identifies shortcomings of the industry as regards fragmentation of markets, insufficient size of companies, low rate of cross-border programme distribution, the spiral of chronic deficits and the inability of the sector to attract financial resources (Commission of the European Community, 1995a). On 10 July and 22 December 1995 the Council of Ministers adopted the three elements of MEDIA II (development, distribution and training; published in the *Official Journal of the European Communities*, 30 December 1995, no. L321/25-38).

In its decisions, the Council stressed the need for improvement in the circulation prospects of cinematographic works and emphasized the encouragement of cooperation between distributors, cinema owners and producers of audiovisual works. By the same token, cooperation between broadcasters and producers should be encouraged and support should be given to concerted action to promote common programming measures at the European level. Media concentration, evidently, is considered an appropriate means for overcoming the misery of an enormous media trade deficit with the USA (3.6 billion US dollars according to the Commission of the European Community, 1995a: 5) and lost audiences for European films.

This rather diverse picture of Community policy (leaving aside pertinent decisions by the Court of Justice) illustrates the lack of internal coherence. Also at the level of the Council of Europe no clear indication has been made so far on how to proceed with media concentration which is limiting freedom of expression. As more and more member states of the Council of Europe join, in one way or the other, the European Union (full membership, Party to the European Economic Area, Association Agreements), measures are taken only in close cooperation with the Union in politically sensitive areas like media concentration.

The only international body with a clear position appears to be the European Parliament, demanding on several occasions the adoption of legislation to limit media concentration on a European scale. In its resolution on the Commission Green Paper 1992, the Parliament declares its concern 'that the control of a large audience share within a particular area by one individual or company poses a danger to pluralism, cultural diversity and the quality of the media, by lessening media autonomy and independence'. The Parliament calls on the Commission to submit the proposal for a directive harmonizing national restrictions on media concentration and enabling the Commission to intervene in the event of concentration endangering pluralism (Parliament of the European Union, 1994: 177).

Time works for increasing concentration. Many international media mergers in the 1990s might have been enacted in order to avoid restrictions at a later stage by rigid legislation. Ironically, the current legal situation in Europe favours transnational media conglomerates, while small and medium enterprises are bound by sometimes very strict national legislation. So far the European Union has not presented a concept to balance this competition disadvantage.

New deal in media concentrations: the audience limit model

Limitations on media concentration and their long and controversial history show no record of success. At the transnational level all attempts to impose binding rules have so far failed; at the national level the anti-trust legislation has largely proved inadequate to regulate the media sector. As shown above, most national rules aim at the owner of television and radio stations and at the publisher of newspapers and limit their operations beyond a certain threshold. The licensing of private operators in the radio and television sector has multiplied the number of media companies and media conglomerates. In parallel with the rising number, media conglomerates entered into highly sophisticated company networks, leaving regulators behind in severe difficulties investigating their ownership structure.

Increasing competition and non-transparent transnational ownership structures have indicated a need to re-establish the basic concept of anti-trust rules for the media. The higher number of actors on the media markets and the reasoning behind anti-trust legislation suggests a new approach. More emphasis on content diversity and less media power allocated to each media conglomerate are objectives shared widely among legislators in Europe. The new approach follows the example of other trade and industry anti-trust regulations by defining the position of economic actors within the relevant consumer markets. Ownership should no longer function as a point of departure but the market penetration of the media.

This model has been suggested by the European Commission during the painful process of elaborating a European strategy for media concentration. At the national level, the United Kingdom was the first to introduce audience limits in the 1996 broadcasting act. Germany followed suit with the *Rundfunkstaatsvertrag* 1996 which establishes as the main criterion for safeguarding pluralism in private television an anti-trust model based on audience markets. In both cases, legal consequences are triggered when media companies reach a defined share of the market.

In the case of the United Kingdom, numerical limits on the holdings of television licences have been abolished, but holdings are restricted to 15 per cent of the total national television audience. Public service television is exempted from this rule but their audience share is taken into account when calculating the audience shares of others. In the case of Germany, the brakes are put on a television broadcaster when it controls 30 per cent of the national audience. In that case the law supposes a dominant position for that television broadcaster.

There are, however, a number of problems associated with the audience limit model for media concentration:

- Where is the audience share limit? While for the United Kingdom 15 per cent of the audience establishes a dominant position, diversity and pluralism are jeopardized in Germany only at the level of a 30 per cent market share. In both cases there is no explanation or legitimization for the supposed level.
- The audience limit model does not solve the problem of ownership transparency. In order to allocate market shares to the different media holdings, a sophisticated model has to be established for calculating the influence shareholders might have on the media under scrutiny. The German example illustrates the problem: shareholding is taken into account only above a minimum participation of 25 per cent in a given television channel. The Springer holding, one of the largest publishers and an influential partner in a number of television joint ventures, would be completely neglected because it holds just 24.9 per cent in the German sports channel and 20 per cent in SAT1 (Röper, 1996: 612).
- Limits to the growth of holdings are strong legal tools. The justification for such measures needs to be equally strong and convincing. The market limit model refers to audience research data as a starting point for legal action. Audience research is a rather weak instrument developed to satisfy the needs of advertisers rather than the demands of courts. Manipulation of audience research data is difficult to prevent.
- There is an intrinsic contradiction within the market share model in competing markets. Growth is one of the paradigms of the market economy. The audience share model does not approve growth but sets limits to it. Organic growth and economic success might drive companies beyond the audience limits. The audience limit model pushes successful companies towards extending their influence beyond their nucleus of activities, thus enhancing concentration rather than competition.

In general, the audience limit model creates new problems and does not solve the traditional ones. Ownership transparency has to be established as a prerequisite of any legal action and arbitrary limits reflect rather consolidated market realities than political considerations on how to re-establish plurality and content diversity.

Conclusion

National media policy has so far addressed vertical concentration and incompatibilities between different media actors in the same local, regional and national market. There are no coherent concepts as regards horizontal, multimedia and diagonal concentration as yet. At the European level, media concentration at the entrepreneurial level increases while regulatory attempts have failed so far, with the notable exception of competition law which became in the 1990s the only effective transnational regulation by taking the initiative.

But competition law does not necessarily correspond directly with quality and content diversity. Policy instruments safeguarding these notions are absent or inefficient. While joint horizontal, vertical, diagonal and multi-media operations foster the profitability of media enterprises, the public interest tends to disappear entirely from their priority agenda. Although most negative effects of media concentration on the public interest have not successfully been caged by legislation for analog media, rapid technology innovation demands new political and legal capacity to respond to the digital challenge.

Bibliography

Commission of the European Community (1992) 'Pluralism and media concentration in the internal market – an assessment of the need for Community action', Commission Green Paper, COM(92)480 final. Brussels, 23 December.

Commission of the European Community (1994a) 'Europe's way to the information society – an action plan', Document COM(94)347 final. Brussels, 19 July.

Commission of the European Community (1994b) 'Follow-up to the consultation process relating to the Green Paper on "Pluralism and media concentration in the internal market – an assessment of the need for Community action"', Communication from the Commission to the Council and the European Parliament, Document COM(94)353 final. Brussels, 5 October.

Commission of the European Community (1995a) 'Audiovisual policy: stimulating dynamic growth in the European programme industry (MEDIA II – 1996–2000)', Document COM(94)523 final. Brussels, 8 February.

Commission of the European Community (1995b) 'Report on application of Directive 89/552/EEC and Proposal for a European Parliament and Council Directive amending Council Directive 89/552/EEC on the coordination of certain provisions laid down by law, regulation or administrative action in Member States concerning the pursuit of television broadcasting activities', Document COM(95)86 final. Brussels, 31 May.

Council of Europe (1995) 'European Ministerial Conferences on mass media policy: texts adopted', Strasbourg: Council of Europe.

Eaman, Ross A. (1987) *The Media Society: Basic Issues and Controversies*. Toronto and Vancouver: Butterworths.

Entman, R.M. (1985) 'Newspaper competition and First Amendment ideals: does monopoly matter?' *Journal of Communication*, 35 (3): 147–65.

European Broadcasting Union (1993) 'Pluralism and media concentration in the internal market', EBU comments on Commission Green Paper, 23 April.

Henle, Victor (1997) 'Fingerzeige aus London: das neue britische Rundfunkgesetz', epd medien. 14: 4–8.

Humphreys, Peter J. (1996) *Mass Media and Media Policy in Western Europe*. Manchester and New York: Manchester University Press.

Kaitatzi-Whitlock, Sophia (1996) 'Pluralism and media concentration in Europe: media policy as industrial policy', *European Journal of Communication*, 11 (4): 453–83.

Kogler, Michael and Traimer, Matthias (1997) *Privatrundfunkgesetze: Regionalradiogesetz, Kabel- und Satelliten-Rundfunkgesetz. Kurzkommentar*. Vienna: Medien & Recht.

Negroponte, Nicholas (1995) *Being Digital: The Road Map for Survival on the Information Superhighway*. London: Hodder & Stoughton.

Parliament of the European Union (1994) 'Resolution A3-0435/93 on the Commission Green Paper "Pluralism and media concentration in the internal market"', *Official Journal of the European Communities*, C44/177ff, 14 February.

Röper, Horst (1996) 'Mehr Spielraum für Konzentration und Cross Ownership im Mediensektor. Analyse der Vielfaltsicherung des neuen Rundfunkstaatsvertrages mit Beispielrechnungen', *Media Perspektiven*, 12: 610–20.

Sánchez-Tabernero, Alfonso (1993) *Media Concentration in Europe: Commercial Enterprise and the Public Interest*. Dusseldorf: European Institute for the Media.

Thiel, Michael (1992) *Presseunternehmen in der Fusionskontrolle*. Munich: Verlag v. Florentz.

Wessely, Karin (1994) 'Die Entstehung oder Verstärkung einer marktbeherrschenden Stellung durch einen Medienzusammenschluss', *Medien und Recht*, 3: 88–95.

Wessely, Karin (1997) 'Medienkonzentrationskontrolle in Österreich. Rechtliche Bestimmungen gegen Medienkonzentration', *Medien Journal*, 2: 26–37.

14

European Policy Initiatives

Mario Hirsch and Vibeke G. Petersen

Regulation of the media at the European level took off in 1989 with the adoption of the EU directive 'Television without Frontiers' and the Council of Europe Convention on transborder television. After nearly a decade of increasing activity in this field it can safely be said that the originators of the prolonged discussions hit upon the salient issues.

Prominent among them was the quota of European content; that is, the requirement that over half of all programmes (not counting news and sports) shown on European TV must be European works, which is designed to boost the European film and television industry in the battle with the all-powerful US industry. It is fuelled by the fear of American dominance on European screens – at the cost of European cultural identity. This was particularly evident in the negotiations over the General Agreement on Trade in Services during the Uruguay Round (finalized in 1993), and it was the most contentious point in the efforts to revise the television directive.

New items have been added to the 1989 agenda. Media concentration has been investigated and analysed since the end of 1992 as preparation for an EU directive, and competition legislation has been put to the test in the media field. The planning of the information society of the future has given rise to numerous Community-level initiatives, many of which touch upon the traditional media. It is evident that technological development and the increase in international competition for software, for the viewers' money and time, and for new sources of income are an international rather than a national challenge. It is, however, also evident that media policy is fitted into the international regulatory schemes only with difficulty.

Of the mixture of economic, industrial and cultural elements that makes up media policy, the cultural aspects are most closely tied to traditional national values, not least to language, and therefore to a high degree perceived as within the domain of national politics. To this should be added the issue of freedom of speech and information, requiring legislators to respect the editorial independence of the media. European regulation in the media field, on the other hand, is mainly based on economic and industrial policies, set up to create the single market.

Implementation of the television directive

When the EU directive 'Television without Frontiers' was adopted in 1989, member states were given two years to implement it in their national legislation and a further two years to report on the extent to which the TV stations under their jurisdiction had fulfilled the quota requirements on European content. Not surprisingly, the report issued by the Commission in 1994 on the first years in the life of the directive showed that the established national broadcasters – among them the public service broadcasters – lived up to the goals, whereas many new commercial TV stations – among them especially satellite broadcasters – did not. In all, about two-thirds of the total of 105 stations complied with the requirements. The next report, published in 1996, shows that 91 out of 148 stations in Europe (including Norway) broadcast a minimum of 51 per cent European productions and 119 stations complied with the requirement of broadcasting a minimum of 10 per cent European works by independent producers.

It was clear from the outset that the quota issue had not been settled once and for all in 1989. The formulation that the quota was to be met 'where practicable' was a compromise, making it possible for quota supporters as well as opponents to accept the directive. The subsequent reports on the attained levels of European works have been used by both sides in arguments over whether to strengthen the quota by removing the 'where practicable' or abolish it altogether.

GATS: Europe v. USA

The ideological battle over whether or not quotas were the proper instrument for furthering the European audiovisual industry became a global issue during the final weeks of the GATT negotiations on trade in services (GATS) in 1993. The audiovisual sector (film and TV) was included in the GATS: this was agreed on very early on in the Uruguay Round, but because of the sensitive nature of cultural issues serious negotiations did not start until a few weeks before the deadline of 15 December.

The USA and the EC confronted each other in a media war with leading actors from the American and the French film industries in the main roles. The arguments put forward by the two sides were clear and simple. Europeans should be given the freedom to choose for themselves what they wanted to watch in the cinema and on the TV screen (it being understood that they would continue to choose American products over any other foreign films) versus the argument that Europeans have a right and a duty to protect their culture from American cultural imperialism.

The Commission, in charge of the negotiations on behalf of the member states, played the difficult role of arbitrator in the internal EC disagreement over the issue. Inspired by the exclusion of culture in the recent North

American trade agreement (NAFTA) between the USA and Canada, the French sought a similar exclusion. The Commission, backed by a majority of member states (many of whom were against quotas in the broadcasting sector), opted for the more pragmatic method whereby appropriate clauses in the agreement provided the desired protection of discriminatory cultural regulation. And after a last-minute showdown between the USA and the EC, the matter was resolved. Both sides won: the audiovisual sector remained included in the GATS, but was accompanied by exemptions so as to keep it outside the agreement for all practical purposes.

Revising 'Television without Frontiers'

Encouraged by the results of the GATS, the European audiovisual industry, led by the French and with backing from the Commission, renewed the effort to win over the quota-sceptics in the upcoming discussions on a revision of the television directive. This revision was, as stipulated in the directive itself, due to take place five years after its implementation. As preparation for the negotiations, the Commission issued a Green Paper on the state of the audiovisual sector, 'Strategy options to strengthen the European programme industry in the context of the audiovisual policy of the European Union'. It also invited the industry to submit its proposals for the policy changes necessary to strengthen its position in global competition. Not surprisingly, the proposals gave enthusiastic support to strong and binding quotas.

The Green Paper, the proposals from the industry and the results of continuing talks among member states and the Commission on the need for a revised directive all served as background for the Commission's proposal for revision, submitted to the Council and the European Parliament at the end of May 1995. In spite of the overwhelming and often repeated rejection of more restrictive quota rules by a large majority of the Council, the Commission's proposal included new measures to secure observance of the quota regulations, including the removal of 'where practicable'. Part of the reasoning behind the proposal is that different national quota regulations in member states constitute a barrier to free trade.

As could be expected, this did not find favour with the anti-quota majority in the Council. The ministers for culture and audiovisual affairs put it plainly to the Commission at the Council meeting in November 1995, when they reached a political agreement to leave the existing quota clause untouched in the revised directive. According to the rules of procedure in the EU, the Council cannot agree on a formal common position until the Parliament has given its opinion on the document. This opinion was still not on the table. The Council unanimity was greeted with displeasure by a Parliament which saw the increased power given it in the Maastricht Treaty challenged.

When the parliamentary opinion came a couple of months later, it gave full support to the Commission's proposals to change the quota rules. In addition, the European Parliament proposed a number of revisions of its own, among them stronger and more precise rules to protect minors against harmful TV programmes (pornography and gratuitous violence) and the inclusion of new services such as video-on-demand in the directive. In its formal common position on the revision of the directive, the Council rejected these proposals in July 1996. About half of all the parliamentary proposals were, however, accepted by the Council.

It should be noted that the Council and the Commission agree on a number of changes in the directive, among them the inclusion of rules for tele-shopping and the continued exclusion of telecommunications services such as video-on-demand. Most importantly, the fundamental principle of the directive, namely that a broadcasting company has to comply with the laws of the country where it is established and not with those of the country, or countries, where the programmes are received, is to be spelled out in greater detail so as to avoid cases of disputed jurisdiction. This principle is seen as a prerequisite for the free flow of television programmes throughout the Union. Only one derogation is permitted: a receiving country can temporarily stop broadcasts that it finds in breach of the clauses protecting minors. The derogation was included in the directive in recognition of the differences among member states in the perception of what constitutes harmful programmes, especially pornography.

During the discussions leading up to the revision of the directive it has become clear, however, that several member states accept this principle of jurisdiction more easily in theory than in practice. The fact that national legislation may be more restrictive than the directive in an area such as advertising has given rise to accusations of unfair competition and to anxiety over the difficulty for a country to uphold its own (strict) standards in the face of more liberal competition from across the border.

The revised television directive was adopted in June of 1997. As an interesting novelty, the European Parliament succesfully proposed to add a clause securing that big sports events, such as the Olympic Games, are shown on national free TV. The new clause enables national legislators to ban exclusive rights to broadcast such events on pay TV, and it is intended to counter the steep increase in the prices of sports rights in recent years.

This initiative can be seen as an expression of the European Parliament's support for public service broadcasting and its efforts to protect the viewers against what it perceives as the harmful effects of an increasing commercialization of the audiovisual media.

The role of the European Court of Justice

The variety in national regulations and in member states' interpretation of the rules of the directive has led to a number of cases at the European

Court of Justice. In one such case, brought by the Commission against the UK for failure to implement the directive's clauses on jurisdiction correctly, the Court upheld (in 1996) the principle of establishment as decisive for allocating jurisdiction over a broadcaster. In another ruling, Belgium was instructed to drop its practice of requiring cable networks to obtain an official authorization to retransmit foreign broadcasts.

Other court rulings are on the way, deciding for instance whether Sweden can prevent foreign broadcasters from carrying advertising directed towards children in Sweden (where such advertising is banned); whether the European Broadcasting Union, an association of public service broad- casters, is in breach of EU competition rules when it buys collective rights to sports events; whether the licence fee can be considered a form of state aid and therefore anti-competitive.

Media concentration

It is a slow process to make the European countries agree on the regulation of television. The difficulty is inherent in the threefold role of television: as the primary channel of information with a claim to editorial independence, as a conveyor of culture, and as big business. The same characteristics are shared by the written press, and it is to be expected that Commission plans for initiatives in this field meet with similar obstacles to efforts at harmonization.

The Commission took the first such step with the Green Paper 'Pluralism and media concentration in the internal market – an assessment of the need for Community action' in December 1992. The rationale for action was growing media concentration and the problems for the implementation of the single market posed by individual national regulations of this threat to media pluralism. The sufficiency of ordinary EU competition regulation to deal with the problems was questioned. The Green Paper posed the question: is there a need for Community action and, if yes, should this action aim at harmonization of national rules or merely at requiring trans- parency of media ownership? After a series of hearings among professionals and governments, the Commission came to the conclusion that the answer to the first question was indeed yes. The answer to the second question is (as of mid-1997) not yet available.

No explanation has been offered publicly for the lack of agreement in the Commission. But it can be assumed that the opposing views expressed by the industry are reflected in Brussels. Publishers have traditionally objected to public interference in their affairs, whether business or editorial ones. With the rise of global competition, media owners in Europe point to the disadvantage they experience because of their comparatively small size. Governments and (parts of) the public point to the potentially harmful effects on media pluralism of concentration of media ownership. Public service broadcasters point to their internal pluralism, in all countries required by law, thus making the case for their exclusion from any Community regulation in this field. They all point to their right to freedom of expression.

The information society

The growing convergence between telecommunications, computer and broadcasting technologies greatly complicates regulation in the European, as well as the national, context. Traditionally, these fields have been dealt with in very different regulatory schemes, with only broadcasting being subjected to content regulation. Common sense suggests that convergence of technologies must be followed up by convergence of regulation. In its Green Paper from 1994, 'Europe's way to the information society', the Commission states that, in the field of audiovisual services, the aim is to ensure the free movement of such services within the Union. This is a response to the opportunities for growth in this sector opened up by new technologies and taking account of the specific nature of audiovisual programmes, regardless of their mode of transmission.

The difficulty in carrying out this principle became apparent early on, however. The Commission did not propose the inclusion of new services, such as video-on-demand, in its draft revision of the directive 'Television without Frontiers' in spite of the fact that, among the new audiovisual services in the offing, none is more like traditional television programmes than video-on-demand. Instead, the Commission promised to publish a Green Paper on the development of new audiovisual services. According to press accounts, this solution was a compromise between different commissioners, some of whom look to the information society as the great boost to European industry, not to be hampered by over-regulation, others worry more about the cultural and social impact of new, unregulated services.

In its report on the application of the directive and proposal for a revision, the Commission itself put it this way:

> It was not felt to be advisable to extend the scope of the Directive to the new point-to-point services because of the specific nature of the problems they present. . . . The Commission is of the opinion that it is too early and too risky to try establishing now what the future Community regulations might look like, since there is inadequate information about the problems these services may generate and the proper Community response to them . . . . (EU Commission, 1995: 25)

The promised Green Paper was approved by the Commission in mid-October 1996. It has been caught up in the increasing public anxiety over the proliferation of pornographic material on the Internet. Industry ministers, telecommunications ministers, culture and audiovisual ministers and the different Commissioners responsible for these fields all discuss the problems of illegal Internet traffic. Together with the Green Paper, a communication on the same issue has been presented. This communication concludes that the answer to the challenge in the short term will be a combination of self-control of the service providers, new technical solutions such as rating systems and filtering software, better information for users and international cooperation. The Green Paper launches a consultation process on ways to protect minors from material on the Internet and new television services such as video-on-demand and is aimed at finding medium- to long-term solutions.

Green Papers and subsequent proposals for directives are issued at an increasing rate by the Brussels bureaucracy. The European Parliament is eager to augment its role in the decision-making process. This leaves national governments with a smaller and smaller turf of their own. In the fields of telecommunications, copyright and commercial communication, new and old broadcasting services initiatives are taken at the Community level, often interfering with specific national solutions that are built on traditions and political consensus.

It is a moot question, however, whether the development of media has overtaken the viability of national regulation. In some cases this is obviously so because of the global nature of the media. In others it is less clear. To what extent and in what ways the wide variety of European cultures, as expressed in the media, is affected by European harmonization efforts remains to be seen.

Regulation or subsidy

There are, obviously, other ways of approaching problems in the media field than by regulating the market from a competition point of view. It has all along been part of EU policy to advocate financial support for the audiovisual industry in areas where market forces are seen to be insufficient. The MEDIA I and II support programmes for initiatives in, for example, education, script development, independent productions and new technology have been established with the aim of making the fragmented European industry more competitive on the global market. The current MEDIA II programme has about 310 million ecu to spend for the period 1996–9.

For the work done by the Council of Europe in the media field, the point of departure is the human rights aspect as expressed in Article 10 of the Convention for the Protection of Human Rights and Fundamental Freedoms. Through its interpretations of this convention, the European Court of Human Rights has an increasing role in defining the boundaries of media regulation in Europe.

Convergence favours a commercial logic

Regulation of broadcasting and communication services in general has a strong and old tradition in Europe, owing to the public service and public interest philosophy. This well-entrenched approach has, however, led to a reappraisal of regulation as such with attempts at deregulation and the retreat of governments from all-encompassing regulation. Many, and especially the European Commission, have come to realize that over-regulation might collide with the need to encourage the emergence of globally competitive players in telecommunications, electronic media and communication markets.

This is most notable in the field of telecommunications where a complete deregulation and varying degrees of privatization of former monopolies have been achieved by the beginning of 1998. This has, of course, given an enormous push to commercial expansion and developments of all sorts that inevitably spills over to the broadcasting sector. It would seem that in the whole field the logic of commerce has taken over and governments are on the retreat, left with making regulatory concessions across the board. The 1989 EC directive 'Television without Frontiers', revised in 1997, reflects the new mood by aiming primarily at achieving a large, unified audiovisual market. But it retained at the same time some elements of the old approach, notably the quota provisions.

Despite this tribute to the old order, it is in essence an internal market measure to provide freedom of services for TV broadcasts and it rests somehow on the assumption that some kind of regulation is needed to help give birth to a strong private sector, be it only to dismantle barriers to free circulation of audiovisual services. Proponents of liberalization and deregulation are confident that once a market has been established and gained enough strength, it can be 'hands off' as far as regulation is concerned. Needless to say, this view is not shared by those who put the emphasis on content regulation.

Despite the many ambiguities in the European approach, for all practical purposes an environment ripe for a more business-like approach to what is called the cultural industries has emerged over the years. The name of the game is now channel multiplication and television abundance, fostered both by cable and satellite. It remains to be seen what digital television will bring, but a good bet would be that it is likely to reinforce these trends.

However, the tendency to argue 'let the market sort it out' has not really taken over for the obvious reason that in Europe the market does not yet exist. Europe is still faced with the problem of scattered and divided markets, characterized by contrasting cultural traditions, language barriers, different needs and value systems. In telecommunications, Europe is on the verge of establishing a genuine common market but in the media field this basically remains to be done.

New technology requires flexible rules

Convergence is, however, pushing in that direction. So do satellites which turned out to be the preferred means of delivery for audiovisual services on the continental scale. Unlike cable or digital terrestrial television, satellites have developed in an extra-regulatory way. They have been the primary drivers of dramatic media changes in Europe. This had considerable bearing on attempts by regulators to keep track of developments. It would now seem that the main task of regulation is to ensure that network operators cannot raise discriminatory barriers to access. These realities explain also why regulation at the European and national level tends increasingly to be guided by considerations of efficiency, enabling operators to optimize their activities by the full exploitation of economies of scale and scope, rather than by the all-encompassing regulatory approach which somehow does not seem to work any more.

While it is still true that Europe does not live by the First Amendment and that its attitude to regulation is quite different from that in the United States, it is widely recognized that regulation and technological development do not necessarily go hand in hand. Society, it is still felt, needs to be protected in certain ways and the public interest preserved. But nevertheless most people are now prepared to take into consideration that change is so fast that regulation has to be flexible in order not to be counterproductive.

Most European regulatory attempts to bridle or to steer technological developments have proved failures. This is most notable as regards EC attempts between 1986 and 1993 to adopt a common HDTV policy as well as a common digital policy in the following years. In both cases it became obvious that it was impossible to reach agreement on a common standard. As far as digital video broadcasting is concerned, only a common interface was agreed upon, but only on a voluntary basis, leaving the digital television sector deeply divided over decoders.

Competition policy

There remains, of course, a case to be made for the avoidance of market dominance. This is especially relevant in the case of digital television with the risk of 'digital gatekeepers' emerging who might use their proprietary decoders to dominate the new markets, control service provider and customer access and drive up prices. Market players must be stopped from monopolizing both content and conduit to the market. EC competition and anti-trust policy is now accepted as the most appropriate instrument for regulating information markets, able as it is to encourage new entrants and restricting dominant players. The European Commission has repeatedly indicated that it is determined to apply the essential principles of anti-trust (Articles 85 and 86 of the Treaty of Rome) to shape the information highway and enforce a set of market rules. A good illustration of this new approach is the 1994 decision by the Commission to block the planned MSG digital services group, a classic gatekeeper case with undue power.

At the same time there is an ongoing debate within the Commission that opposes its competition policy directorate (headed by Commissioner Karel

Van Miert) against the industrial policy directorate (headed by Commissioner Martin Bangemann). The latter tends to argue that principles of market competition and competitive conditions among market players could very well constitute an obstacle in the development of the broadband network and multimedia services. According to this view, the information highway is thought to be better served by a so-called 'tear up the rule books' argument for sweeping withdrawal of regulatory restrictions. Market realities favouring market concentration and consolidation, obvious in the field of digital television where two large alliances carve up the market between themselves for all practical purposes, would seem to confirm the Bangemann approach.

Global pressure to liberalize

In the end, anti-trust policy could very well be displaced by radical liberalization. Competition rules emphasize the public interest in discouraging unfair distortions, uneven development and unacceptable domination by a few players whereas liberalization is in line with globalization, favouring the break-up of public service monopolies while simultaneously replacing them with private monopolies. In view of what goes on at the global level, there is of course a strong pressure on Europe to release its communications industries both from public interest obligations as well as ownership barriers into a state of oligopolistic meanderings likely to enable them to position themselves and retain a competitive edge in the battle over global market shares. These views have been explicitly outlined in the 1994 report 'Europe and the global information society' drawn up by a task force chaired by Martin Bangemann. This extremely liberal view, which is basically a credo to guarantee freedom from regulation for European players eager to compete successfully in the global market, does not yet correspond completely to EC philosophy. It is being opposed by all those who object to a purely commercial approach to audiovisual matters.

But competition policy, now understood to be the primary weapon for regulating markets, is bound to change considerably under global pressure. It is confronted already by some very difficult issues: how to define markets sensibly and to what extent the prime criterion to look out for should be ownership or behaviour. There is also the question of the 'cultural' grounds for making exceptions (for example, for public broadcasters) as regards privileged treatment of some actors which might be otherwise perceived as distorting the market.

As far as regulation is concerned, Europe has come a long way. Digital developments and global competition will add further pressure on what is left of the old order. It is already acknowledged to a large extent that regulation should follow the technology rather than try to influence it or predict its course. Time and again legislation which tried to lead new technologies has been found to be, at best, ineffective. Thus, legislation should allow some time to pass before trying to regulate a new technology, the implications of which are only gradually becoming apparent. Digitalization, coupled with satellite TV and the Internet, is likely to make it increasingly difficult to define exactly who the producer and who the consumer are. Present legislation and regulation are based on a territorial concept which the digital environment puts into question. In all of these instances the global availability of the content raises anyway the issue of the practicality of the territorial application of national or European regulations.

These considerations and many others make it likely that Europe is heading for much more restraint in regulation, basically contenting itself with an over-arching competition policy instead of sector-specific regulatory policies. The regulation agenda will be dominated by new issues such as intellectual property, privacy and data protection. The solutions will have to be both global in nature and flexible enough to cope with the digital world.

Bibliography

EU Commission (1992) 'Pluralism and media concentration in the internal market – an assessment of the need for Community action' (COM(92)480).

EU Commission (1994a) 'Europe's way to the information society: an action plan' (COM(94)347).

EU Commission (1994b) 'Strategy options to strengthen the European programme industry in the context of the audiovisual policy of the European Union' (COM(94)96).

EU Commission (1995) 'Report on Application of Directive 89/552/EEC and Proposal for a European Parliament and Council Directive amending Council Directive 89/552/EEC on the coordination of certain provisions laid down by law, regulation or administrative action in Member States concerning the pursuit of television broadcasting activities' (COM(95)86).

EU Commission (1996) 'Communication from the Commission to the Council and the European Parliament on the application of Articles 4 and 5 of Directive 89/552/EEC "Television without Frontiers"' (COM(96)302).

CONCLUSION

15

Looking to the Future

Denis McQuail

Calm before or after the storm?

There is much news daily from Europe about new commercial developments, initiatives, take-overs and new technologies, especially affecting the
future of older public broadcasting monopolies and new telecommunications businesses. There is much public debate and political concern about
new or increased dangers to society and youth from pornography, violence
and excessive commercialism. There are anxieties about the role of the
media in democratic political processes. Nevertheless, we have not found
abundant evidence of fundamental changes in the European landscape,
with major foreseeable outcomes, in the recent past or currently under way.
This is in contrast to the situation 10 years ago, when electronic media were
in a state of flux and uncertainty and the media landscape appeared on the
brink of radical transformation.

Of course, much has in fact already changed and it may be that we are in
a phase of consolidation and adaptation to the new structures of competitive television and the alternative distribution channels which have
become available. The impact of economic and technological change is
finding expression at last in relative abundance, more consumer choice and
in changes of audiovisual culture. European-level rules relating to television
have been in force for several years and appear to be accepted, with the
accountability procedures working quite well. We can expect the scope of
European regulation to widen. While there continue to be anxieties about
increased concentration and loss of diversity affecting all sectors of the
media, and there is significant concentration already, the worst-case scenarios that have been envisaged have not materialized. No new mechanisms
have yet been instituted at either national or European level to counter the
threat.

The impression of calm is open to more than one interpretation. Two
main alternatives present themselves. Either this situation reflects the
maturation of television as a mass medium, after 50 years of development,

and the basic stability of national media systems or it is a preface to a new storm which will expose the vulnerability and artificiality of the present compromise. If one takes the first, more complacent, view then one is likely to emphasize the apparent public and political consensus about media systems which seem to offer a suitable mixture of amusement and reality and combine some cultural freedom with political diversity. In this view, the existing (adapted) systems are responsive to market forces, still largely serve the needs of democracy and are not drifting out of the control of society. If one suspects the calm to be illusory, one can emphasize the revolutionary capacity of technology still to be developed into consumer products, the insatiable ambitions of old and new media companies, the subordination of national to global forces and the uneasy compromises which keep the present system in place.

Towards a new order

One thing that is fairly clear is that the old European broadcasting order has been effectively transformed, even if basic structures and old principles remain in place all over Europe. In its place, we can discern a new *European model of electronic media*, with some distinctive features. It is clearly a hybrid or mixed model but it might generally qualify for the label of a 'restrained capitalist model'. One of its distinctive features is a continuing politicized or political element. This is partly the price exacted for the transformation from full public control, but it also reflects something distinctive and enduring about European political and media culture(s). The form of politicization adopted also remains variable between national societies.

This new model is likely to be dominant in the electronic media sphere in Europe generally and become the new norm or status quo. Smaller countries will have more freedom than larger countries to deviate from it and to retain a more distinctive, less globalized, variant. On the other hand, they may not be able to afford deviations because of the high cost of maintaining a strong public sector and generally of subsidizing culture. In practice, this freedom will be difficult to exercise, since small country markets will frequently be overwhelmed by cross-border products and services which cannot be kept out. This will apply especially where there is a dominant neighbour sharing the same language (for instance, Ireland, Austria or Belgium).

In the new model, there will be a framework of fairly loose regulation, developed out of existing national legislation and the present European directive, with some new provisions expected in relation to structure, ownership and competition. The model will accommodate various public service requirements and also contain some protected enclaves for particular social needs, especially for politically relevant information, culture, education and the claims of various special interest groups, including the regions. The size, scope and functions of these enclaves will depend on local (i.e. national) political influence. Political deals will be made to neutralize open partisan influences in the new arrangements.

It is still unclear what the typical form of a national media (TV) structure will look like, in terms of balance of content provision, but the safest bet for quite a long time is a continuation of approximately the present system, with any major changes or additions to the 'national' system, whatever the means of distribution, requiring political sanction and fitting into some system of accountability. There will continue to be rather few popular general news/entertainment channels (still broadcast or cabled), coupled with a range of specialist channels and many other services provided by a variety of distribution technologies, including multimedia and the Internet. There will be a mixture of public and commercial providers with a continuing effort to maintain at least one public channel with a significant share of the audience and not primarily dependent on advertising revenue. Subscription on a programme or channel basis is likely to develop as a significant alternative source of funding to the licence fee, advertising or sponsorship. The licence fee in its present form has only a limited life, but no obviously superior and politically acceptable alternative has yet emerged.

Many factors have combined to favour the emergence of a much more commercial electronic media sector in Europe and the result does not represent the realization of any plan. Change has been accomplished in a somewhat haphazard way, although the first steps which opened broadcasting to competition from cable and satellite were certainly planned in some countries. Growing abundance of channel capacity and increased competition for audiences fundamentally altered the operating conditions of public broadcasters. Public broadcasting has approached a condition of implosion, accelerating the advance of commercial operators. The outcome of change has not been quite as predicted by the visionaries of the early days of new media. We have not arrived at the once-feared state of commercialized American media, nor has regulation really withered away.

The new media have not really proved to be 'technologies of freedom', except perhaps in the sense of increasing competition and extending the scope of the free market. Few would claim that there is more freedom of expression in European television as a result of change and expansion. The new order is free to expand in extent as far as the market allows and some of the barriers between media sectors are lowered in the interests of competition and convergence. But it is held back from more fundamental changes to its traditional social and cultural role by political forces. These forces include European regional economic and political interests as well as various national political claims, often backed by public opinion.

The continuation of public broadcasting is one distinctive feature, retained on the basis of public support as well as by the choice of political elites who see it variously as an instrument for some political, social and cultural purposes, an aid to maintaining certain journalistic and cultural standards and a guarantee of some structural diversity and limits to private monopoly. There are still influential voices arguing persuasively for the need to retain a strong public media sector for political, social and cultural reasons (Atkinson and Raboy, 1997; Graham and Davis, 1997). One of the strongest arguments relates to the need to preserve a space for public expression and debate, free from commercial pressures and the control of powerful media corporations (see Schulz, 1997). One of the few dependable guarantees of true media diversity is the continued existence of a public sector.

Convergent systems?

The concept of media technological convergence was introduced in the early 1980s in recognition of the fact that computer digitalization had already abolished the difference between written word, sound and picture, whether moving or still. In practice, there has been little evidence of the impact of convergence at the level of structure. Technological innovations are still mainly launched in order to compete with existing technologies rather than converge on them, especially where distribution is involved. Some combinations of different technologies are increasingly found in the home, but they represent expansion rather than contraction in the alternatives for carrying and transmitting messages. It is true that policy, nationally and internationally, does tend to encourage regulatory convergence, although there are counter trends in restrictions on cross-media ownership.

Nevertheless, there are some general arguments to support the thesis that European electronic media systems are, in fact, converging even if current tendencies to regard the process as both inevitable and calling for celebration are open to question (CEC, 1997). By some criteria, for instance, the large distinctions which were found even 20 years ago between European countries are much less evident. Then one could distinguish quite sharply between large and smaller countries, between north and south, between those countries true to the public service tradition and those with significant commercialism. Some countries were nationally exclusive, while others were partially transnationalized. Few such sharp distinctions are valid today.

In very broad terms, it seems as if European countries share much the same kind of system of television and related services. The common form taken is of a basic service of three to five national general channels, accounting for 70 per cent or more of audience share, with numerous additional options available on cable and satellite (or by video) to cater for minority tastes and special interests. Television experience is still overwhelmingly national, despite the potential and availability of numerous transnational services. Media experience has not become significantly more

American or more cosmopolitan, although there is probably more shared cultural experience by way of an international media culture and the continuing borrowing of formats and standards. This basic structure of provision is the immediate outcome of the end of public monopoly and the expansion of the industry.

These arguments in support of a greater policy and system convergence between European countries do not seem to apply to the print media. As we have seen, press systems seem to remain very nationally distinctive on several dimensions, despite some common trends inspired by technology and market pressures. These trends include stylistic changes and trends towards 'tabloidization' and also de-politicization of content and control.

In general, the pattern of television described is not a specifically European phenomenon, since a similar pattern can be found in North America and developed Asian countries (for example, Japan). The term 'maturing' used above may just reflect the delayed arrival at a particular point of media market equilibrium position which fits the producer and consumer practices of the time. These may or may not be stable, but the arguments are about equally balanced. What may be distinctive about Europe is the prominent share in most countries which public broadcasting still takes in the system, even if it is declining. Economically and legally, European systems are all dual or multiple in terms of finance and regulation. While the internal inconsistency of 'regimes' might seem to imply some potential instability, many other societal arrangements are equally lacking in a consistent logic, but are stable outcomes of past experience and management of conflicting interests in society.

In respect of economics, there is also an increased similarity between European countries in terms of the broad balance between public and private finance of electronic media and public sectors are very similar, based on a compulsory licence fee of about the same type and level nearly everywhere. Behind economic convergence lies integration of markets and similarities of living standards in Western Europe. However, the structure of private ownership differs a good deal from one country to another for historic reasons and also because of differences in market size.

The smaller countries have generally less-developed private sectors, but some do have a dominant economic actor. Among the larger countries, Britain has probably the most diversified private sector, with France, Spain and Germany relatively oligopolistic and Italy dominated by one company, Fininvest. The general pattern of dominance by originally national media companies remains. The probable trend is towards continuing or greater oligopoly (as in Britain). But the effect of participation by national telecommunications monopolies is hard to predict, as is the degree of increase of American participation in the future. Another uncertain factor will be any effect of European regulation for diversity, although there is not likely to be any major resistance to market forces.

The continuing relative and, in some cases, absolute decline of the public broadcasting sector in terms of audience share and income is a feature shared by most European countries, and may also be viewed as evidence of convergence, but the end result may be a return to larger inter-country differences, with some countries having no public sector in the original sense of broadcasting based on a compulsory licence or 'tax'.

It looks as if European-level regulation (especially the directive), and also participation in transnational bodies, such as the Council of Europe, the European Broadcasting Union and the World Trade Organization, do, in general, exert a pressure towards similar standards, norms, policies and practices. Everywhere, the same technological innovations, media industrial trends, and the shared global environment in which Europe as an economic and political region finds itself, will also increase similarities.

Continuing aspects of differentiation

The remarks about public broadcasting are a reminder that we are still dealing with countries which have very varied histories and different cultures, in social and political terms. The media markets are also very different and so are the media systems (especially the press) and the circumstances affecting advertising. In general, media entrepreneurs, especially those operating on the international stage, do not necessarily favour convergence, since they like differentiation for market reasons. Despite the common exposure to economic, technological and global environmental forces, there will always be scope for different cultural policies which will influence decisions about broadcasting, in the light of social conditions.

We have also emphasized the limits to the power of technology to determine change and the degree to which audiences are determinant according to social and cultural needs and experiences. Cultural policy differences in the widest sense (thus covering politics as well as language, education, the arts, regionalism, tourism and the environment) will remain. Convergence will meet resistance, as it obviously has already at national and linguistic frontiers. For the foreseeable future there is no storm warning in force and, if one should be sounded, the winds will not blow everywhere with equal strength.

The future for media policy

Although there has been a fundamental change in the general conditions for media policy in Europe, as a result of the decline of the public broadcasting model, the emergence of entirely new media, the fundamental rearrangement of 'old media' such as the telephone and the complex trends of globalization, media policy as such is not going to disappear. The issues are changing, the values invoked are different and the forums in which they are discussed are also different, but media remain very much a political concern, in the widest sense. Within national societies, there is no less debate about the cultural quality of the media and no less concern by politicians to maintain some control over the conditions of media operation, if not the details of what is published and disseminated, although even here questions of privacy, decency and the harmful effects of the media are hotly debated in public arenas. If anything, the scope of concern has widened because of the arrival of new media.

The directly political activities of the media are closely scrutinized and the relations between the media and politics continue to be regulated. The quality of performance of the media in informing citizens still matters a great deal for democracy. Issues of concentration, diversity and national cultural and minority integrity are still hotly debated. More importance will probably be attached to questions of equity in the distribution of access to the new communication channels, just because we are living in an information society.

The greatly increased globalization of media ownership, activity and audience experience has changed and enlarged the terms of debate, but not put an end to it. It is quite clear that less can be achieved by independent national regulation, and that the capacity directly to control the media at source is much lower. Even monitoring the media for its failings has ceased to be realistic without the active collaboration of the media themselves. The early model of broadcasting policy as limited permission, close monitoring and severe restraint has collapsed.

A largely new era of media policy is opening up in which economic, social, cultural and political issues carry equal weight and for which the concept of an information society provides a central organizing pillar. The new era of policy will be characterized by more internationalism, market realism, technical and administrative complexity and large components of media industry self-regulation designed to reconcile public, private and commercial interests. Media policy in the future will need more than ever to be informed by imaginative and independent research, rather than relying, as in the past, on ideologically based principles and strong political action.

Bibliography

Atkinson, D. and Raboy, M. (eds) (1997) *Public Service Broadcasting: The Challenges of the 21st Century*. Paris: UNESCO.

CEC (1997) 'Commission of the European Communities: Green Paper on the convergence of the telecom, media and information technology sectors and the implications for regulation – towards an information society approach', Document COM(97)623 final, 3 December 1997.

Graham, A. and Davis, G. (1997) *Broadcasting, Society and Policy in the Multi-media Age*. Luton: University of Luton Press.

Schulz, W. (1997) 'Changes of the mass media and the public sphere', *The Public/Javnost*, 4 (2): 57–70.

Index